New York Longshoremen

WORKING IN THE AMERICAS

UNIVERSITY PRESS OF FLORIDA

Florida A&M University, Tallahassee
Florida Atlantic University, Boca Raton
Florida Gulf Coast University, Ft. Myers
Florida International University, Miami
Florida State University, Tallahassee
New College of Florida, Sarasota
University of Central Florida, Orlando
University of Florida, Gainesville
University of North Florida, Jacksonville
University of South Florida, Tampa
University of West Florida, Pensacola

WORKING IN THE AMERICAS
Edited by Richard Greenwald, Drew University, and Timothy J. Minchin, LaTrobe University

Working in the Americas is devoted to publishing important works in labor history and working-class studies in the Americas. This series seeks work that uses traditional as well as innovative, interdisciplinary, or transnational approaches. Its focus is the Americas and the lives of its workers.

Florida's Working-Class Past: Current Perspectives on Labor, Race, and Gender from Spanish Florida to the New Immigration, edited by Robert Cassanello and Melanie Shell-Weiss (2009; first paperback edition, 2011)

The New Economy and the Modern South, by Michael Dennis (2009)

Film Noir, American Workers, and Postwar Hollywood, by Dennis Broe (2009)

Americanization in the States: Immigrant Social Welfare Policy, Citizenship, and National Identity in the United States, 1908-1929, by Christina A. Ziegler-McPherson (2009)

Black Labor Migration in Caribbean Guatemala, 1882-1923, by Frederick Douglass Opie (2009)

Migration and the Transformation of the Southern Workplace since 1945, edited by Robert Cassanello and Colin J. Davis (2009)

American Railroad Labor and the Genesis of the New Deal, 1919-1935, by Jon R. Huibregtse (2010)

Seated by the Sea: The Maritime History of Portland, Maine, and Its Irish Longshoremen, by Michael C. Connolly (2010; first paperback edition, 2011)

Strike! The Radical Insurrections of Ellen Dawson, by David Lee McMullen (2010)

New York Longshoremen: Class and Power on the Docks, by William J. Mello (2010; first paperback edition, 2011)

Life and Labor in the New New South, by Robert H. Zieger (2011)

New York Longshoremen

Class and Power on the Docks

William J. Mello

Foreword by Richard Greenwald and Timothy J. Minchin

University Press of Florida

Gainesville/Tallahassee/Tampa/Boca Raton

Pensacola/Orlando/Miami/Jacksonville/Ft. Myers/Sarasota

Copyright 2010 by William J. Mello
Printed in the United States of America. This book is printed on Glatfelter
Natures Book, a paper certified under the standards of the Forestry
Stewardship Council (FSC). It is a recycled stock that contains 30 percent
post-consumer waste and is acid-free.

First cloth printing 2010
First paperback printing, 2011

Library of Congress Cataloging-in-Publication Data
Mello, William J.
New York longshoremen : class and power on the docks / William J. Mello;
foreword by Richard Greenwald and Timothy J. Minchin.
p. cm.—(Working in the Americas)
Includes bibliographical references and index.
ISBN 978-0-8130-3489-8 (alk. paper); ISBN 978-0-8130-3977-0
1. Stevedores—New York (State)—New York. 2. Stevedores—Labor unions—
New York (State)—New York. 3. Working class—New York (State)—New York.
I. Title.
HD8039.L82U6547 2010
322.'2097471—dc22   2010005489

The University Press of Florida is the scholarly publishing agency for the State
University System of Florida, comprising Florida A&M University, Florida
Atlantic University, Florida Gulf Coast University, Florida International Uni-
versity, Florida State University, New College of Florida, University of Central
Florida, University of Florida, University of North Florida, University of South
Florida, and University of West Florida.

University Press of Florida
15 Northwest 15th Street
Gainesville, FL 32611-2079
http://www.upf.com

This book is dedicated to the memory of my father, Servio Mello, to my mother, Anna Mello, and to my daughters, Anna, Maria, Gabriela, and Elizabeth, for their immeasurable support.

Contents

Illustrations

Illustrations follow page 104

Foreword

The New York waterfront—once a teeming economic hub that employed tens of thousands of longshoremen—is now a place of luxury high-rises and recreation. We seldom remember the world of the working waterfront. That world comes alive in William Mello's telling account. Mello reminds us that the New York waterfront is more than the film *On the Waterfront.* Mello's waterfront avoids the typical stereotypes of organized crime, globalization, and workers as defeated, passive victims. Instead, under Mello's ethnographer's gaze, longshoremen are active, engaged makers of history. They are a force to be taken seriously, one we can learn from in today's complicated world.

Mello uncovers this world through a foundation of oral histories and a close reading of all the available primary and secondary material. Through this amassed collection of data, Mello focuses his attention on the story of longshoremen's lives and struggles. We gain access to their world, following the thick description of Clifford Gertz. Mello challenges us to lose ourselves in this world. This series has been dedicated to understanding, through an interdisciplinary lens, the changing world of work and workers. Mello's work moves knowledge forward. Those wishing to understand the waterfront, workers' self activity, and globalization will now have to contend with a new scholar's voice.

Richard Greenwald and Timothy J. Minchin
Series Editors

Acknowledgments

My interest in the dockworkers' reform movement began with discussions I had with two longtime friends and fellow historians: Paul Mishler, Indiana University, who patiently discussed the project as it progressed over the years, and Richard Greenwald, Drew University, whose encouragement was important for the successful conclusion of this book. My interest in the waterfront labor process continued to evolve during my graduate studies at the Graduate Faculty of the New School for Social Research. The GF faculty in Historical Studies was essential in shaping the present project, particularly Professors Louise Tilly and Michael Hanagan. Professors David Plotke, Adolph Reed Jr., and Victoria Hattam in the Political Science Department and Professor Orville Lee in Sociology all made many comments and suggestions, reading and analyzing earlier versions. The GF faculty continuously provided intellectual motivation for this book. It is important to acknowledge the encouragement of Richard Greenwald, who likewise read earlier versions.

This study draws on the seminal investigations of Professor Vernon Jensen and his book *Strife on the Waterfront*. Access to his collection was an essential part of my research of the dock labor process. My unrestrained access to the Jensen Archives was made possible with the help of Patrizia Scione, who provided immeasurable assistance during my visit to the Catherwood Library at Cornell University. Similarly, I would like to thank Bruce Nelson for important comments made during earlier work on this project. Without a doubt, the editorial and practical work of my dear friends Susan Browne and Patrick Hill and the indexing and last-stage proofreading of Jim O'Brien were vital. I would also like to acknowledge the help provided by longshoremen Pete Bel, Servio Mello, and Arthur Peicoro, who read individual chapters and made important suggestions, besides providing me with access to their documents, newsletters, and pamphlets. Their long years of relentless activism helped shape important notions of life and work on the docks. Finally, this project would not have been possible without the support of my daughters, Anna, Maria, Gabriela, and Elizabeth, who had to put up with my time constraints and absences as the manuscript progressed over the years.

Many people helped along the way, and if I failed to mention anyone, please accept my sincere apologies. As always, even though I received the support of many, any error or failure in this work is my sole responsibility.

Introduction

Any debate about labor's revival must take into account the historical implications that have influenced the organization and mobilization of the American working class. The constraints placed on organized labor immediately following World War II demand greater attention, and the rebellion of New York's dockworkers was an intricate part of this process. Beginning in 1945 and for almost thirty years thereafter, the Port of New York was the site of intense class conflict. Striking longshoremen frequently battled the shipping companies, the police, federal and state political authorities, and their own union leadership simultaneously. Through a series of strikes and protests, New York's dockworkers made their presence felt, paralyzing the transportation of goods, both domestically and abroad, and imposing the financial loss of billions of dollars in U.S. business. At the center of this conflict was the struggle for workplace control—a battle that continually fanned the flames of rebellion on the docks.

When exploring the waterfront conflict, two questions emerge. First, what were the limits imposed by business elites and political authorities against the rebellious dockworkers? Second, what was the longshoremen's political capacity to succeed given the limits to class action? In spite of the rebellious movement, systemic limits introduced into the American political process based on the social and economic stratification of workers offset any demand for working-class participation in the dock labor process. Response to the longshore rebellion melded ideological, judicial, economic, and political constraints that allowed the interests of business elites and political authorities to prevail. The fundamental conflict that characterized this process was the longshoremen's claims for a greater role in the decision-making process and control of the dock labor process. Working-class power on the docks was shaped by the political and economic importance of the New York waterfront, and it was reinforced by the nature of waterfront work that rapidly transformed even basic economic demands into a highly charged political conflict. Given the distinct characteristics of the dock labor process, the struggle for control of the International Longshoremen's Association (ILA) became synonymous with the dockworkers' demand for control of the waterfront. In this sense, the two claims—for control of their union and the dock labor process—were inseparable.

The importance and implications of this study are twofold. First, when the political effectiveness of organized labor and union density continue at an all-time low, it seems pertinent to assert that much of labor's present quandary reflects the historical influence of postwar labor politics and the limits imposed on labor. The process that unfolded on the Port of New York was a harbinger that would subsequently redefine labor's political power. Second, despite the political constraints imposed on New York's dockworkers, their capability to depart from traditional concepts of employment by demanding a guaranteed income limited the employers' ability to dispose of workers at will. In a moment when neoliberal globalization destroys communities and decimates entire industries, the docks serve as a model that reinforces labor's claim that employment is a right of citizenship.

A significant aspect of the waterfront reform process reflected the longshoremen's response to the struggle for control of the waterfront. Class organization and mobilization emerged through both formal and informal political action and organization and was an essential component of the dock labor process. The informal organization of the dockworkers' rank-and-file movement involved many politically distinct groups of labor activists. Their activity on the port illustrated both the complex relations they constructed in response to the shifting local interests and the broader political and economic context of the period. This is not to say this relationship was always harmonious. That would be far from the truth. In this sense, the "popular front" paradigm of political alliances was short-lived, if it existed at all. This process also reflected the changing characteristics and structure of the formal organization of dockworkers, the ILA, and the recurring intersection of class mobilization and conflict informed by the broader political process in course.[1] The transformations of the ILA (imposed or not) mirrored the longshoremen's ability to transform their formal representation and to expand their participation within the sphere of local and national politics. Finally, waterfront reform was also shaped by the actions and interests of competing political forces and shipping employers who likewise sought to gain greater control over the Port of New York.

Working-class activism in the United States and particularly on the Port of New York reflects a process in which power, class organization, and elite interests intersect in American politics. On the docks, the power of local and regional political authorities and the interests of the shipping industry are an intricate component where the interests of some working-class organizations consistently intersect with those of business. New York's shipping interests far outweighed those of other elite sectors because of their role in the national economy and their direct relationship with the European economy. Shipping was not as dependent on regional and local commercial schemes as were other industries. Without sharing this view of an elite-driven, conspiratorial notion of American politics, the rebellious dockworkers' movement provides greater insight into how class conflict and politics converged to redefine the basic structure of organized labor.

At some, albeit few, important moments during the process of waterfront reform, elite and working-class interests coincided and stood in opposition to the growing demands for control of the docks by federal authorities. In the process, political alliances and interests were constantly in flux, power was fragmented, and consensus among reform groups never emerged. At the end of the day, elite interests prevailed and the central demand of New York's dockworkers for greater control and participation in the waterfront labor process remained elusive and unresolved, but not without changing the nature and conditions of work on the waterfront. To date, the achievement of New York's dockworkers remains beyond the reach of other sectors of the American working class.

This study is historical in substance and political in essence. It combines discussions of power and politics with the empirical exploration of class collective action, illustrating the unique way in which workers negotiated power relations. The historical reexamination of class conflict helps rethink the way class expands the location in which politics and conflict serve to continuously redefine the American political process.[2] The introduction of agency into the study of power is important because power relations emerging from class issues come to light in a more direct and unstructured (noninstitutional) form, and this allows the concept of political process to move in a "free-flowing" fashion, unrestrained by simple narrative.[3]

Chapter 1 examines the role of class in the process of political change and the limits to working-class action. Neither the pluralist nor the elite domination models of power entirely explain political change; they are partial accounts at best. In a historical perspective, the distinct ways in which power and politics shaped each other in the East Coast unions illustrates the deeper conflict of how power relations reshaped working-class political participation, introducing historical evidence and the debate of class and power in American political development.

Subsequent chapters focus on the empirical and historical conditions that served as the basis for power relations on the Port of New York as well as the nature of resistance and the reform movement initiated during the mid-1930s by left-wing dockworkers. This historical overview connects the development of the waterfront labor process and the emergence of longshore trade unionism to the subculture of resistance developed by dockworkers. As waterfront unions became increasingly intertwined in the local political structure, the resistance of dockworkers emerged, based on a shared identity of class and the division of labor. Power relations on the waterfront reflected high levels of elite domination that relied on the active support of the corrupt union leadership and the acquiescence of the local political structure. The longshoremen's incipient attempts to resist were defeated with the use of physical violence and exclusion from the decision-making process, where elite domination appears prevalent. While this process occurred largely prior to World War II, it is important because it enables us to understand why the Port of New York became the center of political contention in the postwar period.

The escalating political conflict between dockworkers, their union, political authorities, and shipping companies over apparently local demands had broader political, economic, and social implications. Between 1953 and 1960, the attempt to eradicate the ILA from the Port of New York melded the political, economic, and ideological constraints that characterized the process of waterfront reform. The demands for labor reform and for greater internal democracy in the ILA had far-reaching effects in state and national politics because of the political influence of the corrupt union leadership and the underlying effects on the national economy. As a result, the structures of power on the docks shift from the elite domination model of the prewar period to one where mounting legislative and institutional constraints suppress the longshore reform movement. Increasingly, the location from which power is negotiated moves away from the docks to more complex and inaccessible spheres of political decision-making. The longshoremen's demand for participation in the waterfront labor process was met with a growing array of judicial, economic, and political measures where the interests of shipping companies and political authorities converged.

The rank-and-file movement's struggle to transform the docks was increasingly complicated by the growing process of waterfront automation. During this period, institutional structures converged and the spheres of decision-making became permanent components of the dock labor process, thus narrowing the political alternatives available to the reform movement. Although the importance of the Port of New York slowly declined because of containerization and the transfer of the shipping industry to Port Elizabeth, the rebellious movement persisted. After 1960, the rank and file, especially through the *Dockers News* group, continued to contest the antidemocratic structure of the ILA and the mounting intervention of state and federal authorities in waterfront life. Despite the fact that control of waterfront unions remained in the hands of those who drew upon the legacy of violence and corruption, the rank-and-file movement worked both inside and outside the formal labor structure, making significant gains and advancing the dockworkers' demands. The distinct way in which power was conceived shaped diverse expressions and forms of working-class political action.

The movement to reform the labor process melded the political aspirations of longshoremen for democratic control of the waterfront with their most basic economic demands. In doing so, the longshoremen's ability to impose financial losses and resist mounting political pressure did not lead to greater decision-making. Despite some highly significant victories, the dockworkers' battle for control was lost.

This project draws on archival documents, past and current literature, oral histories of waterfront activists archived in the Tamiment labor archives, and interviews I conducted early in my research. Two of the three interviewees requested that their names be withheld for personal reasons, and I have respected their request.

1

History as Class Politics on the Docks

*In so far as decisions are made, the problem of who is involved
in making them is the basic problem of power.*
—C. Wright Mills

On the cover of the June 1, 1901, edition of *Harper's Weekly*, the images of labor and industry are characterized as men, both equally strong and ready to fight, with the caption "Come brothers, you have grown so big you cannot afford to quarrel."[1] More than just the Progressive Era depiction of antagonistic social forces, the magazine's cover reflects a long-standing misconception that labor and business are equal in strength and power—a notion that has pervaded pluralist accounts of American political development and history. The expansive power attributed to labor in the magazine's characterization has a deeper significance; such an attribution of power implies that labor, in American society, has an equally high level of autonomy and thus participation in the political process.

High levels of employer resistance to labor organizing as a significant factor throughout American history, however, are indicative that something else is going on—that industry and labor are far from equal. In a historical perspective, the limits of class organization and mobilization reflect a long-term process where organized labor became increasingly less autonomous, imposing boundaries on working-class action and constraining the ability of workers to intercede effectively in the essential aspects of working-class life. The limits of class reflect the social stratification of political relations, where embedded institutional constraints constructed over time provide the historical conditions where non-decision-making becomes the dominant form of political exclusion.[2] As a result of this process, some groups systematically prevail in relation to others based on their location in society. This problem not only speaks to the immediate discussion of the role of labor within the American political process but also has underlying consequences about the characteristics of labor's power in American political development and history.

The dilemma of power and class in American history emerges when one attempts an encompassing definition that can explain the way in which power is exercised and its influence on the dominant political structure. Exclusion implies the existence of mechanisms of coercion. With regard to class organization, how does coercion occur in American society? It is important to acknowledge that class constraints occur through both institutional and noninstitutional spheres of political engagement.[3] These questions remain the subject of continuous debate because they conflict with the notion of a society based on free political exchange among citizens with equal rights.[4] In a historical context the inability of workers, as such, to access full democratic participation is a cornerstone of this conflict.

Labor's political power is restricted by the limited possibilities available to workers, but more importantly, these limits reshape and reorganize the nature of the movement itself. Labor's limited political power, constructed over time, was informed by the structural, ideological, and economic coercion of business elites in the American political process. This conflicts with the notion that much of the weakness of today's labor movement is the result of decisions made by workers and their leaders in the interaction of political forces. Since the early 1900s, through regulation and coercion, business elites have continuously sought to reshape the labor movement in their own image, a process that gained greater momentum after World War II. The shifting characteristics of American trade unionism represent a process where the demands for industrial democracy, from earlier historical periods to its present stage of weakness, reflect a process where labor organizations were consistently reconfigured by political, economic, and institutional constraints.[5] In this sense, the traditional argument of an existing postwar labor-management agreement, where workers traded rights for greater economic affluence, was not the result of mutual acquiescence. The political limits of labor emerge in the postwar period, after years of labor's social movement activism initiated in the Progressive and New Deal eras.[6]

The struggles of New York's dockworkers appear as the harbinger for a process whereby labor's political power in the United States became radically limited; from very early on, power for dockworkers became increasingly more elusive. For New York's longshoremen, the process of political constraint was reflected in the highly repressive waterfront labor process. That is, while years of dockworker rank-and-file activism demanded greater control of the longshore labor process, by the early 1960s the result was much the same as for other sectors of labor. It was a process marked by restrictions and regulations that limited the role of class organization in American political life. Even though waterfront workers had distinct struggles and demands, the results were similar.

The centrality of the New York waterfront in the national economy provided local economic elites the basis for expansive influence in the spheres of political decision-making. Power was expressed through high levels of physical and ideological coercion embedded within the waterfront labor process. This system of power became analogous with waterfront unionism. Who controls the union and subsequently the waterfront labor process defines the limits of class power on the docks. The mechanisms for exclusion comprised institutional as well as informal and ideological devices construed upon deep-rooted relations with authorities linked to the local political order. Key aspects of the waterfront labor process were regulated by formal as well as informal understandings developed over time between the ILA leadership and the New York Shipping Association (NYSA). For example, in the 1930s, ideological constraints drew on high levels of anti-communism and later found greater political expression in McCarthyism. The impact of these constraints was far-reaching and not just a momentary "blip" in shifting union leaderships. This not only weakened rank-and-file insurgency but subsequently redefined the alliances among distinct groups active on the waterfront and the ability of the movement to reform the dock labor process. The waterfront labor process was molded to the benefit of the interests of NYSA and ILA leadership. If elites prevailed because of their expansive influence within the local political power structure, this could only occur with the acquiescence of local and state authorities with ties to the spheres of national politics.[7]

Postwar Concepts of Labor Power

Concepts of democratic participation helped define the alternatives available to organized labor and subsequently influenced its future. Developed during a period of momentary upsurge in working-class mobilization, pluralists sought to relocate the role of labor in the power scheme of American politics.[8] Postwar pluralists argued that the historical trajectory of politics was a process where rising entrepreneurs, and later people from the middle and lower strata, ultimately replaced the old dominant elite. They saw power as an intricate part of the local political structure whereby the premises of democracy provide the conditions for stability and political change.[9] For postwar pluralists, politics reflected the reciprocal influence among leaders, subleaders, and the constituency, which is the product of shifting coalitions and interests.[10] The scope of political power varies, depending upon resources such as cash, jobs, and information, which are considered only as the potentials for power because their implementation depends upon how expertly they are employed.

The problem with this argument, however, is that the spheres of influence that controlled the New York waterfront were not exercised only through the institutional and formal political structure. The interaction of social relations from which power was exercised on the docks was not centered on a single branch of government and gave little if any attention to the relations between the community and the decision-making process; there is no consensus.

The experience of New York's longshoremen reflected neither consensus nor stability for any long period of time. Most of the conditions over which they bargained were not simple reflexes of the local political structure.[11] Rather, they were the product of a broader political universe of economic and political interests at the state and national levels. This expansive political scope is in large part a reflection of interregional development and dependency of the American political economy that ultimately limited the power of the local political structure.[12] In this sense, the willingness or refusal of shipping employers to bargain was not entirely decided by the local power structure.

The predominant postwar view considered the role of unions in American political life as "monopolies of the labor force."[13] They argued that labor's "monopoly power" required strong regulation, without which they could become disruptive elements of democracy. Regulation, however, is not simply a set of rules and laws; rather, the political participation of workers was reconfigured by "responsible unionism."[14] Expanding, centralizing, and regulating trade union activity would keep the actions of "disruptive unions" in check if they failed to acquiesce to the orientation of mainstream labor organizations. Unions are viewed as corporate organizations and the means by which class conflict is shrouded from American political life, labor peace is achieved, and inequality is minimized.[15]

This view minimizes the historical impact of employer resistance to trade union organization as a significant factor that systemically contained labor's participation in American politics. In this process the nature of the conflict is primarily for higher wages, which receives little employer resistance since control of the workplace remains unaltered.[16] This argument is a limited view of how class interests are conceived and fails to see the zero-sum basis of class conflict because it does not account for alternative forms of political activity and class-based group formation that emerge and exist outside of the interaction of political institutions. This can be seen in the way in which class action and conflict emerged and many times advanced the claims of important sectors of the American working class. Workers, organized around class interests, frequently waged intense battles that catapulted them to the center of major political struggles for policy reforms, ultimately reshaping elite and popular alliances.

Unclear in this argument are the social forces that drive the political process and how long-term results of the regulatory measures (enacted primarily after World War II) redefined the basic nature of organized labor. Significantly, the Taft-Hartley Act and the Landrum-Griffin Act, placed within the context of the Cold War hysteria of McCarthyism, had a deadening effect on working-class organization. That is, the postwar period signaled the pinnacle of a process where labor's political containment and subsequent structural reconfiguration, driven by the interests of business elites, were transformed into an enduring political relation.[17] For labor, the political effect of the newly enacted regulatory measures ensured the process through which the political influence of labor shifted from its New Deal social activist platform to one where the claims for democratic participation were relegated to the norms of collective bargaining.[18]

The historical development of labor's limited political expression is not merely the result of chance; rather, it is a reflection of structural and systemic constraints based on the division of labor within a triadic structure of power. In this sense the division of labor is not simply the expression of economic relations but the consequence of social and political interaction that emerges as a result of the economic process. This is important if we are to understand how power is exercised on the waterfront, where control of the labor process and power were synonymous. This is also a reflection of a broader recurrent conflict throughout the development of American political life between the institutional framework and how economic elites achieve their interests and the way by which competing political and economic interests shape class relations in contemporary society.[19] In this context, class power emerges as the outcome of broader social interaction among competing political and economic groups within a single dominant political order.

Power is not the result of consent, since power is never equally distributed. Rather, it is the limited submission to further competing interests constructed through the interaction of groups structured by a dominant social hierarchy. In this scheme social alignments are the realm in which organized groups in society coordinate a common practice. Power is not static.[20] In a class perspective, the combined interests of employers enable them to limit the options available to workers through regulated employment practices.[21] In this sense, the way in which power limits class organization is a reflection of a set of social, political, and economic relations that are systemically reproduced and developed over longer periods of time. As a result of this process, business elites prevail in setting the limits of class activity in the political process. If the limits of class participation are the result of power relations structured within a socially stratified society, then the class location of social forces is an important factor in determining who makes the decisions and how they are made.[22]

Labor conflicts, more often than not, tend to have deeper economic and political implications that place the center of the conflict beyond the immediate demands and grievances presented by workers. Waterfront work stoppages paralyzed trucking and embargoed railroads. In many cases, dock strikes had a ripple effect on business, economic, and political forces with only indirect interests in the docks; however, it expanded the political sphere in which negotiation and decision-making occurred. The systemic devices of constraint and the underlying interests may not be readily in evidence.

One direct result of this process is that non-decision-making becomes the main component through which class interests are contained.[23] For the most part, non-decision-making reflects the ability of power holders to determine outcomes through causal devices not necessarily related to the objective question of conflict. Non-decision-making does not always reflect acquiescence, consent, or indifference. Given the social location of a group, some positions may not be available or express the direct interests in a tactical manner.[24] In this context, the constraints on class mobilization and organization reflect the cumulative effects of long-term social and economic inequality that directly and indirectly limit political action of some and favor others. Political conflicts may occur outside of the direct and larger sphere of conflicting interests, and they may be displaced onto secondary policy interests, smaller in scale and scope, that only come into evidence when examined within the broader historical context.[25] Thus the capacity of elite groups to sustain conflict over longer periods and in multiple political terrains concurrently and to distribute their efforts to shape social policy is superior to the efforts of those who have fewer resources, skills, and political capability.[26]

The expansive social, political, and economic context under which power relations emerge as the outcome of social stratification and inequality suggests a triadic structure in the exchange among social forces from both the decision-making and non-decision-making perspectives of power. The social hierarchies that compose the triadic structure of power relations serve as systemic constraints that drive the mobilization of bias and decisions.[27]

This process is especially relevant for a historical analysis of labor.[28] In this structure, equality remains illusive when viewed as a result of citizenship, while the components of socioeconomic inequality become embedded components that comprise the structure of class constraints. The economic interests of the market system outweigh the rights of citizenship where political institutions are dependent on business for revenue. The associational capacity of workers and their organizations is defined and limited by institutional constraints and compounded by education, skills, and social location, all of which provide a structural advantage and access to the institutions of power for some and not for others.[29] Social stratification provides the structure through which inequality pervades power relations in both ways and means. Far from being unbiased, "systemic constraints" provide the framework from which elite interests are transformed into political achievements.

An "Arsenal of Weapons"

Systemic limits to labor's political power imply that some social forces are, over time, effectively constrained from achieving reasonable political demands. That is, workers and their organizations are unable to transcend systemic barriers because of limits embedded within the political process.

As a result, social stratification affords greater political power and resources to some and limits access to others, thus creating a highly skewed political playing field. On the docks this process combined rules, regulatory devices, and institutional structures that were derived from the excessive power of the shipping companies in alliance with political authorities. Systemic limits reflect the capacity of business elites to set the rules and subsequently determine the agenda of the political battle. This affords business elites the power to limit the possible outcomes of immediate and long-term political conflicts. It defines the context in which conflict will occur as well as the boundaries within which workers will act.

The ability to define the agenda for conflict on the waterfront imbued shipping elites with the capacity to decide which rules may or may not be modified and to what extent political transformation may occur and when it will not. In most political processes, the accumulative effects of rules and regulatory devices set in place are not easily visible. They are, however, essential aspects that limit possible outcomes and not simply functions of the administrative structure or devised solely in the interest of preserving the dominant political order. In the case of the waterfront labor structure, devices were melded into an administrative structure, thus creating the framework for a singular process of systemic constraint driven by elite political interests. This, in turn, limited the choices available to longshoremen. In this sense, workers and their organizations are limited to reacting to immediate conflicts. In a conflict of this nature, distinct social forces appear to be talking at rather than to one another, negotiations are ineffective, and political conflict produces highly disparate results.

Political choices, made in the heat of battle, are not conceived in a void. Those available to workers are limited by the social forces that exercise power. The field of political contest is skewed because laws and regulatory devices effectively limit the political bargaining power of labor, allowing political and business elites to define strategic long-term outcomes.

Specifically, a twofold process was set in place to constrain waterfront activism. In the first phase, high levels of violence by gangster union officials with the support of shipping employers and acquiescent political authorities drove the process that severely constrained the dockworkers' reform movement. Immediately following World War II, violence and coercion dominated waterfront politics. This system was carried over from the prewar years. In a second phase, the ability of shipping elites to limit waterfront activists was reflected by their expansive political influence and

ability to mount and continuously refine an arsenal of institutional mechanisms with the support of regional judicial and political authorities. The
shifting devices of systemic constraints of waterfront labor mirrored the
changing political context of the decade following World War II and the
way in which elites sought to contain mounting labor mobilization while
achieving both immediate and long-term objectives.

This process proved to be a harbinger of how business elites and political authorities would deal with American labor. By the early 1960s, economic elites and congressional representatives of both the Democratic
and Republican parties began demanding that President Kennedy initiate a major overhaul of labor legislation. They argued that the prevailing
regulation was inadequate to contain the mounting onslaught of striking
workers. Fearing that such a position would detract from issues deemed
more important at the time, such as tariff reform, Kennedy proposed a
strategy whereby political authorities would gradually construct an "arsenal of weapons" to contain and limit the demands and political power of
labor. The "arsenal of weapons" strategy, as a deterrent to labor's increasing
mobilization, illustrates how the business elites, in alliance with political
authorities, exercised their influence to draw on multiple laws, regulatory
devices, and institutions to obligate labor's compliance.

Particularly on the Port of New York, the process drew on violence,
economic power, ideological coercion, and acquiescent legal and political authorities; however, these characteristics were not always equally relevant. That is, during different phases, one or more of the four dominant
features drove the process of waterfront labor politics. This does not mean
that the other factors ceased to influence the process. Rather, their preva-
lence waxed and waned in response to a broader political context. While
there was no clear sequential structure to the arsenal, some appeared with
greater frequency while others shifted from a primary to a secondary role
at different phases of the reform process. For example, ideological constraints are constant over different phases. In the 1930s and 1940s, the ILA
collected money from employers for its Anticommunist Fighting Fund
and used the money to pay for hired thugs to purge activists from the
docks. By the 1950s, McCarthyism and all of the legal devices it entailed
had become a more successful mechanism. Up until the early 1960s, ideological pressures significantly limited and informed the actions of dock
labor activists. On the other hand, while political violence never ceased to

be a possible threat, it was less prevalent as the rank-and-file movement gained larger expression on the docks.

After the passage of the Taft-Hartley Act in 1947, political constraints against waterfront labor were increasingly institutional in nature and signaled the onset of a variety of new devices to limit labor activism. The process was driven by the expansive political influence of shipping elites to constitute an arsenal of legal devices that not only limited the mobilization of rebellious longshoremen but reshaped the nature of their claims. This process was structured upon a legal framework of labor regulation set in place between 1947 and 1960, initiated with the passage of the Taft-Hartley Act with its power to prohibit strikes and boycotts. In 1953 it was followed up with the creation of the Bi-State Waterfront Commission and its stringent regulatory actions and policing of the waterfront. The Commission assumed control of all major aspects of the dock labor process. The passage of the Bi-State Waterfront Compact signaled the de facto preemption of the fundamental premises of the Wagner Act, which was supposed to foster collective bargaining between workers and employers. The creation of the Waterfront Commission radically transformed the relations between shipping employers and dockworkers because it represented a shift in the location of the decision-making process, moving it away from the direct intervention of the longshoremen. Attempts by the ILA to have the compact declared unconstitutional proved fruitless, and its permanence brought state political authorities into the struggle for control of the waterfront. The final major systemic transformation of labor was the passage of the Landrum-Griffin Act in 1959, which further refined the institutional boundaries of labor's power that were originally set forth with Taft-Hartley. During this period, the process of containment was further reinforced by myriad regional commercial regulations and the ideological flavor of McCarthyism, which on the waterfront gained practical expression with the use of various investigative agencies and loyalty programs directed primarily against rank-and-file activists.

The second phase of this process had two distinct strands. In one strand state political authorities sought to construct an alternative to the ILA with the support of the conservative AFL. When that effort proved ineffective, shipping companies constrained the actions of rebellious dockworkers through legal measures that limited the scale and scope of the reform movement. Even though at one point both strands were interwoven, the second phase relied primarily on the extensive political influence of shipping elites and the support of local and regional authorities to redefine legal understandings, as well as their authority to rapidly enact new ones. In this process shipping employers were just as likely to use the NLRB to file claims against rebellious workers as was the union to file claims against the shipping companies. A good example was the dockworkers' claim for coast-wide bargaining.

Dockworkers sought to expand their control of the waterfront labor process by negotiating a single contract for the entire East Coast. When employers refused to even consider the matter, a long strike ensued. Shipping employers moved swiftly against the dock union. The NLRB decided that the demand for a coast-wide agreement was an "unfair labor practice" and that any attempt to make such a claim would give employers the right to request a federal injunction against the ILA. This decision severely limited not only the union's immediate power but also the scope in which collective bargaining could occur in the future. Thus it became a permanent restriction that employers revived every time negotiations went in an unfavorable direction. The denial of a coast-wide contract limited the demands that dockworkers could make and their power at the most basic level. Even though coast-wide bargaining was practiced unofficially, the effect of this NLRB decision laid the groundwork for a process that constrained the rights of workers to such a point that even the longshoremen's refusal to approve a contract proposal was considered an "unfair labor practice" and subject to federal injunction.

Power and Conflict on the Docks

Power on the waterfront was not monolithic. It was slowly but increasingly contested and fragmented after 1945, indicating how the broader political process helped shape power relations and contain the political aspirations of dockworkers. On one hand, within the framework of the institutions of the waterfront labor process, power was exercised based on formal relations between the ILA and the NYSA. On the East Coast, formal class representation (the relationship between the ILA and dockworkers) was weak and based on high levels of coercion and violence. In spite of this, workers confronted the violence inherent in the waterfront labor process and created informal yet politically resilient forms of organization that contested domination at the most basic level—pier by pier. The informal means of organization and protest, which were the longshoremen's initial response to organized and institutionally sanctioned coercion, became an alternative form of negotiating power relations, often moving the forum of negotiation outside of the institutional framework.

An equally important component of the process of waterfront reform was the activity of liberal political reformers. Through the organization of "citizens groups" as well as the actions of the Roman Catholic Church, liberals interceded and minimized what they viewed as the growing communist influence among dockworkers. This was achieved by moving the decision-making process away from the direct sphere of influence to the more distant and complex sphere of institutional politics. In this way class power is not simply the reflection of distinct geopolitical systems but rather an illustration of a single process of political development. Even though New York longshoremen continued to elect the same unscrupulous union officials who were entrenched in state and local politics, they were able to construct an alternative to their powerlessness outside of the formal labor process that allowed them to advance their claims.

Even though dockworkers contested and wrested varying degrees of control from employers, they were unable to prevent the transfer of the decision-making center from the docks to institutional spheres where they exercised little control or influence. By weaving the process of industrialization into the broader political structure, New York's waterfront employers were able to circumvent long-standing political institutions and reconfigure the way in which power was conceived.

Elite Interests, Coercion, and Non-Decision-Making

The ability of shipping elites to shape the waterfront labor process was not simply a reflection of economic and political influence to impose their will. It was also the political expression of local and state authorities, embedded within the economic structure and their ability to reshape the basic structure of the division of labor. Elites, in this sense, are not an autonomous group; they do not exist independently of the prevailing political order. Rather, their presence reflects the combination of political interests and economic wherewithal interwoven within the broader political structure. Because of this, their presence and political influence cannot be viewed merely as the conflict of competing interest groups. The labor process that emerged on the Port of New York as a result of this perverse reshaping of the political order draws, in part, on the concept of corporativism.[30] On the New York waterfront, shipping employers made the longshore labor process a junction where national and local political and economic interests intertwined in ways that afforded them the power to redefine the local and regional political structure.

The emergence of economic elites resulted from the process of industrialization at the turn of the century. They made their dominance felt in national politics, and those connected to the New York waterfront held a particularly prominent role.[31] The Port of New York employed a large part of the city's workforce (both directly and indirectly) and was the mainstay of much of New York's economic activity.[32] This made them less dependent on more typical regional development processes that were unfolding in other U.S. cities.[33] Moreover, it allowed New York's elites to bypass many of the economic incumbencies that were common to other large manufacturing centers, demonstrating a high level of political independence. At the time, New York was the largest manufacturing center in the nation. While other regions were constricted by regional protectionist policies, the city's elites exercised their political clout and were able to bypass these regulations because of their ties to the world economic market.[34]

Early on, the city's economic elites, connected directly or indirectly to the shipping industry, expanded their influence into the national political sphere, melding economic and political power. The gold standard linked international trade and the national financial market to the regulation of the wealth of the nation and thereby empowered New York's shipping entrepreneurs with expansive political wherewithal. The power of New York's shipping employers can be viewed not as an anomaly but, rather, as the capacity of the political structure to reproduce inequality. There is an analogy between economic and political power, where those in the lower strata are continuously undercut by the "systemic advantage" held by economic elites.[35]

The prominence of New York's economic and political elites, many of whom were connected in some shape or fashion to the shipping industry, drew upon their expansive political power to subjugate the demands of dockworkers and thus set them apart from other sectors of the working class. Elite interests, however, did not just rely on economic power; it also drew on ideological and political concepts deeply embedded in American society to enforce their control of the docks. Specifically, ideological coercion and extremely high levels of political repression were two other significant aspects of waterfront life.

The Politics of Coercion

Not surprisingly, anticommunism gained greater influence in American political life during the same period when the process of industrialization consolidated the convergence of elite political and economic power. Anticommunism is not just the repression of radical political tendencies, such as the Palmer Raids or McCarthyism, but also the ideological construction around which economic elites sought to define the conflict between the broad democratic promises of political equality and the expanding economic inequality and elite redesign of American political life. Within the context of laissez-faire economics, the growing claims for economic and social reform led to conflicting notions of democracy and laid the foundation for the repression of labor as a permanent aspect of American politics.[36] Political and economic elites perceived that the demands of the working class (particularly prominent in non-Anglo-Saxon communities) were "the disease of impossible expectations"[37] In this sense, anticommunism became an important component of the daily exercise of power by elites over labor. Anticommunism was the ideological foundation upon which businesses and industries developed mechanisms of political coercion to contain and limit the egalitarian demands of workers as well as shape the political alternatives available to them.

Political repression in the United States often occurred through informal albeit state-sanctioned ancillary organizations.[38] Shipping authorities used informal devices to limit and contain contesting claims to the status quo. This holds particularly true with regard to the use of political violence on the waterfront.[39] Contrary to many historical accounts that limit the existence of political repression to specific and usually exceptional periods of politics, the disproportionate coercion of labor unions was a permanent facet of American society. The constraint of labor organizations was a particularly significant factor during the 1920s when the convergence of economic and political interests of elites gained significant expression.[40] The conflict between elite economic interests and labor's democratic aspirations served to limit the ability of workers to translate economic demands into broader political power. The conflict was carried forward into the 1930s and 1940s, even if with greater or lesser visibility.

During the 1930s, even though President Franklin D. Roosevelt was primarily recognized for the New Deal's transformation of American social policy, with regard to the increasingly conservative political designs of elites, his role was at best dubious or arguably ineffective. The conflict between New Deal social policy and business interests and the Democrats' support for a conservative political agenda with regard to labor is a clear indication that underlying political interests moved beyond party affiliation and the more immediate tasks of the economy.[41] Notwithstanding the first two years of the Roosevelt administration, business interests laid the boundaries of the New Deal's impact on policy. In spite of the claims of business elites that FDR was "soft on communism," Roosevelt continued to support and expand the capacity of the FBI and J. Edgar Hoover's crusade against political dissenters. The speed with which McCarthyism gripped American political life by 1950 is an indication that, even though not easily visible during the 1930s and throughout the war, conservative political forces allied with economic elites were constructing new institutional ideological devices to constrain labor and its supporters.[42]

The creation of the Dies Committee in 1938, which was later transformed into the House Un-American Activities Committee (HUAC), illustrates the ideological constraints developed in the heyday of the New Deal. By 1945 the committee had been transformed into a permanent organization of Congress that would continue to exist well into the 1970s. For the first two years of its existence, the Dies Committee focused on right-wing activity. Then it switched its attention to the labor movement.[43]

Much along the same vein was the approval of the Smith Act. Enacted in 1941, the Smith Act was an essential piece of legislation that later enabled the federal government to jail and coerce political opposition. Significantly, it was initially used against labor. The institutional devices of political repression were well in place before the beginning of the Cold War. In this context, McCarthyism was a moment in American political life when the repression of labor became most notable. It was not simply the domestic shift toward Cold War politics. For labor the emergence of McCarthyism represented how elites pursued their interests in labor politics, a process that had been in the making for some time.[44] For political coercion to succeed on the scale and scope of McCarthyism, the convergence of the political interests of federal political authorities with economic elites was essential. In this sense, mechanisms of the federal political structure became devices for coercion and intimidation, drastically weakening labor's power.[45]

The deeper interests of economic elites in the national anticommunist campaign and its benefits for business are evident in the policy bulletin of the U.S. Chamber of Commerce. The organ of business elites argued: "From the larger point of view, the cleansing of the labor movement of communism will have important results for the entire country. It will lead to sounder, more peaceful, and more reasonable labor relations." Of the four main areas of activity analyzed in the report, labor is considered a fundamental area of concern.[46] For economic elites, the institutional incentive to carry forth the "un-American" purges was political expediency, necessary for the protection and expansion of their interests.

The political repression of labor unions was coordinated through legislation and regulation. Major expressions of this strategy were the Taft-Hartley Act in 1947 and the Landrum-Griffin Act in 1959. Among its many provisions, the Taft-Hartley Act restricted many of the advances made by unions during the New Deal, principally in the area of organization and bargaining. This was accomplished by expanding the injunction power of the federal government and denying legal recourse of the National Labor Relations Board to unions where suspected communists held leadership positions. It reflected a broad consensus of political and economic elites in both political parties to contain labor's broader political demands. Democrats and Republicans alike supported the Act.[47]

The same political alliance would approve the Labor-Management Reporting and Disclosure Act of 1959, also known as the Landrum-Griffin Act, further constricting labor's effectiveness by imposing a rigid regulatory structure and federal control over labor organizations. Politically, the approval of the measure reflected the alliance of business elites (with the broad support of Democrats and Republicans alike) to limit the power of labor, both politically and economically, by redefining its priorities.[48] In both cases, in spite of the labor movement's political ally, the Democratic Party, and its strong representation in Congress, economic elite interests were able to reshape the original configuration of labor legislation proposed in the Wagner Act, placing further constraints on class organization. With regard to New York's longshore rank-and-file movement, both measures were disastrous, limiting not only their bargaining power and the terms of negotiation but also the ability of dockworkers to effectively transform their unions.

The impact of McCarthyism and Cold War politics for the labor movement cannot be underestimated. It was a wholesale ideological attack by economic elites and the national state, which helped reconfigure the way in which labor participated in American politics. Relying on myriad security-loyalty programs, employers sought to purge the most active sectors of the labor movement.[49] New York's longshoremen were among the hardest hit. The main reason for this was the importance of the New York waterfront for the U.S. economy. The political influence of New York's shipping companies was essential for the maintenance of the highly lucrative waterfront labor process where the unregulated hiring process called the "shape-up" was still in existence. The hiring of dockworkers in New York remained under the control of the shipping companies and the ILA. The East Coast contrasted sharply with the West Coast, where since the General Strike of 1934 the ILWU had attained control of the hiring process, which was regulated by a seniority system that made political blacklisting harder to impose. Many longshoremen screened off the East Coast docks found their way out west, where they joined the ranks of the ILWU. Different from other sectors of the economy, on the waterfront, economic demands could rapidly take on a highly political connotation impacting on domestic as well as foreign policy. The federal government was relentless in following the movement of longshore labor activists on the East and West Coasts, particularly the latter, since the union had demonstrated high levels of political independence and militancy. As early as 1936, J. Edgar Hoover repeatedly alerted FDR to the dangers of the ILWU and Harry Bridges and the threat of "communist control" of the labor movement, which remained the focus of Hoover's attentions for most of the period.[50]

After the war, U.S. foreign policy and elite economic interests in Europe and Asia continued to drive the process of control and repression of dock labor activists. As the Korean War became a reality, so did the scrutiny and control of waterfront labor. Claiming the preservation of national interests and the war effort, the federal government began to tighten security measures and purge labor activists from the docks. The shipping industry found themselves with an "unfriendly union" on the West Coast and the growing inability of the ILA to control dockworkers on the Port of New York, which was repeatedly gripped by wildcat strikes. Riding the wave of the un-Americanism hysteria, the shipping companies "screened" dockworkers for their political allegiances using the threat of economic sanctions to foster "better labor relations." Moreover, the heightened security of the waterfront did not apply only to those ports directly involved in war transportation. Under pressure from the shipping employers and conservative union officials, the port security plan was still being implemented long after the Korean War had ended, in such out-of-the-way locations as the Mississippi River.[51]

For conservative unions the port security programs had an added attraction: by diminishing the effectiveness of left-led unions and rank-and-file movements, they could expand their jurisdiction and weaken any threat of a challenge from below. Mechanisms of the federal government were the centerpiece of the process of political repression.[52] In this way, relying on devices of institutional political power, elites purged activists from the docks and sought to reshape labor politics according to their own interests during what is considered by most to be one of the darkest moments in American political life.

Power and Political Violence

The repression of labor as a means of ensuring elite interests was accomplished through the use of economic sanctions—that is, by threatening to fire dockworkers.[53] On the New York waterfront, political violence sanctioned by local authorities became the norm. Widespread violence reflected the ability of economic elites to control rebellious dockworkers and influence rank-and-file demands for reform.

The relations between employers and the ILA depended on the union's ability to continuously coerce and contain the dock labor force. Repression of activists allowed the shipping companies to stem the tide of contestation and reinforce the union's control over the docks. This in turn permitted the NYSA to continue to regulate labor through the shape-up system and to regulate shipping costs through the constant oversupply of workers on the docks, a central contention of New York's dockworkers. Furthermore, the long-lasting reign of violence exercised by the ILA existed in large part because state and city political authorities made no real attempt to enforce the rule of law. Violence permeated waterfront unionism because authorities either "turned a blind eye," failing to properly investigate charges, or covered up crimes in one of the most violent sectors of American trade unionism.

The feeble attempts on the part of the local and state officials to pros-
ecute gangster union officials reflected a deeper understanding of an informal sanction of the ILA's repressive rule: the role of political violence
within the context of waterfront unionism and its relation to the dominant
political order.[54] Violence was not just a means of containing rebellious
dockworkers. It was also an intricate part of economic activity, the way
of "doing business." As far back as the early 1920s, success in the business
world relied increasingly on the use of violence.[55]

Elite interests, reflected in the perverse bonding of the shipping companies with gangster union officials in the ILA and local political authorities,
not only limited the ability of New York's longshoremen to control their
union but subsequently reshaped their perception of "them and us" and
helped to construct a movement where class issues and economic interests
converged. The distinct nature of waterfront activism became an important catalyst for reshaping the local political order. Ultimately, the effect of
political repression in any and all of its forms, independent of the number
of individuals directly victimized, has a much broader reach. The chilling
effect of combined economic sanctions and the threat of physical violence
against rebellious dockworkers went beyond those directly affected and
was well known to the thousands of workers who made their livelihood
on the waterfront. The notion of class among dockworkers is significant in
that it provides the basis for alternative concepts and forms of organization
that emerged from the longshore labor process, becoming a device of permanent contention between dockworkers, elites, and political authorities.

Class, Power, and Resistance

For New York's longshoremen, the notion of class served as the basis for
a culture of resistance that resulted from the specific conditions that developed within the dock labor process and was compounded by the waterfront's predominant role in the political economy. The dockworkers'
subculture of resistance is particularly significant given the complexity of
how class and power were conceived and subsequently how longshoremen
developed their response to societal constraints.[56] Specifically, the characteristics of the dockworkers' subculture of resistance reflected the general
conditions of the waterfront labor process; casual employment with no at-
tachment to a single employer, brutal and dangerous working conditions,

the lack of occupational mobility, and the shared belief that they are at the lower strata of the working class—all of which help strengthen notions of group and occupational solidarity.[57]

Traditional Marxist analysis views the role of class in the political process fundamentally as a device through which the increasing class consciousness of workers within the process of capitalist economic development is a catalyst for a political movement that would inevitably seize control and transform the structures of power. In broad terms, they view elites as the "ruling class" bound by emerging interests that originate in the process of capitalist economic development.[58]

Class and power are never purely the result of economic activity. They also reflect the sociopolitical and cultural interaction between different groups with competing interests. In this process, political and economic interests cut across societal hierarchies and define the parameters for conflict. Essential to understanding how class functions within the broader political structure is the process through which class issues are transformed into political conflict. On the docks, the division of labor was a central mechanism for class formation because it is through this process that groups with similar interests converge and through which longshoremen organized resistance to the ILA leadership and the NYSA.[59]

Class, however, is not a static concept, and for longshoremen, notions of class were constantly reshaped at work and at home.[60] Class activity on the waterfront emerged from the interchange at multiple levels of the political process, and it provides an alternative to institutional class constraints.

The unique culture of resistance peculiar to longshoremen, while based on their shared interests, was not just tradition; rather, it was closely linked to their particular experience at work and the waterfront's insertion in the political economy.[61] Shared interests, however, are not the center from which notions of class emerged. Although they are important, shared interests are but one of the many devices through which social, political, and economic interchange occurs. The political spectrum under which notions of class are constructed is much broader.

On the docks, class interests wove together the longshoremen's claim for reform with the demands of local political and economic elites organized in the NYSA. The broad political context from which the movement for reform of the waterfront emerged produced both progressive and conservative class responses to the longshoremen's demand for reform.[62] Class consciousness and power as conditions for collective action on the docks reflect the interaction between distinct social forces that produce multiple alternatives in the heat of struggle.

Class interests on the waterfront quickly transformed what at first appeared to be economic claims into a broad political conflict, melding the economic and political characteristics of the longshore reform movement. During much of the conflict, purely economic issues were more easily resolved whereas the longshoremen's claim for greater control of the dock labor process remained highly contentious, thus demonstrating a correlation among political and economic elite interests. Political and economic democracy is not a distinct characteristic of American society. Class, as an organizing concept, is at the center of how working-class power gains greater expression, and it is the platform from which economic issues quickly gained expansive political expression.[63]

The growing process of waterfront mobilization, strikes, and political struggle illustrates how New York's dockworkers conceived a political process driven by class interests but bounded by formal and informal institutional constraints. The prominent role of class interests in the movement for waterfront reform and the way in which class interaction and conflict are permanent, if not always visible, are critical aspects of working-class life on the Port of New York.

2

Who Controls the Waterfront?

The initial stage of postwar waterfront reform reflected the growing challenge by New York's dockworkers to the system of domination carried over from the prewar period characterized by high levels of political violence and intimidation. This process laid the groundwork for the transition to a formalized institutional structure of control, which joined the actions of state and federal political authorities, business elites, and conservative trade unionists. Shipping elites controlled the dock labor force through their alliance with the ILA leadership and the acquiescence of local political authorities, leaving few alternatives for reform outside of open rebellion. The rank-and-file response during the initial years of this phase mirrored the popular front paradigm of political alliances. That is, reformers sought to construct a broad alliance of distinct and often conflicting political forces. They were united by the central objective to reform the waterfront labor process and the democratic transformation of the ILA. Both the system of domination and the political alliances of those in favor of reform, however, were rapidly changed as business elites sought to contain the mounting longshore revolt.

Two years of tumultuous wildcat strikes on the port, between 1945 and 1947, signaled the growing incapacity of the ILA leadership to continue controlling dock labor through traditional devices of domination. Shipping elites, with the recently passed Taft-Hartley Act as the centerpiece, began mounting an arsenal of weapons of their own. During this period shipping elites and state political authorities constructed the framework for a long-term strategy that sought, over time, not only to contain the rebellious movement of longshoremen but also to reconfigure its characteristics and set the agenda for future conflict. A major characteristic of this process required expanding the power of state and federal political authorities who, working in conjunction with conservative forces within the trade union movement, defined the terms of conflict. In this process, latent ideological constraints within the dock labor force were enhanced, resulting in the fragmentation of traditional political alliances. The campaign to "free the waterfront of its criminal elements" led by then New York governor Thomas Dewey served as the point of convergence where conservative political forces staked their claim in the struggle for control of the waterfront. Drawing primarily on the support of disaffected forces within the ILA and the AFL leadership, state-sponsored intervention into the process of waterfront reform added new forces, the most significant of which were the state political authorities of New York and New Jersey.

In October 1945, just five months after the end of World War Two, New York's dockworkers staged a wildcat strike, a grassroots initiative that would turn into a highly politicized and contentious movement. Challenging the ILA leadership and demanding greater democracy in the decision-making process, rank-and-file dockworkers were in fact making a claim for greater control. Even though Local 791, on the Chelsea piers of Manhattan, started the strike, informal organizations led by left-wing dockworkers quickly expanded their role. In this sense, the wildcat strike would increasingly reflect competing political forces that made their presence felt. This process of political alignment united distinct political forces with ties to New York's political elites who viewed the growing contention on the docks as a signal that the traditional alliances with the ILA leadership would not survive. They sought to reposition themselves, legitimize their presence in the reform movement, and ultimately influence the way in which reform would occur.

Before examining the post–World War Two wildcat strikes, it is important, if only briefly, to review the framework upon which longshoremen constructed their contentious movement. Long years of sustained collective action challenged the dominant view that New York's dockworkers were a conservative or restrained sector of the working class. While social movements are not simply the rebellious actions of social groups, in the case of New York's dockworkers, rebellious actions were an important aspect of cumulative collective experience, which shaped the activity of the organized reform movement. Independent action was not just something that happened sporadically on the docks. It was a way of life and means of survival.

Shape-up and Casual Work

The characteristics that consolidated the waterfront labor process are indicative of the dialectical nature of power and work. Control over the workforce was vital. Longshoremen were one of the most controlled sectors of the working class.[1] Fundamentally, whoever controlled the hiring of dock labor literally controlled the waterfront. Moreover, the hiring of dock labor defined relations between workers and employers in two distinct ways. On one hand, it was a coercive device. But over time, it also served as a vehicle through which dockworkers would construct notions of group solidarity fundamental for the rank-and-file movement. A central aspect was the form in which dock labor was hired; the labor-intensive characteristics of longshore work were regulated by the shape-up. This was a process where dockworkers would congregate in front of the piers three times daily, at 7 A.M., at noon, and then at 7 P.M., to compete for work. They were paid an hourly rate with no guaranteed work period. Work could last one hour or twenty, and longshoremen often faced long stints of unemployment in between jobs. Their survival depended exclusively on the needs of the shipping companies.[2]

Within the shape-up, some variation in hiring practices did occur: some piers would hire on a weekly basis while others would give priority to hiring longshoremen by the gang. What united all longshoremen, in whatever form the shape-up took, was the infrequency of work, given the constant oversupply of dock labor. The uncertainty and insecurity created by the shape-up permeated the process from the foremen to the dockworker in the hold of the ship.[3]

According to the records of the 1910 Wainwright Commission on Unemployment, there was great disparity in hiring practices. The hiring of one stevedore company examined over a nine-week period fluctuated between 22,890 and 44,878 man-hours worked.[4] This placed the competition for work as an intricate part of the waterfront labor process and a means of direct control of any incipient rebellion. With 120,000 longshoremen in the United States in 1930, it is estimated that 50,000 worked on the Port of New York.[5] The waterfront labor process led to a highly coercive and corrupt work environment based on the daily concession of work.

However "casual" dock labor may be, it was not unskilled labor, as the ship owners had long contended.[6] The particular knowledge necessary for dock work led to the formation of permanent work gangs. Moreover, the collective nature of dock work and workers' reliance on each other would later help consolidate the rank-and-file movement.[7] The "system" also provided the power by which the ILA and the shipping companies exercised their iron-fisted control over longshoremen.[8] This relationship affected elites and dockworkers alike. While the shape-up and the casual nature of work were devices through which the shipping companies and the ILA leadership exercised control over the labor force, it also served as a catalyst which in time helped consolidate the unique concept of collective solidarity and framed the conditions for the rank-and-file revolt beginning in 1939.

As early as 1874, strikes sporadically paralyzed the Port of New York, many times erupting into massive protests. In 1907, Brooklyn dockworkers had walked off the ships protesting their mistreatment by foremen. This strike, which came to be known as the Italian May Day of Brooklyn, united dockworkers and warehouse workers from Brooklyn and lower Manhattan, many of whom did not belong to any formal labor organization.[9] While most of the earlier sporadic strike movements were defeated, they became emblematic of the growing notion of group solidarity among dockworkers based on shared interests consolidated by the distinct nature of work and was expressed through direct action. During the early part of the century, the Port of New York continued to be the scene of sporadic and unorganized conflict against the highly oppressive working conditions.

By the 1930s, independent rank-and-file activity on the waterfront had become an extremely difficult endeavor—not that it was any easier during other periods. Activists simultaneously confronted the union under the leadership of Joe Ryan, president, and Emil Camarda, vice president, the shipping companies, and the local political structure represented by state and city politicians. It was an environment where a rebellious longshoreman could lose his livelihood and his life. The characteristics of waterfront unionism consisted of corruption, violence, and political patronage that left longshoremen to their own devices when they wanted to better their conditions. These attributes set New York waterfront unions apart from the expanding industrial trade union movement in the United States organized around notions of mutual solidarity. The concept of mutual solidarity for waterfront workers came not from the union but from the rank and file and its informal organization.

The political wherewithal of the ILA and its supremacy over longshoremen pointed to two distinct aspects of life on the waterfront. Their domination was both economic and political and had far-reaching connections to New York's Democratic Party. Longshore political patronage was administered through the "City Democratic Club," organized by Emil Camarda's brother and other ILA officials.[10] Another form of political articulation was the Joseph P. Ryan Annual Dinner Committee, and other informal devices such as contributions to Ryan's "Anti-Communist Fighting Fund." Illustrative of the alliance between employers, the ILA, and the local political structure, William J. McCormick was the chairman of the Arrangements Committee for the annual dinner organization. He was a waterfront employer with personal relations with FDR and strong ties to the New York State Democratic Party. Among the many guests of the waterfront union leaders, between 1931 and 1951, were Governor Franklin D. Roosevelt, Mayor James Walker, Mayor Fiorello LaGuardia, and Police Commissioner Edward Mulroony, as well as the district attorneys for Manhattan, the Bronx, Brooklyn, and Queens.[11]

The alliance between the ILA leadership and the local political structure involved heavy campaign contributions in exchange for protection of the pier rackets, facilitating pier leases, and the use of the waterfront for job patronage. Just days before the New York State Crime Commission hearings to investigate corruption on the waterfront, Borough President Robert Wagner, vice president for the Annual Dinner, consorted with gangsters like John "Cockeyed" Dunn. Dunn received the support of New York City Councilman Adam Clayton Powell Jr. and Congressman George Tinkham of Massachusetts, who helped him obtain early parole from a previous coercion conviction.[12] Later convicted for the murder of a longshoreman, Dunn was executed by the state of New York. The waterfront union leadership had the political influence necessary to stall or restrain any investigation into the claims of corruption and violence.

It was the brutality of longshore work and the perverse relations between dockworkers and their unions that laid the basis for independent action. The newsletters and rank-and-file groups that continuously appeared in spite of the repressive nature of waterfront unionism on the East Coast illustrate the strong notion of independent action among dockworkers that existed through permanent, albeit informal, means of organization. Over different periods, distinct rank-and-file groups were organized; they assumed the same characteristics, presented similar demands, and relied on similar devices and concepts of independent action. Rank-and-file activism on the docks of New York and Brooklyn indicates a notion of class that was different from that of most American workers. The fact that workplace control was administered not only by employers but also by the unions, and later by the government, shaped the nature of collective action among dockworkers. In this context, the notion of mutual solidarity, a characteristic traditionally developed by labor organizations, i.e., formal union organizations, for New York dockworkers came from the actions of the rank-and-file activists and their informal means of organization outside of the formal union structure.

On the waterfront, informal means of organization and communication assumed the political space traditionally occupied by the union. In this sense, the culture of independent action and their informal organization are central characteristics of class identity among dockworkers. The traditional notion of class division, "them and us," where "them" means the employers and "us" signifies the working class, was fundamentally different in the case of the longshoremen. "Them" meant the employers, the government, and the union; "us" meant the dockworkers and their different devices for survival. Early on, the union assumed the characteristics of a supplier of labor and an administrator of the work process rather than a defender of the exploited workforce.

By redefining the dockworkers' recurring mobilizations as a social movement, long-term class objectives of both workers and elites gain greater clarity and allow for a more precise view of the interaction of conflicting forces. On the waterfront, the collective challenge of longshoremen appears through wildcat strikes and pier mobilizations as a means of negotiating both long- and short-term demands. An essential moment in the collective challenge is the ability of movement leaders to combine intermittently formal and informal methods of collective action.[13]

Starting in 1939, the notion of "common purpose" gained greater clarity and organized expression with the longshoremen's initial movement for reform when the demand to end the shape-up provoked large-scale mobilization. It was the first organized rank-and-file movement to appear on the waterfront interconnecting economic and political demands. This movement ultimately created a permanent common denominator that laid the basis for constructing the collective identity of New York's dockworkers and shaped the parameters for their unique notion of "them and us."

Greater evidence of the emerging reform movement crystallizes in 1945, when longshoremen began combining formal and informal means of organization and collective action within the wildcat strike movement. The third component of a social movement reflected the ability of rank-and-file activists to maintain a protracted movement for waterfront reform that began in 1939 and continued into the early 1970s.[14]

The possibilities for reform, however, depended not only on the longshoremen's sustained mobilization but also on the actions of elites, who were increasingly unable to control the waterfront through traditional means.[15] Their movement brought to the forefront economic demands that were politically significant. Even though short-lived, their experience during the 1930s became emblematic of waterfront unionism in New York after World War Two.

The Brooklyn Rank and File Committee and Pete Panto

Unfortunately, the assassination of rank-and-file labor leaders was not uncommon in the history of the American working class, particularly during the accentuated class struggles of the 1930s and 1940s. In 1935, dockworkers in Brooklyn began organizing the first broad movement for waterfront reform. Class politics and culture were reflected in the struggle between those who controlled the unions and those led by Pete Panto, who organized open resistance to the corrupt union leadership. More than just a case of political violence and corruption, the movement initiated by Panto and the Brooklyn Rank and File Committee was a microcosm of the growing culture of independent action among East Coast dockworkers. The factors that shaped this culture were the casual nature of longshore work, the incessant need for brute force, the extremely low wages,[16] and a common understanding that outside of their distinct community there was no formal means for redress. Since their emergence on the waterfront, longshoremen were at the lowest level of the American working class. Culture in this context is not only a particular occupational community of workers but a common identity of shared interests based on ideological, socioeconomic, and political factors. The importance of the Pete Panto case was that for the first time the notion of independent action and informal organization were combined simultaneously, giving the movement the unprecedented ability to mobilize dockworkers outside of general movements for higher wages. In this case the principal grievance of the dockworkers was for democracy and not higher wages. Democracy for Panto and the committee could only be achieved by contesting the "shape-up" hiring system, which was a central mechanism that determined who controlled the waterfront. By contesting the existence of the shape-up, they not only questioned the very nature of the New York waterfront structure but the relations of the gangster union officials to local political structure as well.

Panto was a radical Italian longshoreman who was murdered in the summer of 1939 by gangsters who controlled the ILA in Brooklyn. Sixty years after his death there are still people in the Red Hook section of Brooklyn who remember the case. This also illustrates the chilling effect that political repression and violence have as a deterrent for collective action. It was not uncommon for activists on the docks to disappear.[17]

In the mid-1930s, a group of radical dockworkers with political ties to the American Labor Party and the Communist Party formed the Brooklyn Rank and File Committee, influenced by the sweeping changes that were occurring on the West Coast waterfront under the leadership of Harry Bridges. The Committee sought to transform working conditions on the Brooklyn docks. They contested the shape-up hiring system that encouraged corruption. Longshoremen often had to kick back as much as 25 percent of their salary.[18] The antidemocratic nature of the waterfront unions, the extremely harsh working conditions, particularly in Brooklyn,[19] and the casual nature of dock labor were used to control longshoremen.

Twenty-eight-year-old Pete Panto was at the center of the Rank and File Committee. Its initial activities included a newsletter called *Shape-Up*. The bulletin served to organize and invigorate longshoremen who were already growing dissatisfied with the gangster-dominated union. Brooklyn's dockworkers were forced to give salary kickbacks to guarantee steady work and contribute to fictitious banquets and dinner dances organized by the union officials. Other forms of extortion consisted of paying for haircuts and shaves at a local barber shop without ever receiving either, as well as being forced to shop at certain grocery stores in the Red Hook section, where the prices were usually higher than normal. As one longshoreman reported to the newspapers of that period: "I haven't worked in six weeks now . . . not a day, because I paid one kick back, and a few hours later another fellow came along and demanded more. I refused. I haven't worked since."[20]

The political control of the Italian American working-class community was another important aspect of the domination exerted by waterfront union officials over Brooklyn dockworkers. As another longshoreman from Brooklyn pointed out: "They check up on us, after the votes are counted in the Italian neighborhood they can figure out pretty much what percentage of the men voted as they were told. If too many men voted the other way a lot of men from that neighborhood found themselves without work just as a warning."[21]

Panto and the Committee directed the struggle against the ILA leadership. They continually contested the actions of the union leadership and, as the movement grew, opened an office at 186 Remsen Street in Brooklyn. Their newsletter began publishing letters from longshoremen on different piers complaining of the brutal working conditions, discrimination in the shape-up, and even the existence of professional gamblers in the leadership of local unions.

The growing discontent among longshoremen became evident as Panto began to organize open-air meetings in front of the piers. At one of the first large meetings, in Brooklyn in June 1939, 800 longshoremen participated. CIO organizer Sam Madell reported that the open meetings "were a tremendous success. . . . The whole neighborhood resounded with the enthusiasm and cheering of the longshoremen. . . . Every time union hiring hall and rotary hiring was mentioned the longshoremen went wild."[22] This was an unprecedented event that helped lay the groundwork for the anti-Ryan rally held on July 3, where more than 1,500 dockworkers gathered to show their support.[23] The massive public demonstration of dockworkers for a democratic union in such an organized form had never been witnessed before. The radical longshoremen counted on the support of Congressman Vito Marcantonio of the American Labor Party (ALP), who spoke at the rally.[24] Friends, however, continually warned Panto of the growing danger, to which he responded that he would not be frightened.[25] Others were more skeptical, as Sam Kovnat, a CIO field organizer, remembered: "It would be a slow process, because in spite of the enthusiasm of the men, we are yet to see how they react when [gangster] Camarda's gunmen start to work."[26]

Pete Panto's organizing activity did not go unnoticed by the union officials. At first they tried to weaken the growing support for the reform movement by spreading the word: "he's a Red, he's a radical, he'll get you and the union in trouble." When that failed, they tried to bribe him, and finally they resorted to threatening him. It was said that he often reacted by grinning at the gangsters who were sent to threaten him and would continue to tell the dockworkers, "We are strong. . . . All we have to do is stand up and fight."[27]

One of the last threats he received came shortly before his disappearance. Camarda told Panto: "The boys don't like what you're doing so lay off." After returning from work at 5 P.M. on July 14, 1939, Panto seemed worried. Friends who saw him leave work declared later that before going home Pete confided that he was "going to meet two guys he didn't trust."[28] Leaving his rented room at 11 North Elliott Place two hours later, Pete told Michael Maffia, his fiancée's brother, that if he did not return by ten the next morning they should call the police. Pete never returned home.

Later testimony by Abe Reles, member of Murder, Inc., to the Brooklyn district attorney described the way Panto was taken to the house of waterfront gangster Jim Ferraco. Albert "the Enforcer" Anastasia and Mendy Weiss met them inside the house. On Albert's orders, Mendy Weiss strangled Panto and dumped his body in a lime pit in Lyndhurst, New Jersey.[29]

On February 17, 1941, Albert Tannenbaum, a Murder Inc. associate, in testimony to Assistant District Attorney Heffernan, gave a more detailed account of the Panto assassination. He revealed a discussion he had with Mendy Weiss shortly after Panto's disappearance. Tannenbaum declared: "He [Mendy Weiss] goes on to tell me that Ferraco, Anastasia, and himself were in a house waiting for somebody to bring some Wop [sic]. There they were supposed to kill and bury him. He said the guy just stepped into the door and must have realized what was about to happen and tried to get out. He almost got out. It's a lucky thing I was there. . . . It's Panto, some guy Albert had a lot of trouble with down on the waterfront and was threatening to get Albert into a lot of trouble. . . . He tried all sorts of ways to win him over and quiet him down, but he couldn't do anything with him. He had to kill him."[30]

Assistant District Attorney Burton Turkus narrated the struggle between Pete Panto and the waterfront thugs: "He gave them a terrific battle. Mendy was a 200-pounder, built like an ox. The labor crusader was a slim 163. He struggled with the desperation of a man fighting for his life. Somehow he managed to get his teeth around one of Mendy's stumpy fingers, and came close to chewing the digit clear off."[31] Immediately after Panto's disappearance, the ILA union officials appointed a new "hiring boss" (Panto's job), who took over the shape-up on the Moore McCormick pier and refused to hire men connected to the Rank and File Committee or friendly with Panto.[32]

Panto's death spurred extensive political action among progressives and trade unionists. In the aftermath of Panto's disappearance, an organization of progressives was formed called the "Pete Panto Memorial Committee." The Committee united intellectuals, trade unionists, and progressive politicians. Their strategy was to mobilize public opinion in order to compel the police and local government to find those responsible for Panto's disappearance. The executive board of the Pete Panto Memorial Committee included Richard Wright (author), Michael Quill (president of the Transport Workers Union), Ruth McKenny (author), Vito Marcantonio (ALP congressman), Frederick Myers (field organizer, National Maritime Union), Rev. Reginald Bass (Park Community Church), Nat Einhorn (Newspaper Guild), Dr. Bella Dodd (Teachers Union Local 3), and Mary Testa (editor of *L'Unità del Popolo*). The Rank and File Committee of Brooklyn longshoremen immediately launched an informational campaign about Panto's disappearance, seeking to pressure the union and local politicians. A few days later, the question "dovè Panto?" ("Where is Panto?") began to appear on the pier walls as well as in pamphlets distributed by the Committee.[33]

Early in the investigation of Panto's disappearance, both the special prosecutor, Herlands, and his investigator, Roland Sala, kept promising the rank-and-file activists "sensational developments," but nothing ever came of it. In January 1940, in a meeting with the Committee, the newly appointed district attorney, William O'Dwyer, also promised action. Almost a year after Panto's disappearance, in June 1940, during an open meeting of the Rank and File Committee (Local 929), union delegate and Camarda goon Johnny Erato responded to heckling by workers who questioned the whereabouts of Panto by stating: "He was misled by the wrong guys, if he had listened to the right guys nothing would have happened to him. If he had been smart, Pete Panto wouldn't have gotten his." The Committee sent this information to O'Dwyer, who never admitted to receiving the letter, nor did he take any action after he was given the new information. At a second meeting between O'Dwyer and the Panto Committee in October 1940, the district attorney admitted that Panto had been murdered but refused to reveal the source of that information. When the Committee declared that ultimately the deeper question concerning Panto's death was the corrupt gangster-dominated waterfront unions, O'Dwyer stated that he had "cleaned up waterfront gangsterism."[34]

At the same time, political and physical violence continued to mount against other waterfront activists. At the October 9, 1940, Rank and File Committee meeting, Pete Mazzei and other activists were severely beaten by Gus Camaniti, Nino Camarda, and Johnny Erato, who attempted to break up the meeting. Even though police protection was requested earlier, the police did not respond until after the assault had taken place and the meeting hall had been destroyed.[35] The three gangsters were arrested only to be acquitted months later. The reluctance of the police and local authorities to intervene allowed the union to repress longshore activists until it was almost impossible for activists to hold public meetings, thus driving them underground. Various attempts to find a meeting place were fruitless because the hall owners always backed down under pressure from the gangsters.

Pressure to investigate the Panto assassination came from the docks as well. Shortly before January 1941, Italian longshoremen in Brooklyn organized "Il Circolo Educativo Pete Panto" (Pete Panto Educational Club). It was a means of keeping his memory alive and organizing dockworkers. The club's first president was Gennaro Sasso, a short, stocky man and longtime member of the Communist Party. With the cynicism common among longshoremen, Sasso understood that only independent action would change the situation. The honorary chairman of the Pete Panto Educational Club was Vito Marcantonio. At one of the first meetings, Mike Mazzola, representing Marcantonio, read the following message: "I greet the people who are interested in the Pete Panto case. This case is of vital importance to organized labor. The members of organized labor and the people of the City of New York in general are not only interested in the apprehension of the killers of Pete Panto, but they are concerned in the apprehension and bringing to justice of those who hired the killers. Until those who were behind the assassination of Pete Panto are punished no rank and file member of organized labor is safe."[36]

Both O'Dwyer and the assistant district attorney, Edward Heffernan, deliberately refused to act in spite of the information they continued to receive regarding Panto's death. This coincided with a campaign of terror waged by goons associated with the ILA. The consequences of O'Dwyer and Heffernan's inaction combined with gangster violence served to gradually demoralize the once growing rank-and-file movement on the Brooklyn waterfront. It is also alleged that Emil Camarda was the godfather to one of Heffernan's children.[37] A subsequent review of O'Dwyer and Heffernan's role in the Panto investigation confirmed the allegations. A Kings County grand jury declared: "The indisputable proof is that William O'Dwyer and Edward Heffernan, the Assistant District Attorney, were in possession of competent legal evidence that Anastasia was guilty of first degree murder. . . . We find the 'perfect murder case' was presented and almost completed to the Kings County Grand Jury in May of 1940 by Heffernan who then suspended and abandoned the case. He stated that the case was dropped on instructions from his superiors."[38]

In his January 1940 meeting with the Panto Memorial Committee, O'Dwyer did not mention any knowledge of the case, and only in October 1940 did he acknowledge that Panto had been murdered. But as the grand jury investigation indicated, by May 1940 O'Dwyer's office had almost completed its investigation, which then should have been presented for further legal action. O'Dwyer had had concrete information about the Panto murder since March 1940, when Abe Reles testified before him. In November 1941, Reles, the principal witness for the district attorney, mysteriously "fell" out of a window at a Coney Island hotel where he was being held under police protection. Shortly afterward, the Panto case was closed.[39]

The immediate effect of the Panto assassination was also a message sent to all who attempted to organize New York's longshoremen. After Panto's death, the Rank and File Committee was quickly isolated. Hounded by gangsters and receiving no protection from local authorities, the Committee found little solidarity in the surrounding community that had initially supported Panto. Sam Madell recalled the Red Hook community's reaction to Panto's assassination: "The Brooklyn waterfront was terrorized. . . . The doors that were opened to me previously, closed. You couldn't get anyone to talk."[40] Most of their political support after Panto's death came from progressives outside the Red Hook neighborhood. If the mass mobilization among dockworkers was unprecedented, Panto's murder sent the rank-and-file movement into hiding, a condition from which it would never fully emerge.

The Resurgence of Rank-and-File Mobilization, 1945

Four years after the demise of the Brooklyn Rank and File Committee, longshoremen on the Port of New York and Brooklyn reignited intense class conflict. Once again dockworkers simultaneously battled the NYSA, the state and local authorities, and their union, the ILA. Different rank-and-file groups present on the waterfront organized the wildcat strikes that erupted after World War Two. The movement paralyzed the transportation of goods and military troops, both domestically and abroad. Over a seven-year period, they initiated a process through which they continuously imposed financial losses in the millions of dollars and mobilized thousands of workers. The wildcat strike movement that expanded over several years was the resurgence of reform activism but with a much broader political composition, which allowed greater diversity in strategies and tactics. This movement eventually consolidated the activists' presence on the waterfront, constructing an alternative that contested the formal labor structure organized around the ILA.

The resurgence of the rebellious movement, however, is more complex and more far-reaching. The broad political and social implications of the dockworkers' wildcat strike movement help us understand the role of class in American politics, where the interaction between elite groups and organized labor is not so straightforward. As a result of the insurgent dockworkers' movement, sectors of local political elites with ties to the Democratic Party were forced to reconfigure their alliances and restructure their relations with local economic elites. The dockworkers' reform movement helped reshape the relations between organized labor and the political structure in one of the major urban centers of the United States.

A deeper understanding of the waterfront labor process and the extent of its political influence, however, requires a comprehension of both labor and politics, not as discrete categories but as components of a single process linked by the interaction of workers, unions, and economic elites embedded in the political structure. Given the economic importance of the Port of New York and the implications that control of the waterfront unions had for the national economy, the longshoremen were able to expand the realm and consequences of their actions. In this sense, class-based informal action was synonymous with a reform movement that had broad political consequences surpassing the immediate and localized economic demands put forth by the rebellious workers.

The Postwar Political Economy of the Waterfront

The Port of New York had a particularly important role because of the magnitude that the export of manufactured goods (necessary to bolster the transition from wartime to a peace economy) played in the overall U.S. economy.[41] This process melded political and economic elite interests, making control of the waterfront a decisive factor.

The immediate effect of the transition from a war to a peacetime economy in the United States was reflected in an output reduction on the order of $82 billion, most of which was due to the decrease in government spending. In contrast, private-sector production decreased by only 3 percent, or $12 billion, and the almost immediate return to the production of consumer goods, housing construction, and the expansion of exports to Europe and Japan account for the relative stability of private-sector output. A fundamental ingredient for the postwar recovery of the United States depended on the success of such programs as the Marshall Plan and the Economic Recovery Plan for Japan, which stimulated the expansion of U.S. exports of manufactured goods. Economically the United States needed Europe almost as much as Europe needed U.S. economic aid. Moreover, the effect of the growing export economy was not limited to its direct impact on the Gross Domestic Product (GDP) alone; U.S. exports after the war had a far-reaching effect on the economy, in many cases indirectly, and even though not visible numerically, nonetheless highly significant.[42]

For the Marshall Plan to prevail, however, it was also necessary to gain the acquiescence of labor, particularly control of the Port of New York, the exit route from which a majority of U.S. exports sailed to Europe. It was no accident that the Taft-Hartley Act and the ideological purge of the labor movement coincided with the expansive economic growth experienced after World War Two. This conservative movement found an increasingly warm reception and led many labor organizations to retreat from their initial opposition to the act and to purge the more militant activists and leaders from their ranks. It was in this context that the CIO moved swiftly to adapt to the new policy toward labor. Secretary of State George C. Marshall addressed the 1947 convention of the CIO, which was in the midst of its own purges (realized just four months after the passage of the Taft-Hartley Act).[43] He was received with great pomp, including a military band.

Specifically with regard to the waterfront, the CIO went far beyond acceptance of Taft-Hartley and was essential in organizing and administering port security programs that were the result of a meeting of the Truman administration, the shipping companies, and conservative maritime unions in the summer of 1950.[44] It was in this complex and often highly adverse context that New York's dockworkers would challenge the union leadership and local regional political structure over the next ten years. In contrast to early rank-and-file activity that was dominated by left-wing organizations, groups with distinct political orientations and claims emerged after World War Two and found ready activists among the soldiers returning to civilian life seeking employment on the Port of New York. Behind the longshoremen's movement for higher wages was an intricate, class-based organization with ties to local politics, conceived by distinct class-oriented political organizations of workers, with accumulated years of experience and corresponding claims that originated in the mid-1930s with the Brooklyn Rank and File Committee.

The *Dockers News* group, political heir of the Brooklyn Rank and File Committee, illustrates how longshoremen perceived their situation. In the first issue of their newsletter, distributed on the Port of New York, they argued: "We dockworkers earn our money the hard way. Our work is the hardest, most backbreaking work you can find. The longshore industry has the second highest accident rate in the country, yet we don't have adequate safety regulations, or an adequate medical, pension or welfare plan. . . . The official figures of our employers, the New York Shipping Association, shows that three out of four longshoremen earn $10.00 a week or less."[45] Further studies indicate that between October 1950 and September 1951, approximately 41,000 longshoremen worked on the Port of New York, of which 11,000 workers were employed for 100 hours or less, 3,000 were employed between 100 and 200 hours, and some worked up to 3,000 hours per year. This indicates that the composition of the workforce was divided between those who found steady employment and a second group that was highly casual. During the same period, shipping companies made high net profits. For the fiscal year of 1951–52, one of the largest New York stevedore companies, Moore-McCormick, reported a net profit of approximately $19 million. Other shipping companies, such as the

U.S. Lines, reported a profit of $18 million, and even smaller companies, such as American Export Lines, reported net profits of almost $5 million.[46] The workers' claims went beyond the pure and simple demand for wage increases and included proposals that sought to transform relations with their unions as well as with economic groups influential in the state and local political structure.

The complex waterfront labor process that emerged after World War Two was shaped by four distinct factors: first, the shifting alliances of economic groups embedded within the local political structure; second, the antagonistic relations between dockworkers and their unions; third, competing forces within the national labor movement that disputed control of New York's waterfront unions; and fourth, the emergence of state authorities as a political force on the waterfront. Federal and state governments expanded their spheres of influence in regulating both the waterfront workforce and the labor process, while severely restricting the alternatives available to longshoremen to reform the docks.

The Rank and File

The ILA's structure comprised approximately seventy organized local unions on the docks of Manhattan, Brooklyn, and New Jersey, reflecting a highly diverse and segmented workforce.[47] While data pertaining to the ethnic composition of the waterfront labor force of this period is scarce, the ethnic predominance of local union leaders implies that they were mostly first- and second-generation Irish and Italian Americans. African American and Scandinavian ethnic groups also appear in notable concentrations, although they were decidedly smaller than Irish and Italian groups. Among the waterfront rank and file, both ethnic and racial polarizations were additional factors with which the movement contended.

The *Dockers News* group was the most enduring on the waterfront. Organized by the Communist Party in the late 1940s, its influence remained primarily on the Brooklyn docks. The group became a nucleus for the organization of radical longshoremen, and their presence on the waterfront was both respected and contested by other rank-and-file organizations. Local 791, led by Gene Sampson, was highly influential. Located on the Chelsea piers, its participation illustrates how the reform movement combined formal organization with informal methods of collective action. While it was a formal organization of the ILA, it was the dockworkers of Local 791 who first walked off the ships, spurring the first port-wide wildcat strike of 1945. Sampson's leadership reflected conflicting interests within the rank and file. Activists point out that the participation of Local 791 in the waterfront rebellion also reflected Sampson's individual interests; he was a frequent contender for the presidency of the ILA and the brother of Frank Sampson, an ex–Tammany Hall leader with strong ties to New York's political elite. As the movement for reform of the waterfront grew, Sampson rode the anticommunist hysteria of the McCarthy era and associated his demands for reform with strong anticommunist rhetoric, thus disassociating himself from other, left-led rank-and-file groups on the waterfront.

Another group came from Local 968 in Brooklyn, which had held a charter from the ILA since 1917. Known as the "Black Local," it was a Jim Crow union of black longshoremen set up by the ILA. Unlike other ILA locals, however, Local 968 had been assigned no pier jurisdiction, forcing members to seek work with other local unions along the port. Counting a comparatively small membership of 500, only 100 of the local's members were able to find regular employment on the waterfront.[48] Led by Cleophas Jacobs, the actions of Local 968 were also restricted due to long-standing racial divisions within the waterfront labor process.

The Catholic Church also sought to influence the rebellious dockworkers. Led by Father John Corridan, director of the Xavier School for Labor Studies, the Catholic Church aspired to mobilize the Irish longshoremen on the West Side of Manhattan. The Church sought to expose the evils of the waterfront labor process, and it staunchly opposed the increasing influence of communists in the labor movement seeking to redirect the way in which waterfront reform would occur. In spite of the growing presence of the church in waterfront affairs, up until 1948 it was the communists and their allies who took the lead in organizing opposition to the ILA leadership.[49]

The Citizens' Waterfront Committee brought religious congregations, middle-class reformers, and businessmen into the fray, seeking to slow down the political influence of the left. Organized informally in December 1946 and formally in September 1955, the CWC Executive Committee included William Schieffelin, chairman; Mary Sukhovitch and Rev. Russell Bowie, vice chairs; Rev. Paul Rischell, secretary; Joseph Lorenz, treasurer, and Mary Van Kleeck.[50] The Committee was highly critical of Ryan and the ILA, but sought reform by raising public awareness of the problems of the docks in the hopes of expanding the control of the waterfront by public authorities. As they explained: "Because our Committee has no official status or governmental authority, it must rely for acceptance and approbation (and for effective service on behalf of the public in general and labor and management in particular) upon its own good-will and impartially on the humanity of its approach."[51]

The emergence of groups, both within and outside the ILA, reflected the distinct and frequently competing political interests of dockworkers. In this sense, the unity in favor of waterfront reform represented the broadest and most basic claims that were either rejected or ignored by the ILA leadership and the shipping companies. The central demands that united the rank-and-file activists were greater safety regulations (such as weight limits on sling loads), higher wages, and democratic unions. Demands for reform escalated to one of labor's most explosive moments in the postwar period. As Sam Madell pointed out, "The men would go along with all of these terrible things for a period of time, and then there would be an explosion, and the docks would be all tied up."[52]

"No Contract—No Work!"

Just five months after receiving commendations for their productivity and vital support for the war effort, longshoremen staged the first in a long series of wildcat strikes that gripped the Port of New York. The wildcat strikes demonstrated great similarity to previous rank-and-file movements in both methods and claims. Striking dockworkers systematically attempted to shift the center of the contract negotiations from within the sphere of the closely knit relations between the ILA and the NYSA, thus compelling the inclusion of a third force not accounted for: the rank and file.

In October 1945, after Ryan announced a tentative agreement between the ILA and the NYSA, the longshoremen of Local 791 walked off the six piers under its jurisdiction. They protested the failure of the ILA and its Wage and Scale Committee to negotiate a reduction in the weight limits on sling loads.[53] In response to the walkout, Ryan, with the support of the ILA district council, called for an end to the work stoppage, which further enraged the rebellious dockworkers. The following day, the entire Port of New York was paralyzed. Rank-and-file groups in Brooklyn and Manhattan rapidly organized meetings along the waterfront and increased the number of their demands, forcing Ryan to place more grievances before the bargaining committee.[54] The *New York Times* reported: "The strike spread from its starting point in Manhattan, it took in the long Brooklyn waterfront including the huge Bush Terminal. . . . It took in the Jersey shoreline from Bayonne to the Hoboken piers. . . . It spread to Staten Island, Newark Bay, the Army's Caven Point Terminal to the naval base at Leonardo, N.J."[55] Approximately 350 ships remained idle. Although the *Times* estimated that there were 30,000 striking workers, according to Jack Gerst, secretary-treasurer of Local 791, the number was closer to 60,000: 46,000 longshoremen and 14,000 ancillary dockworkers such as checkers, carpenters, etc. The workers demanded reduction of the duration of collective bargaining agreements to one year; reduction in the number of shape-ups, from three to two per day; four hours guaranteed pay for hired longshoremen; and time and a half pay when working through the lunch period.[56] The strikers also demanded the reduction and limit of the sling load to 2,240 lbs. (1 ton) and an end to the shape-up. The rebellious dockworkers claimed that the unlimited sling load many times went as high as 7,000 lbs.[57] The claims of the strikers quickly shifted from the initial grievances and sought to transform the waterfront labor process, including the resignation of "King Joe Ryan."

On the third day of the strike, the Labor Department issued a statement declaring that "the strike had reached dangerous proportions," and Captain Hewlett Bishop, Atlantic Coast director for the War Shipping Administration (WSA), said that the situation was "growing more serious."[58] The impact of the strike on domestic and foreign trade was almost immediate. By the tenth day of the strike, the NYSA reported that 110,000 tons of European relief cargo and U.S. military supplies were sitting idle on the port. This included 37,000 tons of Army cargo, of which 8,000 tons were meat. Moreover, 13,000 U.S. troops stationed in Europe were awaiting redeployment to the United States because seventeen cargo-Liberty ships were held up by the strike.[59]

While Ryan and the ILA exhorted the longshoremen to return to work, the insurgent strike movement gained the support of other maritime unions. The West Coast Longshoremen of the ILWU quickly gave their support, as did the National Maritime Union (NMU), by donating $2,500 and distributing leaflets. Ryan dismissed the endorsements for the insurgent workers as a communist attempt to control the waterfront and the ILA, a diatribe he would frequently use over the years to explain the enduring and vocal opposition to his leadership of the union.[60] The long-shoremen contested the verbal agreement between the ILA and the NYSA. In a vote held by the District Council, from which most longshoremen were excluded, the agreement was approved.

However, the strike continued to gain momentum. Initially the employers expressed "surprise" at the wildcat strike. In a public statement, John V. Lyons, chairman of the NYSA, declared: "At no time in the history of the collective bargaining between the employers and employees in this port had there been a work stoppage once the respective committees had orally agreed on the terms of renewal. . . . The employers will live up to the terms agreed upon."[61] The wildcat strike upset the traditional relations between the ILA and the NYSA, and as the strike lengthened, doubts about the ILA's ability to control the waterfront workforce began to set in. Seeing no end to the strike, the employers soon reversed their opinion and agreed to reopen negotiations with the ILA if the striking longshoremen would return to work. In response, the activists refused the employers' proposal and began structuring their own negotiating committee.[62]

The rebellious longshoremen's movement also contested the autocratic structure of the ILA organization and its alliance with the shipping companies. That is, while the demands of the wildcat strike were predominantly economic, the method the workers employed of mass assemblies along the waterfront advanced the claim for greater worker participation in the decision-making process. On October 10, in a mass meeting held in a vacant lot on the corner of Hicks and President streets near the Brooklyn waterfront, 2,500 dockworkers formalized the rank-and-file committee, elected William Warren as chairman, and then created a steering committee comprising Sal Barone (Local 338), Eurico Ceccarelli (Local 1199), Joseph Alanpi (Local 338–1), and Fred Cerutti and John Susino (Local 338).[63] Later that day the longshoremen attempted to participate in a second meeting called by the ILA. Even though the police barred many of the workers from entering the meeting, the dissatisfaction among dockworkers with the union leadership ran high.[64]

Other rank-and-file groups that were not aligned with Warren or with the ILA leadership also pressed for Ryan's removal. Local 808 members began circulating a petition to the National Labor Relations Board requesting new elections in the ILA. Joe Hucker (Local 808) stated: "The men have lost confidence in Ryan and think the ILA is corrupt because of its close-knit control . . . but even within the machine there are healthy elements. We just need an election for new officers."[65] As the Committee began assuming the leadership of the walkout, mounting dissension soon became apparent between the Committee and some of the initial organizers of the strike. Some of the organizers feared losing control of the movement and the negotiation process. When questioned about the newly formed committee, Gene Sampson of Local 791, who had helped organize the walkout, charged that the "movement influences were communistic."[66]

Even if the Committee was able to paralyze large sectors of the waterfront, their capacity to influence the contract negotiation process was limited. That is, given the political influence of waterfront employers and their alliance with the ILA leadership, their legitimacy was increasingly questioned. Both the employers and the ILA quickly denounced the attempts made by Mayor LaGuardia to influence a settlement between striking dockworkers and the NYSA. After meeting with all sides in the dispute, LaGuardia defended the idea that a significant aspect of the problem originated from a "factional" dispute within the ranks of the ILA, and he proposed that new union elections be held. In an open letter to all parties involved, LaGuardia stated: "The situation in our port is becoming increasingly serious. . . . We must recognize that there is a factional dispute within the International Longshoremen's Association of this port."[67] Responding to LaGuardia, the Rank and File Committee wrote: "In response to your statement in the press this morning, be advised that the Rank and File Committee is ready to meet with you to settle the issues of the strike, as soon as you can guarantee us protection from the goons employed by Ryan to terrorize the rank and file."[68]

The ILA responded by labeling LaGuardia's call for elections "silly." Supporting the ILA's position, the employers also refused to meet with the committee. Responding to LaGuardia, the shipping employers stated that the NYSA "would continue to deal with the ILA's accredited representatives until legal procedures demonstrated that they no longer represented the longshoremen. . . . The Association recognizes that the procedure by which the ILA determines the membership of the negotiation committee is entirely up to the union itself. . . . For that reason we cannot agree to negotiate with any committee not so determined."[69] In this dispute, New York's mayor had little power (if any at all) to negotiate a settlement, even if he recognized the authority of the Rank and File Committee. Ultimately, as the Committee's response to the mayor indicates, the dockworkers also feared the violent repression of their movement, which was all too much a part of life on the docks under Joe Ryan.

Rather than negotiate with the insurgents, Ryan preferred to organize a movement of his own to compete with the Rank and File Committee. Ryan relied on the help of ex-convicts, whom he appointed as union organizers to control the waterfront and impose a reign of terror. In his deposition before the U.S. Senate Subcommittee Hearing on Interstate Commerce, Ryan defended the use of physical coercion to control the workforce, all with the acquiescence of the employers, as well as federal and state authorities. Physical violence, endemic to waterfront unionism, however, was justified within the context of national politics. A small excerpt of Ryan's deposition to the Committee on April 30 1953 illustrates how violence, anticommunism, and corruption converged on the waterfront. Speaking to Downey Rice, counsel for the committee, and Senator John Pastore he argued:

Mr. Rice: What do organizers do? Do they organize the men into locals?

Ryan: No, their main duty is watching other people that come on the waterfront.

Mr. Rice: They are watchdogs?

Ryan: Go into the record of how many times we have had this attack by the communists.

Mr. Rice: These organizers oppose communism, is that the idea?

Ryan: That is part of the idea.

Mr. Rice: They are watchdogs to fight communism?

Ryan: We have had that fight for a while.

Senator Pastore: Don't you think if you wanted to fight communism more effectively, you could do it with a fellow who didn't have such a bad criminal record?

Ryan: Some of these fellows with their bad criminal record were pretty handy out there, when we had to do it the tough way. The employers said it, especially in the case of Staten Island, where there were a few work stoppages. That is one of our big troubles, people trying to take over the organization, infiltrating and trying to start illegal strikes. . . . The commies move in with their paid staff and we need fellows to combat them. . . . The employers had no complaint about that, I can tell you that.

Mr. Rice: You said that it was part of the job of the organizer to fight

communism. You have a "Communist Fighting Fund," do you
not?

Ryan: Yes Sir.

Mr. Rice: Do you lack confidence in the ability of the FBI to do that
job?

Ryan: We have worked with the Department of Justice. We have
worked with the FBI, with the Military and Naval Intelligence in
1943 and in 1947. . . . You say this corruption has existed over many
years. I am telling you that this same organization that we are con-
demning now was praised in its 1947 convention by every official
of this government.

Defining the conflict along ideological lines, as a struggle between patriotic Americans and "evil communists," Ryan set out to isolate the rebellious movement and force the longshoremen to return to work, always
insisting that the strike was the result of "communistic influence." Ryan
rallied the support of conservative trade union organizations, in what was
called the "Back to Work" movement. His action received support from
labor organizations such as the Seafarers International Union (SIU) led by
Harry Lundeberg, as well as the New York Central Labor Council and the
New York State AFL, all of which issued statements supporting Ryan and
the ILA. Ryan's "Back to Work" movement combined high levels of red-
baiting with physical coercion and began taking its toll on the piers where
workers were less organized.[70]

By October 17, the local newspapers announced that approximately
11,500 longshoremen, reinforced by ILA-sanctioned strikebreakers, were
returning to work. The main holdouts continued to be in Brooklyn and
New Jersey. In spite of the growing return to work, 3,000 striking dockworkers marched through the center of Manhattan from 34th Street to
Chelsea along the waterfront, chanting, "Down with Ryan—Down with
the Finks," in reference to the returning workers.[71] In Brooklyn, where the
rank-and-file resistance to return to work was greatest, the ILA recruited
Army veterans as strikebreakers. Some wore their Army coats with ILA
badges pinned on them. They broke through the pickets, claiming: "You
guys made plenty of dough while we were in the Army; now we're going
to get some of it."[72]

In an attempt to attenuate Ryan's pressure on the striking longshoremen
to return to work, the NMU ordered its members to turn off the steam on

the ships and walk off the striking piers in solidarity with the insurgent dockworkers.[73] While the NMU's new effort to support the strike did little to reverse the slow return to work, tensions multiplied on both sides of the conflict. What ensued was combat, both physical and ideological, between striking longshoremen, supported by maritime workers on one side and the supporters of Joe Ryan and the ILA leadership on the other. Striking workers clashed with hired goons and strikebreakers, as well as the local police, organized by Ryan to remove the picket lines and reopen the docks. The fledgling Rank and File Committee, unable to sustain the escalating battle with no apparent solution in sight, on October 18 admitted that the strike had been broken and advised all to return to work. In a statement to the press, Warren declared that the return to work was "to preserve the unity of the longshoremen that had developed during the strike and to continue to build the unity to achieve our economic demands and a clean and democratic union. . . . We make this recommendation because the continuance of the strike at this time in the face of Ryan's gangsterism, the strike breaking of Harry Lundeberg [president of SIU], and the lies in the antilabor press, the active collusion of the ship owners with Ryan and Lundeberg convinces me that the unity of the ILA rank-and-file may suffer."[74]

However, Warren and Barone quickly switched loyalties in the aftermath of the strike. Just three days after making these declarations, they were physically beaten by gangsters in Brooklyn and expelled from the ILA. Unlike the insurgents before him, Warren almost immediately turned on his fellow insurgents and gave his support to Ryan. In a later statement, he declared that they had been "misled," that they had been "wrongly steered into the communist camp," and that in fact they were "just a couple of plain, ordinary longshoremen who wanted a good, strong, honest union . . . and were just being used as dupes" by Rank and File Committee lawyers Nathan Witt and Harold Cammers.[75] Witt responded that it was the beatings Warren suffered that must have "convinced him to work for Ryan."[76] The Rank and File Committee quickly replaced Warren and Barone, appointing John Berg as chairman, Charles Andersen as secretary, and James Glasgow as treasurer. When Ryan was informed of the new leadership, it was reported that he declared Berg and Andersen were "part of a small group that had been boring from within for the communists in the ILA for the past five years."[77]

Even though the demands of the rank and file were defeated, the ILA leadership saw itself forced to allow local unions to conduct elections to vote on the contract proposals. In spite of high levels of physical and ideological coercion, the organized strikebreaking movement, and the haphazard return to work, the membership voted to reject the ILA's contract proposal. The NYSA responded that they would make no further concessions. The Rank and File Committee moved to obtain a restraining order that prevented Ryan from signing a contract without the approval of the membership, thus attempting to continue influencing the negotiation process.

Legal maneuvering by the ILA leadership and the NYSA proved more effective, illustrating the weakness of the dockworkers' informal organization. While the restraining order prevented the NYSA and the ILA from signing a contract, it did not prevent them from continuing negotiations and submitting the proposals to arbitration. Thus the ILA, allied with the employers, successfully bypassed the rank and file's claim for port-wide elections to decide a new contract. As the Rank and File Committee's newsletter argued: "We do not oppose to arbitration as such. We do oppose to any attempt to settle the longshore situation without giving the longshoremen an opportunity to decide democratically and free from coercion what steps shall be taken on our behalf."[78] Despite the dockworkers' claims, the arbitrator quickly approved the proposals submitted by the shipping companies and the ILA; the contract negotiations were over. If Ryan won the battle, however, the conflict was far from over. The 1945 wildcat strike was just the beginning of a reform movement that repeatedly paralyzed the Port of New York for years to come.

Overtime and Back Pay

In tandem with the 1945 wildcat strike, waterfront activists began raising the demand for back pay by filing lawsuits against the Huron Stevedoring Co. and the Bay Ridge Operating Co., in which they demanded $800,000 in unpaid overtime.[79] These lawsuits paved the way for a more expansive lawsuit that was filed in 1947 covering 3,000 longshoremen and demanding $5 million in unpaid overtime. The rush to file this second lawsuit was spurred by the passage of the Portal Pay Act of 1947, which reduced the time frame when workers could enter claims for past overtime from six to two years.[80] The insurgents argued that the collective bargaining agreements between the ILA and the NYSA had violated the 1938 Fair Labor Standards

Act, and as a result, back pay was owed to thousands of longshoremen. They contended that they regularly worked outside of the normal work hours, which were from 8 A.M. to noon and from 1 to 5 P.M., and that many worked through the night without receiving overtime pay. Their attorneys contended that work during the evening hours should be paid at overtime rates above the regular time and a half that was being paid. Madell pointed out that "the men were interested in this thing because it meant millions and millions in back pay would be due the longshoremen."[81]

With the end of the strike, back pay committees were formed in Brooklyn and Hoboken, while African American dockworkers organized their own committee under the auspices of Local 968. The ILWU's Washington representative, William Glazier, remembered that the meetings of the back pay committees were strong and drew as many as 1,800 participants. Unsettled claims of the 1945 wildcat strike and high levels of unemployment in 1947–48 invigorated the growing radicalization of New York's dockworkers and their support for the back pay movement. These demands included reducing the weight of sling loads and an end to the acceleration of the work process, as well as a halt to the already infamous shape-up as a hiring practice.[82]

In the ensuing legal battle, the U.S. Supreme Court sustained the argument of the Rank and File Committee for back pay, reinforcing the role of the insurgent longshoremen in the upcoming collective bargaining negotiations. Despite opposition from the NYSA and the ILA, the Supreme Court decided in favor of the insurgents' demand and set the hourly cost of overtime and night work at 2.62 percent of the hourly wage scale.[83] That was not enough, however, to ensure a victory for the Rank and File Committee. The ILA leadership and the NYSA reacted strongly to the Court's decision and proceeded to lobby Congress, with the support of Representative Fred Hartley Jr., to have the Fair Labor Standards Act amended.[84]

Parallel to the 1947 back pay campaign, the dockworkers of Local 791 once again paralyzed the port between Canal Street and Chelsea in Manhattan. On August 19, 1947, a tentative contract agreement was reached between the ILA and the NYSA that provided for nothing more than a 10 cent hourly wage increase. In reality the ILA and the NYSA were attempting to preempt the Taft-Hartley Act ban on preferential hiring practices by signing the agreement before the legislation was enacted. Informed of what was happening on the same day, Sampson of Local 791 held an "unscheduled meeting" where the members rejected the ILA's contract scheme (before the agreement was even officially announced).[85] In a move similar to what had occurred less than two years earlier, 4,000 longshoremen walked off the piers in Manhattan. Sampson initially denied any knowledge of the wildcat strike, stating: "The men just aren't around for work." However, he ended by declaring that he "supported their actions 100 percent." The demands of the rebellious workers were a 25 cent per hour wage increase, eight hours of guaranteed pay when hired, two weeks of paid vacation, and the reduction of the sling load.[86]

The strike had its greatest impact on passenger ships. It forced the U.S. America Line to withdraw its ships from service, and the company lost thousands of dollars in passenger revenues. The strike, however, also immobilized twelve cargo ships. Compared with the strike of 1945, wide support for the job action was slow and not so forthcoming. The strike received the support of dockworkers from Locals 895 and 1258, also in Manhattan. In Brooklyn, half the piers were paralyzed on the second day of the strike, only to return to normal the following day.[87] After six days on strike, the longshoremen of Manhattan's West Side returned to work. Significantly, the limited support for the strike appears to indicate that conflicts were brewing within the leadership of the rank-and-file movement, between Sampson and the left-led Rank and File Committee. Whatever their differences were, it would not impede the resurgence of the movement in the renewed contract negotiations in the following year. Stated at the outset of the 1948 contract negotiations, the claims of the rank and file, bolstered by the movement for back pay, became the catalyst for the second general wildcat strike on the Port of New York.

Once again the strategy of the Rank and File Committee focused on blocking the ILA's attempt to negotiate a contract without the participation of the dockworkers. The ILA's collusion with the ship owners was obvious. When employers would ask to hear the demands of the ILA, one employer recalls Ryan responding, "Give them a nickel, if they won't take that, give'm a dime,"[88] which earned Ryan a second nickname, "nickel and dime Joe." The employers' control of the ILA permeated all levels of leadership. The deposition of Thomas Maher, superintendent of the Grace Lines shipping company, to the U.S. Senate on March 27, 1953, illustrates the perverse collusion that had developed between the ILA and the shipping companies over the years:

Mr. Maher: Mr. Fortune—he was the vice president of the Huron Stevedoring Company at the time—he told me that there was a check to be carried on the payroll as "Ross" in 1942. It has been carried on the payroll ever since. He told me that Ross was Tim O'Mara [ILA official].

The Chairman: You knew that was crooked?

Mr. Maher: Yes Sir.

The Chairman: Didn't you do anything about it?

Mr. Maher: No sir, I just carried out orders.

Senator Pastore: What good did it do to carry out orders? What was the purpose of all this?

Mr. Maher: The purpose of the thing-the 'brass check,' as far as what I got from Mr. Fortune, and my father, was that he was the man who could settle the strikes along the river front, especially for the Grace Line. They weren't interested in anything except for the Grace Line.

The Chairman: So you know that was stealing?

Mr. Maher: I didn't know that was stealing.

The Chairman: What do you call it?

Mr. Maher: I was only following instructions. . . . The company knew about it all the time.

Senator Potter: We have on record here stating that from 1945 to 1952 payments were made to Tim O'Mara under the name of Ross in an amount totaling $25,604.80.

The willingness of the employers to openly admit to years of corruption and collusion with the leadership of the ILA indicates not only that the employers did not fear legal reprisals but also that, even though their traditional relationship was under fire from political authorities, the transformation of the waterfront labor structure was not going to occur very rapidly if it depended on the NYSA or the ILA. The growing movement for back pay was a clear indicator that contract negotiations were not going to be easy. On August 17, 1948, just four days before the contract was to expire, President Truman, informed of the growing tension on the Port of New York, invoked the recently passed Taft-Hartley Act, in order to halt any strike activity for eighty days. Truman's decision postponed the formal strike date until November 9. By early November, negotiations between the NYSA, the ILA, and government mediators appeared to be arriving at a settlement. On November 6, Ryan informed the press that he did not think an extension was necessary and that at a negotiation meeting to be held on November 8 an agreement would be reached.[89] On November 10, as the ILA announced that it would sign the agreement, the rebellious dockworkers once again walked off the ships. More than just a protest against unresolved grievances between employers and employees, it became increasingly evident that the ILA leadership was unable to represent the collective claims of New York's longshoremen. In contrast, the rank-and-file movement allowed dockworkers to exert a larger influence in the decision-making process, filling the vacuum where the institutional means of representation were highly exclusionary.

Sensing that the movement for back pay reinforced the rank and file, Ryan shifted from the strategy he had used in the previous wildcat strike, and three days after the wildcat strike had begun, he declared the wildcat strike legal. This move paralyzed dockworkers from Portland, Maine, to Hamptons Road, Virginia. He also instructed affiliated dockworkers in Montreal, Halifax, and the Gulf ports not to work on ships diverted from New York. The proposed settlement endorsed by both the ILA and the NYSA had been rejected almost unanimously. The employers responded that they would make no further offer.[90] The ILA's strategy was twofold: first, it attempted to gain control of the rebellious movement by declaring the strike legal; second, it sought to weaken the Rank and File Committee's claim to representation by limiting strike activities, such as picket lines and demonstrations. This strategy kept the bulk of the membership disorganized and uninformed. To reverse the ILA's attempt at co-opting the strike movement, the Rank and File Committee called for a general meeting on November 16 at the ILA's Manhattan Center. Ryan responded with his usual red-baiting tactics, claiming that the meeting was "communist inspired" and that "if the communists interfere with this, our men will throw them in the river."[91] The Rank and File Committee ended the meeting after defining their main demands: a 25 cent per hour wage increase, $3.00 per hour additional pay for work performed at night and on weekends, an employer-financed welfare fund, two weeks of paid vacation, lighter sling loads, and payment for the past years of unpaid overtime. They then closed the meeting with a minute of silence in memory of the slain rank-and-file activist Pete Panto.[92]

As the strike pressed on, mail, cargo, and perishable goods lay on the port. For example in the cargo holds of the idled ships, 150,000 bags of mail were retained on the Westside Port of Manhattan. The strike had become a growing point of contention between longshoremen and the federal government as well, since goods destined for Europe, as part of American support for the Marshall Plan, also lay on the port. It was estimated that 20,000 tons of Marshall Plan exports destined for Europe accumulated daily at a storage cost of $36 million. By November 16, railroads began laying off freight handlers: 742 employees of the New York Central, 150 workers in the New York freight yard, and 200 in Boston. In terms of the financial impact of the strike, the New York Board of Trade executive vice president estimated a daily loss of $25 million between exports and imports.[93]

Federal authorities, the ILA leadership, and the NYSA agreed on one point: the exclusion of the Rank and File Committee from the negotiation process. The Federal Mediation and Conciliation Service (FMCS) pressed for negotiations between the ILA and the NYSA, but excluded the participation of the Rank and File Committee from the process. While the Rank and File Committee had a significantly high level of political legitimacy among the striking workers, confirmed in their ability to immobilize the port, they had little if any control, in the institutional sphere, in the contract negotiation process. On November 25, the ILA and the NYSA signed an agreement that allowed for a 13 cent per hour wage increase, two weeks of paid vacation after 1,350 hours of work, and the organization of the ILA Welfare Fund.[94] Ryan quickly announced that a majority of longshoremen had voted to accept the agreement and return to work. In a meeting at St. Stephen's Hall on the corner of First Place and Hicks Street in Brooklyn, activists decided to wait for the complete election results before deciding whether or not to return to work. In their initial polling, a majority of Brooklyn's dockworkers had voted against the proposed contract, as did the longshoremen of Local 1249 in Jersey City. Speaking at the meeting, activist Mitchell Berensen declared: "Joe Ryan didn't call this strike and we have no faith in his announcement tonight." Paul O'Dwyer (the brother of the mayor and ex-Brooklyn district attorney in the Panto murder, William O'Dwyer) announced that the meeting "was to take whatever action necessary on the outcome of the voting . . . [and] if the majority votes for it we will accept it."[95]

The continued exclusion of the Rank and File Committee from the negotiation process reflected the limits of informal organization in an industry that was increasingly under the scrutiny of the federal authorities. Their inability to mobilize and sustain the active participation of the membership was due to both a lack of resources and institutional legitimacy. Once the ILA had declared the strike legal, it had assumed, at least in the legal sphere, the representation of New York's dockworkers. The 1948 ILA contract fell far short of the rank and file's initial claims. By declaring the strike legal, the ILA had weakened the political initiative of the rank and file. Between August and November 1948, the ILA leadership, relying on far greater resources and institutional political influence, systematically eroded the efforts of the opposition, demobilizing and maintaining compliance among large sectors of the membership that were kept uninformed. The ILA leadership assumed as its own the political initiative of the Rank and File Committee, using it as leverage in its negotiations with the NYSA and the federal government.

The limits of the reform movement reflected the complexity of intersecting formal and informal forms of organization and representation and was compounded by competing interests within the waterfront labor process. While the rank and file appeared highly effective at mobilizing for conflict, both the lack of resources and the lack of institutional legitimacy ultimately curtailed their insertion in the negotiation and decision-making process. On the other hand, strategic maneuvering by the ILA and the NYSA, with the support of the federal government and conservative sectors of the trade union movement, accentuated the ideological differences and weakened the rank and file's claim for political legitimacy. The "competition" was highly unequal, in terms of available resources, political influence, and institutional legitimacy. Added to all that, the effects of high levels of physical coercion compounded the advantages of the ILA and the NYSA further in the conflict.

Moreover, while the wildcat strike of 1948 helped expand the composition of political forces active in the reform movement, this did not lead to greater political legitimacy. That is, in the end, contract negotiations remained under the close scrutiny of the ILA, NYSA, and federal mediators. By legitimizing the strike, the ILA claimed for itself the political initiative of the rank and file. By keeping a large part of the membership demobilized and uninformed, the ILA leadership could continue to maneuver in favor of its own interests and those of the NYSA, which seemed highly compatible. Ultimately, Ryan used the threat of a possible rank-and-file takeover of the East Coast waterfront union, combined with his red-baiting diatribe, to control the ILA for only a few more years. By the time of the Senate subcommittee hearings in 1953, Ryan had been indicted by a New York County grand jury on thirty counts of misapplication of union funds and was under investigation by both the IRS and the FBI.

Before Ryan's subsequent indictment, however, the Port of New York would come to a standstill once more. In 1951, another wildcat strike began when rebellious dockworkers refused to accept a two-year agreement that had been negotiated between the ILA leadership and the NYSA. The longshoremen questioned the validity of the ILA-sponsored contract ratification election. Approximately 25 percent of the estimated 40,000 dockworkers participated in the election. The contract was "approved 2 to 1" in a highly suspicious plebiscite. The rebellious movement, however, continued to demand radical changes in the antidemocratic nature of the union's decision-making process.

As the 1951 contract negotiations neared the October 1 expiration date, Joseph Ryan publicly announced that "considerable progress" was being made toward reaching a new agreement, despite the fact that the NYSA's offer fell far short of the union's original demands. The longshoremen demanded a 25 cent per hour wage increase; a guaranteed day's pay with only one shape-up, and increased contributions to the union's welfare benefits. The employers' counterproposal offered an 11 cent wage increase, a 16.5 cent wage increase for overtime pay, and the promise that improvements to the welfare fund would be submitted to a joint committee for further study.[96]

The proposals of the union and the NYSA continued to be very different, even though Ryan expressed "confidence" that a new accord would be reached.[97] As the deadline approached, minor disagreements between the union and employers emerged, but with the quick intervention of the federal mediation service and a one-week extension of the contract deadline, all was seemingly settled; the ILA announced that they had finalized a new two-year contract with the NYSA. The basic provisions of the new agreement granted dockworkers a 10 cent hourly wage increase, $1.25 per hour increase toward welfare contributions, a reduction of the required work hours necessary for one week of vacation from 800 to 700 hours, one shape-up per day, and four hours guaranteed pay when hired. Despite mounting discontent among longshoremen with the new contract, Ryan and the ship owners assured everyone involved that it would be approved in the upcoming contract ratification election.[98] Ryan's ratification vote, however, would not suffice to gain the longshoremen's acquiescence to the new labor accord.

On October 15, one week after the ILA-sponsored ratification election, where Ryan had boasted of the 2 to 1 margin approving the new contract, a wildcat strike slowly began to immobilize the Port, protesting the election and demanding that Ryan reopen contract negotiations with the NYSA. Members of ILA Local 791 on the Hudson River initiated the strike, but the movement quickly spread to Brooklyn.[99] The dockworkers argued that the ILA voting process was, at best, highly suspicious and that the promiscuous voting process enabled "ballot box stuffing," repeat voting, and a vote-tally system that relied solely on local ILA officials to call in the results after the votes were counted. The rebellious longshoremen demanded a new ratification election supervised by an independent third party.[100]

Hoping to convince striking longshoremen to return to work, Ryan went to the Chelsea Pier, but was immediately rebuffed by the strikers. "They won't listen to me," Ryan stated. "They feel they have a grievance but they have no leader I can deal with." When questioned about the fact that the strike had spread to Brooklyn, Ryan's answer was completely different. Hoping to drive a wedge between Manhattan and Brooklyn longshoreman, he replied, "As for the Brooklyn walkout that's strictly communist inspired. They're riding around Brooklyn in cars now prevailing on the men to walk out. You know [Harry] Bridges was in town last week."[101] Ryan tried to deflect his own incapacity to persuade striking longshoremen to return to work and the growing discontent of dockworkers with the ILA leadership by continuously reinventing a supposed communist plot to dominate the Port of New York. The following day he announced a campaign to rid the port of communist influence. "They [Ryan loyalists] will be armed with circulars explaining how the Commies are seeking to break up our union and they will try to talk to the boys in Brooklyn into returning to work [sic]. If there is any violence it will be Bridges' fault," Ryan declared.[102] Red-baiting, attempting to portray striking dockworkers in Brooklyn as "un-American," was intensified by the fact that the workers had paralyzed the activities of the Brooklyn Army Base embarkation pier. The ILA leadership continuously tried to link the Communist Party's position against the war in Korea to the Brooklyn job action.

In Brooklyn, "tough Tony Anastasia" was making little headway at deterring striking longshoremen, although the ideological pressure placed on rebellious dockworkers by the union leadership did obtain some results. In an attempt to break the strike, Tony Anastasia appeared at the Brooklyn Army Base. Appealing to striking longshoremen he shouted, "I am Anastasia, one of the foremen on the waterfront. This is one place you gotta work. If you don't I supply the men. This Army base is controlled by the United States Army. I was here yesterday and I'm back today as a good American citizen." Even though the dockworkers initially ignored Anastasia's orders, when he ordered approximately seventy-five strikebreakers to move in toward the pier, the climate changed.[103]

Fearing for their jobs, Pier 4 hatch boss Salvatore Brocco climbed up on a truck and responded, "Anyone who calls us Commies is a damned liar. We are patriotic; we have worked this base since before the war. Gene Sampson [Local 791 business agent] is our man and a better leader than Joe Ryan." Then, turning toward Anastasia, Brocco declared, "Get those stooges out of there and we'll go in."[104] Anastasia called off the strikebreakers, and the dockworkers filed back onto the pier. If "Tough Tony" was able to force rebellious longshoremen to return to work at the Army base, he and his brother Gerardo Anastasia were not so successful on other piers in the port of Brooklyn. The piers of Brooklyn remained for the most part paralyzed.

The ILA leadership's attempt to portray the strike as a "communist conspiracy" drew strong criticism from the rank-and-file leaders, their allies, and even from the left. Gene Sampson declared: "I'm sick and tired of these references of communism that emanate from Ryan's headquarters and elsewhere. These men who refuse to work are more patriotic than any of their critics. If the critics were half as patriotic and honest, we would not have this situation."[105] The Association of Catholic Trade Unionists (ACTU) also condemned the ILA's red-baiting tactics, calling Ryan's anti-communist rhetoric a "red herring" and saying that the strike was a "rank-and-file clean house movement" with an anticommunist leadership. Even Harry Bridges called a press conference to deny left-wing involvement in the initiative to strike, even though they were entirely supportive of the movement.[106] Bridges's denial of left-wing leadership of the movement was also an indication of the growing divergence between conservative (i.e., Catholic) and communist rank-and-file activists.

The strike was the initiative of local ILA leaders who had grown disenchanted with Ryan's control of the ILA. Left-wing dockworkers, however, were strong supporters of the movement. By the end of the first week, local ILA leaders appointed Gene Sampson the "strike leader." The implications of Sampson's appointment as spokesman for the striking longshoremen were twofold. First, it was a logical move because his local union had initiated the movement on the first day. His appointment, however, also reflected a deep ideological conflict that was growing among different rank-and-file groups along the waterfront. For example, one strike bulletin carried a picture of the American flag and the caption, "This is not a commy [sic] paper."[107] Second, by appointing Sampson, the conservative rank-and-file leaders sought to diminish the ability of the left to gain influence over the direction of the strike through pier activism as they had done in the previous wildcat movement. Early on, conservative rank-and-file leaders had been circulating a bulletin called *The New Deal*, self-described as "anticommunist and anti-Ryan." The bulletin was an attempt to counter the influence of the left-wing *Dockers News*. In its first edition, the conservative newsletter stated: "The *Dockers News* is a commie rag [sic]. Useful only to Ryan to cry 'communist' when the men rebel against one of his sell outs."[108]

The Communist Party, however, was growing increasingly suspicious of how far Sampson was willing to take the movement, creating an uneasiness between the left and conservative rank-and-file leaders. George Morris's analysis of the strike mirrored the growing distrust among rank-and-file leaders. Writing for the CP's *Weekend Worker*, he argued: "The main pattern seems to be to somehow get an agreement from Sampson and his group to call off the walkout, pending an 'impartially conducted' ballot of longshoremen on the Ryan pact, or deliberations of a Truman fact-finding Board, or some promise to renew negotiations. It amounts to an agreement to disarm while the enemy, armed to the teeth, is considering something or other."[109] As we will see, Morris's predictions were not far off. *Dockers News*, published daily during the strike, continuously demanded that the conservative strike committee take a more aggressive stance. As the progressive journal *March of Labor* recognized: "It is not conceivable that this struggle could have developed without the persistent activities of a small but fighting group of progressive longshoremen. Their rank-and-file paper, *Dockers News*, conducted a vigorous campaign against the evils on the waterfront, against Ryan and his ruinous policies and for militant job action. . . . To them the 30,000 longshoremen owe a debt of gratitude."[110]

The federal government responded to the growing work stoppage on the port by sending federal mediators to New York in the hopes of negotiating a settlement between the ILA leadership and the rebel dockworkers. This coincided with the beginning of the ILA's "Back to Work Campaign,"[111] which received the immediate support of the AFL's Maritime Trades Department, which announced that "all member unions would give their support to the embattled ILA leadership." Ryan remained adamant in his demand that the longshoremen return to their jobs, declaring: "Even if they manage to tie up the entire port we still have a contract. . . . It is now, and would be then an outlaw strike."[112] The ILA's stance not to reopen negotiations was echoed by the NYSA and the federal mediators. Clyde M. Mills, assistant director of the Federal Mediation and Conciliation Service, described the strike as "intolerable" and went on to demand "that the work stoppage be ended and that all employees engaged in the work stoppage return to their respective jobs immediately."[113] After making this statement, Mills abruptly withdrew the participation of the federal service from further negotiations.

With the movement gaining momentum, striking dockworkers showed little possibility for an immediate return to work. At the beginning of the second week into the strike, 90 piers were paralyzed on the Port of New York;[114] by the end of the week 138 piers and 104 ships were immobilized on the port.[115] Moreover, longshoremen in Boston and Baltimore joined the strike.[116] As the *Dockers News* wrote: "Boston is out solid along with the New York–New Jersey region. Philadelphia and Baltimore may join us at any moment. The start of mass picketing at the docks yesterday makes our strike tighter and stronger than ever." Approximately 20,000 longshoremen were actively participating in the job action, and with no solution in sight the American Railroad Association embargoed all cargo headed for the Port of New York.[117] The Commerce and Industry Association estimated that cargo valued at $250 million was piled up on the port and growing at a rate of $25 million per day.[118] This prompted the executive committee of the Chamber of Commerce of the State of New York to request that Governor Dewey appoint a special district attorney "for a complete investigation of the New York waterfront situation."[119] Pressures against the striking longshoremen continued to mount.

At a general meeting of the strike movement held at Manhattan Center, 3,000 dockworkers demanded that the ILA reopen negotiations, and they denounced the growing campaign of intimidation that the union leadership had initiated. At the gathering, ILA Local 808 business agent Frank Norowki charged that some of Anastasia's goons were attempting to intimidate the rank-and-file leaders. Norowki informed the meeting of the ILA's strategy to break the strike in Brooklyn: "There were some well-heeled goons down there and we were in no position to risk bloodshed. If anything happens to me I hold the Anastasia brothers responsible."[120] Sure enough, the following day, while leading a roving picket caravan of sixty cars, Norowki and other activists were attacked by fifty stone-throwing Ryan loyalists, allegedly directed by Gerardo Anastasia, Frank Russo, and Joseph Collazo. The attack injured some of the activists and destroyed their vehicles. Anastasia and Russo were subsequently arrested for the attack.[121]

The withdrawal of federal mediators from the strike discussions, however, did not signify the disengagement of the federal government from the strike; on the contrary, as the federal mediators stepped out, President Truman stepped in, appealing to rebel dockworkers to end their job action. Truman did not invoke the Taft-Hartley Act, despite the effects that the strike was having on the national economy and particularly in the defense industry. Increasingly, sectors of the business elite demanded that the president invoke the act, but he preferred to limit his action to making a direct appeal to the rebel longshoremen. Moreover, it seems that if he were to invoke legal measures against the striking dockworkers, it would also give the longshoremen the legal venue to debate the legitimacy of the ILA agreement, and neither the ILA nor the NYSA wanted to consider reopening the contract. The insurgent dockworkers rejected Truman's appeal. In response to the president, Sampson argued that if the federal government wanted to end the strike, it could invoke the Taft-Hartley Act or have the case referred to the Wage Stabilization Board (WSB), which regulated wages in national defense industries. Both alternatives would have provided a legal forum for the dockworkers to discuss their claims; the ILA leadership and the NYSA wanted no part of it.[122]

Ryan's "back to work" movement seemed to be having little impact, at least initially. He blamed the police for his movement's lack of effectiveness. In a telegram to New York's Mayor Impeliterri, Ryan denounced the lack of police action: "Since the police have refused to give us protection, we have decided not to permit the men to attempt a shape-up tomorrow." Violence between striking dockworkers and Ryan's strikebreakers led him to make strong accusations against the police department for "failing to keep the pickets in line."[123] Ryan had been met by approximately 700 striking dockworkers at the entrance to Pier 92 on West 52 Street when he attempted to bring strikebreakers onto the pier. Violence broke out, and the strikers emerged victorious, forcing Ryan to retreat from the pier. But Ryan's defeat was only temporary.

The following day Ryan announced that he would renew his efforts to reopen the port. In a telegram to President Truman, he declared that the Port of New York was "now open" and that the ILA loyalists would "go through and over" striking dockworkers to open the piers. "The family of the ILA is closing its ranks against these disrupters on our waterfront," Ryan proclaimed. The continued stalemate between striking dockworkers and the ILA leadership, and the fact that rebellious longshoremen found little support for their movement outside of the docks, led strike leaders to search for an alternative. Prompted by Ryan's telegram to Truman, Sampson also sent a telegram to the president, stating that if Truman were to appoint a fact-finding commission to examine the causes of the strike, he "would urge the men to return to work."[124] The rank-and-file leaders' willingness to examine such alternatives was a reflection of the slow but consistent return to work. In Staten Island, for example, Ryan loyalist Alex DiBrizzi successfully forced the dockworkers to return to work on all Army piers. Moreover, Ryan's demand for greater police protection for strikebreakers got results. Increasingly larger numbers of police were being used on the port, forming protective barriers that allowed Ryan's strikebreakers to move onto the piers.[125]

The strikebreaking tactics of the ILA leadership coincided with employers' legal action seeking to restrict the striking longshoremen. The NYSA filed charges with the NLRB against ILA locals 791, 1258, 895, 808, and 968, alleging unfair labor practices for breach of contract.[126] Added to the NYSA's charges, New Jersey shipping operators received a judicial restraining order against New York dockworkers prohibiting them from forming pickets on the piers of New Jersey. As the legal pressure continued to mount, state mediation officials began meeting with the ILA leadership and the dock leaders, hoping to end the three-week debacle.[127]

Edward Corsi, New York State industrial commissioner, appointed a citizens fact-finding commission to examine the waterfront conflict. The commission comprised Professor Martin Catherwood of Cornell University, Dean Alfange of the New York Bar Association, and Monsignor John P. Boland of the NYS Mediation Board.[128]

Despite the dockworkers' resistance, after four weeks on strike, it was noted that Ryan's "back to work" movement, aided by political and legal pressures, was taking its toll. On November 5, the U.S. Customs House reported that 3,000 dockworkers had reported for work on nineteen piers along the Port of New York.[129] Three days later, Sampson advised all dockworkers to return to work despite the fact that a day earlier the NLRB had dismissed the unfair labor practice charges filed by the NYSA.[130] The rebellion had ended.

Even though the strike had negligible results, the dockworkers' claim for greater democracy in the ILA's decision-making process continued to mobilize the waterfront, and rebellions against "King Joe" gathered momentum. The movement was a strong indicator of the mounting disaffection for Ryan among local ILA leaders and their increasing capacity to act independently of the ILA president and respond to the demands of dockworkers. Ryan's diminishing capacity to command the dock union would subsequently lead to his removal as "President for Life" of the ILA. For the budding rank-and-file movement, the strike indicated the widening chasm between the left-wing and politically conservative rank-and-file activists and strategic and tactical divergences between the two factions concerning the direction of a movement that continued to grow.

The citizens fact-finding commission quickly closed its sessions to the public. *Dockers News* asked, "Why the Secrecy?"[131] The radical longshoremen charged that once the commission had uncovered Ryan's vote rigging, the legitimacy of the 1951 collective bargaining agreement could be called into question. The decision to close the hearings, however, was a useful maneuver, since neither the federal and state political authorities nor the ILA or NYSA were in favor of reopening the contract negotiations. After criticizing the ILA structure, the commission suggested the appointment of a permanent waterfront arbitrator to resolve future conflicts.[132] But this solution failed to attend to the dockworkers' demand for democracy and greater control of the waterfront labor process. The dock rebellion was far from over.

The same forces that had given the ILA leadership institutional legitimacy for more than twenty-five years were quickly unraveling. With time, however, the constant threat of rank-and-file action reshaped the relations between dockworkers and their union. While the ILA never became an example of democratic trade unionism, at moments of greater conflict the ILA leadership would find itself forced to negotiate with the informal rank-and-file groups that continued to exist on the waterfront. In this sense, from the rebellious wildcat strikes emerged informal means of representation, which became permanent forms of participation and action, making rank-and-file organization an enduring facet of the waterfront labor process. It was the first time the ILA leadership had been forced to submit its decisions to a port-wide referendum. Although faint, the dictatorial decision-making process had taken a blow.

3

Who Speaks for New York's Dockworkers?

By 1953 the basic elements necessary for the transformation of the waterfront labor process were set in motion. Political authorities and business adopted a twofold strategy with both short- and long-term objectives. Their main goal, to gain control of the New York waterfront, manifested itself in the alliance of state and federal political authorities with conservative sectors of the trade union movement and business elites who acted in unison. Federal injunctions against the ILA and insurgent dockworkers became increasingly common. In its initial stage, the conservative waterfront alliance tactically sought to gain control by challenging the institutional legitimacy of the ILA to represent New York's dockworkers and to replace the union with a labor organization that would acquiesce to the regulatory measures that were being set in place.

This strategy combined the use of legal constraints such as the Taft-Hartley Act and other legal devices with injunctive and punitive power, reinforced by a system of industrywide regulatory measures administered by the Bi-State Waterfront Commission. The conservative alliance justified these stringent measures by shrouding their actions in a moral campaign to "rid the waterfront of its gangster-dominated unions." Even though there was widespread corruption and violence during Ryan's term at the head of the ILA leadership, the conservative reformers were hardly stalwarts of democratic unionism. Nor were they innocent of charges of corruption in their own unions, and still other participants were longtime associates of Joe Ryan and Emil Camarda. In this sense, the objectives of the conservative alliance led by Governor Thomas E. Dewey and the AFL leadership with the support of the U.S. Department of Labor and business elites were more about creating an alternative system of control for the dock labor process than expressing any deep-rooted desire to allow dockworkers greater access and control of the waterfront labor process. Even though the attempt to replace the ILA was unsuccessful, the strategy achieved its principal objective, which was to piece together a system of institutional legal measures to contain the rebellious longshoremen. An important aspect of the process was to shift the location of the decision-making process to a forum away from the docks and the union. The process left the structure of the ILA extremely debilitated. It drained the union's financial resources and left it with a temporary government-appointed trustee to oversee the union's daily administration. Isolated from large sectors of the trade union movement, the embattled ILA rapidly shifted its forms of action by mobilizing increasingly larger sectors of the dock labor force in its political battles (something unheard of under the leadership of Joe Ryan). As a result of the mass mobilizations, the ILA leadership sought and received the support of progressive unions such as the ILWU and the UMWA. Albeit temporary, the tactical shift of the ILA, combined with the growing fragmentation among its leaders, particularly between Brooklyn and the national union, forced the ILA to become more responsive to the demands of the rebellious rank-and-file movement.

The growing convergence of political forces seeking the demise of the ILA was clearly defined. Federal and state political authorities joined by economic elites and conservative sectors of the organized labor movement were all actively involved in the movement to remove the ILA from the docks. How was the dock union able to survive the attacks of a movement with such extensive political and economic influence? What were the complex political alliances dockworkers conceived, and what were the effects of such alliances in the ongoing struggle to control the docks? The 1953 contract negotiations and the mounting tension between the ILA, the NYSA, and longshoremen had become synonymous with the struggle for control of the New York waterfront. The AFL's challenge to the ILA's right to represent New York's longshoremen and the direct participation of federal and state political authorities divided the port-side forces in favor of reform and shipping elites, radically transforming long-standing alliances and practices. This process melded the political and economic conflict between employers and workers in a brutal, often violent campaign, shaped by federal and state political participation in the "inter-union" dispute, undergirded by changing patterns of work and wages. Added to this was mounting federal regulation that sought to control hiring and work practices since control of the waterfront still depended, for the most part, on controlling the workforce. Over the course of three years, dockworkers would go to the polls three times to decide who would represent their interests.

The debate between New Hampshire Republican Charles Tobey and AFL president George Meany during the Senate Subcommittee Hearing on Interstate Commerce investigating waterfront labor conditions set the tone for labor politics on the Port of New York for the next five years. During Meany's testimony, Senator Tobey declared that if need be, federal legislation would be enacted if the AFL failed to clean up the racket-dominated ILA. When asked what the AFL would do, Meany responded: "What we'll do about it is something we'll decide." Pounding his gavel, Tobey quickly answered: "I think we will decide if you don't. We will pass legislation to put the hooks into that crowd up there if you don't. We will do it, God helping."[1] The mechanisms for federal and state regulation, bolstered by the AFL's interest in gaining control of New York's dockworkers, were already in motion as Meany and Tobey argued during the Senate hearing.

In spite of Meany's tone of independence, the AFL leader and federal and state political authorities were drawn closer together in the battles that ensued on the New York waterfront over the next few years. On one hand, the AFL would depend on the federal authorities for political and legislative support in its struggle for control. On the other hand, political authorities viewed the AFL as the answer to their waterfront labor problem—that is, a labor organization that was supportive of government regulation and control of the dock labor process. Over the next four years, both the federal and state governments, in alliance with the AFL, would work to expel the ILA from the waterfront. Even though unsuccessful, their actions were successful in encouraging the already growing division among the competing rank-and-file groups and introducing the framework for a complex labor regulatory system.

The recurring wildcat strikes on the Port of New York between 1945 and 1951 had left business elites and political authorities alike searching for new devices to regain control. Placed within the political context of the period—the centrality of the Marshall Plan for U.S. foreign policy, the Korean War, and the expanding U.S. economic interests overseas—control of the Port of New York continued to be undoubtedly an axiomatic component of deeply embedded elite political and economic interests. Growing opposition to Ryan's domination of the dock union made his control of the waterfront labor process dubious at best. For Ryan's opposition, however, if the mounting demand for democratic unionism galvanized the presence of competing opposition groups along the waterfront, their increasingly tenuous relationship driven by strategic political differences regarding the reform process would rapidly place them in opposing camps. After 1953, any immediate hope for a unified rank-and-file reform movement quickly dissipated as both liberal and left-wing groups took opposing sides. Waterfront reform increasingly became a question that mobilized dockworkers as well as significant sectors of New York's political and economic elites.

Since the onset of postwar wildcat strikes, the Port of New York had been under increasing scrutiny. It became the object of investigation by the New York State Crime Commission Hearings, the Senate Subcommittee Hearings on Interstate Commerce, various presidential boards of inquiry, a sensational series of articles written by journalist Malcolm Johnson for the *New York Sun*, the formation of a Brooklyn Rackets Grand Jury, the Citizens Waterfront Commission, the New York City Anti-Crime Committee headed by former assistant secretary of state Spruille Braden, and the Catholic Church, through the Xavier Labor Institute, led by Father John Corridan. In the public imagination, the docks of New York also gained immense notoriety as the subject of numerous magazine exposés and the 1954 movie *On the Waterfront* starring Marlon Brando, as well as lesser known versions of the same genre such as *Slaughter on 10th Avenue* and *Murder, Inc.*

Because of the complexity and diversity of the political forces favoring reform and the ability of the rank-and-file movement on the port to move rapidly between formal and informal forms of action, controlling workers demanded a much more complex set of regulations. The eighty-day cooling-off period provided by Taft-Hartley was rapidly being incorporated into the dockworkers' strike repertoire. Likewise business and political elites slowly sought to distance themselves from Ryan. They quickly learned, however, that simply changing the figurehead of the ILA would not suffice. Ryan's quick removal from office helped reinforce the power of local groups within the ILA structure, such as Tony Anastasia in Brooklyn. In this sense, the ILA leadership was in no way as monolithic as it appeared under "King Joe." That is, they could no longer depend on the ILA alone to contain the rebellious dockworkers even if the union wished to do so. To expand their sphere of influence into the dockworkers' reform movement, business elites worked simultaneously in various spheres of the regional and federal political structure, creating the legal devices and shaping public opinion. This process ultimately moved the center of the reform movement from the docks to the broader sphere of institutional politics, which implied linking local economic interests with the national political arena. The need for stricter regulation of the waterfront labor process, however, also reflected the underlying economic interest of business elites, even though unknown to many in the reform movement at the time. Since the end of the war, the U.S. Navy had made the technology of containerization of cargo available to shipping companies.

The Waterfront Commission

Of all the legislation and multitude of the public hearings covering the waterfront, the creation of the Waterfront Commission reflected the convergence of political and business elite interests with regard to control of the Port of New York and had a deep impact for the future of rank-and-file activism on the docks. The importance of the Commission on the Port of New York was both political and transformative.

The Waterfront Commission was organized as a result of the recommendations made to Governor Dewey by the New York State Crime Commission Hearings on the New York Waterfront. Moving rapidly through the process of legislative approval, the Commission was enacted in the state legislatures of New York and New Jersey between June 25 and June 30, 1953. Since it was an interstate regulatory commission, the Bi-State Compact was required to seek the approval of Congress, which it received on July 30; it was signed into law by President Eisenhower on August 12 and put into effect on December 1, 1953. Equally important with regard to the formation of the Waterfront Commission is the fact that its operation was not financed by federal or state money but by the shipping companies themselves.[2]

The two main components of the Waterfront Commission's structure were the operation of "Licensing and Information Centers," which controlled the hiring of dock labor, and "Investigation and Enforcement," which enforced the newly enacted regulations. Of the approximately 120 employees hired by the Commission, half were "field investigators." One of the early Commission reports declared: "The Commission was charged with re-establishing the dignity of the longshoremen by freeing them from discrimination in hiring and from kick backs, usury, and other forms of oppression; with restoring ethical practices on the port of management and labor representation by eliminating bribery and extortion."[3] On December 1, as promised, the employment centers of the Commission went into operation, putting an end to the shape-up hiring system, an important mechanism through which the ILA controlled dock labor. This did not signify, however, that the waterfront labor process became more democratic or inclusive or reflective of the interests of the vast majority of dockworkers. The Commission was far from politically impartial to, or economically disinterested in, elite political and economic interests.

The emergence of the Waterfront Commission initially divided employers. Thomas Jefferson Miley, executive vice president of the Commerce and Industry Association of New York, energetically supported the Commission's ratification. He commended "the prompt and resolute action of Governor Dewey and Governor Driscoll in agreeing on a framework for the Bi-State controls to clean up the Port of New York."[4] In contrast, even though the NYSA pledged to adhere to the new regulation, it was repeatedly accused of working against the regulation, which demonstrated at least some resistance to the Bi-State Compact.

Within the broader political context of McCarthyism, control of rank-and-file dockworkers was essential. In this sense, the Waterfront Commission worked in conjunction with the U.S. Coast Guard and the Office of Naval Intelligence, investigating and prosecuting those who did not acquiesce to the new system. By denying them waterfront passes, the Commission could regulate who worked and for how long.[5] The government-sponsored witch hunt included Coast Guard questionnaires that many received as they applied for registration as longshoremen. The questionnaire usually began by asking the infamous question: "Are you now, or have you ever been, an officer, or official, or member, or affiliated or associated with in any way any of the organizations set forth below?"[6] Immediately following the question was a list of 300 organizations, followed by two pages that dealt specifically with communist affiliation. "They would call you down; they held hearings . . . in an inquisition type of fishing expedition. If you didn't answer right they could take your pass away. . . . They tried with me, asking me if I was a member of the American Labor Party (ALP), whether I was a member of the Peace Committee. I had a whole damn hearing. Anybody who didn't face them out, who got scared, they would take your pass away," one activist recalled.[7] Others were not so lucky, and even if you went up against the Commission, the struggle could be long and costly. Pete Bel remembered: "The problem with the Waterfront Commission, the only way you could deal with that was to go public because we could try and influence public opinion. The Waterfront Commission was preventing beefs in a lot of instances from being settled on the piers. If there was a wildcat strike, if there was a disruption, the Waterfront Commission would be the first ones down and they would always threaten to lift your pass. So in essence they were the ship owners' enforcers. They were doing a better job than the union officials. . . . I'll tell you, I testified in June of 1964 at a State Senate Subcommittee against them and in July they took my pass away. It took me $3,000.00 and two and a half years of court fights to get my pass back."[8]

If the Waterfront Commission proved efficient at prosecuting dockworkers, they did not seem to have the same efficiency at eliminating waterfront gangsterism. According to the 1953 New York State Crime Commission report, one-third of the ILA leadership had criminal records. By 1964, however, the inconsistencies between the stated mission of the Commission (of ridding the waterfront of crime) and its actions were apparent. For example, even though loan sharking had long been common on the docks, the Commission could not stop it.[9]

Even if the Waterfront Commission was successful at limiting the infamous shape-up, the ultimate impact was to move the center of conflict and decision-making away from the port. The Commission became the embodiment of a highly repressive structure and regulatory system that ultimately worked to the disadvantage of the average longshoreman.[10] The AFL and a sector of the waterfront reform movement, however, saw in the government's actions a process that could restrain the activity of left-wing longshoremen and eliminate the ILA's control over dockworkers in one single process, thus clearing the way for the AFL's new labor organization on the Port of New York.

Shifting Patterns of Waterfront Employment and the Economy

The impact of the Commission's waterfront employment regulation would only be felt over time. It did, however, have an immediate effect on the growing representational dispute on the docks. That is, the rapid transfer of the employment process from the shape-up to the Commission's employment centers and the regulated longshore registration process imposed an entirely new set of conditions on those who sought employment as dockworkers. If maneuvering the daily shape-up was difficult, the transfer of control over employment to a politically biased, quasi-federal agency financed by the NYSA was no alternative. The introduction of the Commission's employment regulation occurred during a period of decreasing U.S. exports (1952–53), which drastically reduced waterfront employment, giving credence to the argument put forth by the ILA that the AFL with the support of the Commission was working toward eliminating jobs.

In 1952 and 1953, activity on the Port of New York experienced a rapid decrease of export tonnage handled by New York's longshoremen. The 1947 benchmark of waterfront economic activity would not be repeated. In 1947, the Port of New York received 5,051 long tons of import cargo and exported 10,940 long tons of cargo; 15,991 tons of cargo passed through the Port. By 1952, however, while the cargo tonnage of imports remained relatively steady (in fact, slightly higher), export tonnage decreased drastically. In 1952 import tonnage handled on the Port was 6,945 long tons and export cargo handled had dropped to 5,732 long tons, reducing the total amount of cargo handled by longshoremen on the Port to 12,677 long tons. By 1953 the total cargo tonnage handled on the Port had decreased even further to 10,753 long tons.[11]

The reduction of export cargo was followed by a reduction of men employed on the Port. Between October 1946 and September 1947, a total of 54,442 men worked the Port of New York, putting in 37,285,864 manhours. During the same period in 1952–1953, the number of men working the Port had declined to 42,286, working 33,772,248 man-hours, of whom 54.9 percent worked less than 700 hours. This made them ineligible for benefits, but more significantly, it also made them ineligible to participate in the upcoming representational elections, even though this sector of dock labor comprised over 50 percent of the workforce. This disparity in work hours also led to disparate earnings among dockworkers. Those who worked below 700 hours accounted for only 9.2 percent of the average annual earnings of longshoremen distributed by hours worked. In this sense, over half of the waterfront workforce received less than 10 percent of the annual wages earned by dockworkers.[12]

The political effect of the sudden decrease in waterfront employment was an important factor, albeit not the only one, which would shape the way longshoremen would vote in the upcoming elections. The reduction in employment occurred concurrently with the introduction of the Commission's waterfront employment scheme and was aggravated by large numbers of AFL seamen registering for dock work at the new employment centers.[13] Added to this was the limited number of eligible participants, thus reinforcing the ILA's claim during the elections that the AFL wanted to replace the regular longshoremen with unemployed seamen.

Waterfront Wars

On September 25, 1953, as contract negotiations between the ILA and the NYSA were under way, the AFL, at its national convention in St. Louis, expelled the ILA and chartered a new dock union on the Port of New York. The reason for the new organization, the AFL declared, was the inability of the ILA to adhere to its previous promises to "clean house" and remove the criminal elements from its organization. The creation of the new union, the ILA-AFL, set the stage for liberal waterfront reformers to abandon the ILA and join a new union being formed under the auspices of the AFL, the International Brotherhood of Teamsters (IBT), and the Seafarers International Union (SIU). The new dock labor organization also received the support of waterfront priest John Corriden, who viewed the gangsters of the ILA and the radical rank-and-file activists as being equally evil for longshoremen. "As everybody knows," Corriden stated, "one of the reasons I am in the work that I am doing is to fight communist penetration in labor unions. I have plenty of sources of information about what the communists are doing anytime they are active on the waterfront"[14] The three-year jurisdictional dispute that ensued between the AFL and the ILA redefined the nature of the growing conflict for control of the waterfront labor process. The newly organized ILA-AFL represented in large part those who viewed favorably the increasing federal and state control of the New York waterfront, which forced the reconfiguration of the political alliances both within the ILA and the rank-and-file movement. As longshoremen on both sides of the fray went to battle, wage and contract negotiations came to a halt, while political elites, under the direction of Governor Dewey in close touch with President Eisenhower, moved to expand their influence over the newly chartered union.

Purporting to represent the desire of New York's longshoremen for "honest and democratic trade unionism," the AFL executive board appointed IBT president Dave Beck and Paul Hall, secretary-treasurer for the Atlantic and Gulf Coast division of the Seafarers International Union, to lead a five-man trusteeship of the newly chartered AFL organization. The ILA-AFL also counted on the participation of four ILA vice presidents who had abandoned the old union. The new union started its campaign with a war chest of $200,000.[15]

If the rampant corruption and abuse of the old ILA had since become widespread public knowledge, the composition of the "honest and democratic" AFL union was not much better. Head trustee Beck, much like his ILA adversary Ryan, was soon to be the topic of a congressional investigation for the misuse of union funds. It was discovered that he "borrowed" over $250,000 from the IBT's Western Conference treasury for personal use and made payments to a Seattle building contractor to the sum of $146,678, a significant part of which was for the construction of a pool at his home and work done on the homes of other IBT officials. The approval for the expenses could never be verified because, much like what had occurred in the old ILA locals, the financial records had mysteriously disappeared.[16] The ILA-AFL received the support of longtime waterfront reformers and gangsters alike. For example, the union was readily supported by Gene Sampson of the rebellious Local 791 and John Dwyer of Local 895, both on Manhattan's Hudson River. Even though the membership of Local 791 voted overwhelmingly to remain in the old ILA, the members of Local 895 voted to affiliate with the ILA-AFL.[17] In contrast, the AFL dockworkers union also received the immediate adherence of John and Vincent Erato, union officials of Local 1199–1 in Brooklyn, who years earlier had been responsible for leading the persecution and demise of the Brooklyn Rank and File Committee led by Pete Panto.

There were few ideological differences (if any at all) between the ILA and the newly organized AFL dock union. Both unions were highly conservative. Since the early years of Ryan's tenure as president, the ILA had an "anticommunist fighting fund" (that he often used for personal expenses) from which he paid organizers to guard the docks, repressing rank-and-file opposition, which in Ryan's rhetoric was always "communist inspired." The AFL dock union likewise readily embraced cold war rhetoric. At first it was used to distance the ILA-AFL from the CP-led rank-and-file movement that remained particularly influential on the Brooklyn waterfront. For example, in 1953, AFL organizers Gene Sampson and John Dwyer proclaimed in the headline of a pamphlet they distributed concerning the Board of Inquiry Hearings, "This Is Not a Commy Paper. Attention ILA Members."[18] The AFL campaign to reform the waterfront would rapidly embrace the McCarthy era red scare, attempting to discredit the ILA by linking it to the CP and the ILWU.

The resemblance between the two competing dock unions was not only in their composition but in their tactics as well. In its first organizing campaign on the waterfront, according to reports, 300 ILA-AFL sympathizers, comprised mainly of seafarers and teamsters, rode in caravan to the Brooklyn docks, armed with sawed-off baseball bats, pipes, and jack handles, to "recruit" new members to the AFL union. The driver of the car transporting the arsenal was found to be an SIU employee, and he was immediately arrested and charged with possession of dangerous weapons.[19] Similarly, by mid-October 1953, the ILA-AFL filed charges with the NLRB against Brooklyn ILA officials "Tough Tony" Anastasia and his brother Gerardo. One of the main accusations was "threatening to do bodily harm and doing just that."[20]

Violence was a common practice of both organizations. For example, there was the case of 52-year-old hiring boss Mike Brogan of Pier 32, an ILA-AFL supporter. Brogan disappeared after work on September 29, 1953. Anonymous letters to the New York Crime Committee alleged that Brogan's body was in the oil tank of the ship *Moremacreed*. The ship's tank was searched upon its arrival in Rio de Janeiro, but there was no trace of the body. On October 21, however, Brogan's body was found floating in the Hudson River.[21] In actions that in many ways resembled the persecution of old rank-and-file activists, seventy-five ILA-AFL supporters in fifteen cars invaded the headquarters of ILA Local 1235 on Port Street in Newark, badly beating four ILA members and destroying the union hall. Even though it took approximately 100 Port Authority police to remove the AFL activists, no arrests were made.[22] The Port of New York had rapidly been transformed into a war zone.

The main difference between the two dock unions focused on how they viewed reform of the waterfront labor process and subsequently the role of the ILA. The ILA resisted the creation of the Waterfront Commission, viewing its organization and other government activity on the docks as an encroachment on their close-knit relationship with the NYSA. Since the approval of the Commission by Congress, the ILA had gone into federal court challenging the constitutionality of the measures. The reform of the dock union, in their opinion, could be done without external regulatory mechanisms. In contrast, since its inception the ILA-AFL relied heavily on the support of state and federal authorities to bolster its campaign to remove the ILA from the port.

Just one day after his appointment as head of the AFL dock union by George Meany, Dave Beck arranged a meeting with New York governor Thomas E. Dewey. Beck requested the governor's support to pressure shipping employers into not signing a new collective bargaining agreement with the old ILA. Equating the ILA's control of the Port of New York to that of Harry Bridges on the West Coast, Beck argued: "We see every evidence that the New York employers are bent on signing a contract they think will save them money, even though it means freezing racket control of the piers and making honest unionism that much harder. It was exactly that attitude on the part of waterfront employers that gave Harry Bridges his control of the West Coast." Beck's proximity to the governor was viewed as a signal of the new dock unions' support for state and regulatory measures. The *New York Times* reported that Beck's meeting with Dewey was a "sign of the new union's readiness to cooperate with the New York–New Jersey Waterfront Commission," which was scheduled to go into operation on December 1, 1953.[23] As Beck had declared in October: "We are one hundred percent convinced that it is the Commission's desire to recognize, develop and assist in every way the legitimate longshoremen in his employment. . . . We are one hundred percent in accord with the Commission for the elimination of all phases of muscle and corruption in the longshoremen's securing employment."[24]

Likewise, George Meany and the Executive Board of the AFL publicly declared their intention to support federal and state actions on the waterfront as well as seek their support for the ILA-AFL. The statement issued by the AFL executive board was clear: "The primary responsibility for wiping out crime on the waterfront rests upon the federal, state and local law enforcement authorities. We welcome indications that they are now determined to do so and point out that our efforts are being concentrated on the same objective. Therefore we rightfully expect full cooperation from the official authorities."[25]

There was a significant distinction between the campaigns that the two dock unions developed during the electoral process. The ILA-AFL denounced the corrupt practices of the ILA, while the AFL increasingly focused its campaign on portraying the ILA as being dominated by the ILWU and the CP. In contrast, the focus of the ILA's campaign argued that the ultimate goal of the AFL union was to replace the longshoremen who worked the port with Seamen and Teamsters, members of the SIU and IBT. Mounting control and regulation of waterfront employment by state and federal political authorities, combined with the effects of rapidly shifting patterns of employment, hours and wages, ultimately allowed the ILA to gain greater credibility in the upcoming representation elections of 1953–54.

The struggle for representation on the New York waterfront was further complicated because it coincided with the beginning of the 1953 NYSA-ILA contract negotiations. While the tensions created by the recurring wildcat strikes of the previous years had helped advance the demands of rank-and-file longshoremen, the ILA leadership had never readily embraced such tactics. Increasingly, however, the ILA began to use the same tactics employed by rank-and-file activists to deflect the mounting pressure of those who sought its demise. As the NY State Crime Commission prepared for its hearings on corruption in the waterfront labor process, Brooklyn dockworkers staged two wildcat strikes within a week's time. Two hundred dockworkers on Piers 36, 37, and 38 of the Barber Lines walked off the ships protesting a company practice of calling men into the shape-up and only hiring a few. The striking workers thus reiterated their long-standing demand to end the shape-up. In contrast, the previous week had witnessed a wildcat strike of 1,000 North River dockworkers protesting the issuance of subpoenas to the ILA leadership by the New York State Crime Commission. The employers' response to the strikes cut to the center of the upcoming contract negotiations, demanding "punitive action" on the part of the ILA leadership against the striking longshoremen. John V. Lyons, chairman of the NYSA, declared: "Normal management-labor relations cannot continue unless the union takes appropriate steps to live up to the contract."[26]

Similarly, as the conflict between the ILA and the NYSA continued to mount, wildcat strikes broke out on four Jersey City piers. Increasingly apprehensive employers threatened to withdraw from contract negotiations should the work stoppages continue. Even though Ryan was proving to be more and more ineffective, in his usual conciliatory manner he guaranteed shipping employers that there would be no more wildcat strikes. In a letter to the NYSA dated September 4, 1953, he stated: "The illegal strikes that took place on Piers D and F of the American Export Lines and Pier 9 of the American President Line in Jersey City was, of course, wrong and was strongly condemned by the delegates to the Wage and Scale Committee. . . . Work stoppages will not occur while an agreement is being negotiated."[27]

Ryan's incumbency as president of the ILA was becoming increasingly problematic. Under a barrage of indictments for using union funds to pay for personal expenses, even some of his old cohorts were now calling for his resignation. Michael Clemente, an East River ILA official, publicly called for Ryan to resign. According to Clemente, Ryan asked: "But why do you say that to me now when I've got an indictment hanging over my head?" Clemente responded: "What, I've got three indictments hanging over my head." By early October the mechanisms to remove Ryan from the presidency of the ILA were already in place. Within two months, a special convention of the ILA was convened, at which Ryan retired with a $10,000 per year pension and was replaced by ILA vice president William Bradley.[28]

The importance of the 1953 contract negotiations was twofold. First, the demands presented by the ILA sought to compensate for the minimal wage increases of past contracts negotiated under Ryan's leadership. Second, the negotiations were also a race against the growing movement led by the AFL that questioned the ILA's right to represent the longshoremen. That is, if the ILA could renew its agreement with the NYSA, it would retain its right for exclusive representation of New York's dockworkers for another year and thus ward off any pressure by the AFL for a representation election.[29]

Realizing the weakened position of the ILA, the NYSA not only resisted the economic demands, but sought to make structural changes in their relationship with the ILA that would move decision-making away from the piers and ultimately away from the dockworkers themselves. The initial demands put forth by the ILA included a 50 cent hourly wage increase over the existent $2.27 per hour; severance pay; a maximum sling load; the contribution of an additional 10 cents per longshoreman to the welfare fund; and a 20 percent payroll contribution to an unemployment relief fund.[30] The NYSA's counteroffer to the ILA's demands was minimal.

The employers remained steadfast proposing an 8.5 cent hourly wage increase, the appointment of a permanent waterfront arbitrator with "power to penalize," and the demand that the ILA withdraw the demands for severance pay, sling load regulation, the unemployment relief fund, and additional welfare contributions. As the September 30 deadline neared, a stalemate in the contract negotiations seemed inevitable in spite of the declaration from both sides that a contract was imminent. In a last-minute effort to reach an agreement, the ILA radically reduced its demands to a 10 cent hourly wage increase and four guaranteed work hours on Monday and eight hours per day from Tuesday to Friday when a longshoreman was hired on that day.[31]

This last-ditch effort for a contract led to increasing discontent even among those who worked within the ILA. Thomas "Teddy" Gleason, secretary-treasurer of Checkers Local 1346, announced, "This offer is a farce. I wouldn't blame our people for looking for new leadership if we accept it."[32] In contrast, Tony Anastasia in Brooklyn was promising that "there would be no strike in Brooklyn no matter what happens in this contract negotiation."[33] Added to the ILA's internal dissension were those sectors of the ILA aligned with the AFL who declared the contract a "sellout." Internal pressure and the mounting AFL organizing campaign forced a rapid shift in the ILA's contract negotiations. On September 29, just one day before the contract was to expire, the ILA made a final offer proposing a 13 cent per hour wage increase and a 3 cent per hour increase in the contribution to the welfare fund.[34] The NYSA's immediate rejection of the ILA's final offer sealed the fate of the port; the strike was on. The next day, ILA executive vice president Patrick "Packy" Connelly announced: "There will be a strike unless our demands are met."[35]

Up to this moment, mobilization was not a part of the ILA's political repertoire. As the dock union came under attack by the AFL and the state and federal governments, however, its campaign for legitimacy would include massive public demonstrations appealing for public support. In the first of such actions, on October 26, 1953, protesting the interference of state and federal authorities into the waterfront labor dispute, the ILA staged a massive march and rally in Madison Square Garden. Starting at Pier 74 and 34th Street, 15,000 marched down Twelfth Avenue in support of the ILA. Besides dockworkers from New York, the demonstration counted on the participation of delegations from other East Coast ports. Ryan made a quick appearance at the rally, but the event was led by Packy Connelly.[36]

Coinciding with the contract negotiations was the growing campaign by sectors not directly involved in the waterfront labor process seeking to pressure the NYSA into not signing a collective bargaining agreement with the ILA. The AFL, Governor Dewey, and sectors of New York's political elite all reinforced the demand that shipping employers not enter into an agreement with the ILA, no matter how acceptable or lucrative. The logic behind the campaign was that the lack of a contract would ultimately weaken the ILA's claim to exclusive representation and that if they had to choose between certifying the ILA for one more year and the possibility of a strike on the port, the latter was more acceptable.

The underlying belief behind their logic was that even in the event of a strike, the Taft-Hartley Law could always be invoked if the situation became uncontrollable. After a meeting between Beck and Dewey, the topic of which was their mutual interest that the NYSA not sign an agreement with the ILA, the ILA-AFL general organizer John Dwyer (formerly of ILA Local 895) sent a telegram to the NYSA urging them not to sign. In a news conference George Meany noted that given the present division between unions on the waterfront, signing an agreement might not avert a strike, since by doing so, it could lead opposing factions within the ILA to rebel against the ILA leadership's decision. Dave Beck added that if the contract was signed, the piers on which the signing shipping companies operated could be considered the target of a trucking boycott.[37] The position of Dewey and the AFL was reinforced by political reformers such as Spruille Braden of the New York City Anti-Crime Committee. In a statement to the shipping association, Braden urged the employers "not to deal directly or indirectly" with the "mobsters or their puppets in control of the union."[38] Finally, even federal and state mediators involved in the contract negotiations appeared sympathetic with the idea that the NYSA refrain from renewing its contract with the ILA. One daily newspaper covering the negotiation process wrote: "Federal and State mediators had all but given up their efforts to promote a direct wage agreement, in the apparent belief that a strike would be less harmful than a contract that would anchor the racket ridden union to the Port of New York and Atlantic Coast for another year."[39]

While all sides seemed headed for an inevitable strike, as the contract deadline arrived, business elites moved quickly. Even before the strike began, they pressured President Eisenhower to impose the Taft-Hartley Act on the East Coast longshoremen. The September 30 front page of the *New York Times* announced: "Business groups in the affected area from Portland, Me, to Newport News, Va, bombarded the White house with pleas for an eighty-day no strike order under the Taft-Hartley Act." Employer associations, such as the New York Commerce and Industry Association, estimated that a strike by New York's dockworkers would affect as many as 800,000 employees directly and indirectly with a financial loss of approximately $1.5 million per day in New York alone.[40] As the ILA prepared to go on strike, the Waterfront Commission was sending out the first lot of 27,000 employment registration forms.

On October 1, 1953, approximately 50,000 longshoremen walked off the ships. In response, the NYSA stepped up their efforts, pressuring the governors of New York and New Jersey to intercede and demanding that the federal government impose the Taft-Hartley Act. In a telegram to Governor Driscoll of New Jersey and Governor Dewey of New York, NYSA chairman John V. Lyons exhorted state authorities to speed up the issuance of an injunction against the striking dockworkers. He argued: "It is evident that the present interests of the general public and the national welfare and our industry are inseparable. It is therefore of paramount importance that you take prompt action in support of our request for an injunction, as provided under the Taft-Hartley Law." Even though the ILA-AFL promised not to cross the pickets of the striking ILA longshoremen, they added that they would continue to meet with Dewey to coordinate the actions of the state and the AFL to "clean up the waterfront."[41]

Just twelve hours after the strike began, Eisenhower, in response to the demands of the shipping companies and the state political officials, and in compliance with the Taft-Hartley Act, requested an immediate Board of Inquiry into the waterfront labor crisis with the purpose of issuing an injunction against the striking dockworkers. With a speed never before witnessed in other cases, the Board of Inquiry met, and on October 4 Eisenhower issued an eighty-day injunction against the ILA. This, however, was not the traditional "cooling-off" period between employers and workers, which was supposedly the original intent of the law. In fact, state political authorities had little, if any, intention of coming to terms with the ILA.

Political authorities hoped that the injunction would reinforce the campaign of the AFL to dislodge the ILA from the Port of New York. In a press conference held after he had met with Beck and Hall, Governor Dewey made it public that at no time was the state interested in reaching an agreement with the striking workers represented by the ILA. "I am greatly interested," he stated, "that the ship owners do not sign with the old racket controlled union. It would make our job much more difficult: our job is to clean out the racketeers and gangsters from the waterfront."[42] By issuing the measure, however, a conflict between distinct labor regulations emerged. On the one hand, the Taft-Hartley Law states that seventy days into the injunction, federal mediators should attempt to reach an agreement between the parties. Labor legislation under the Wagner Act, however, forbids unions from signing collective bargaining agreements if there are representation issues pending. Thus the AFL's representation request barred the ILA and the NYSA from reaching a settlement.

Even before the injunction was issued, both employers and the federal and state governments had realized this. When asked at the presidential fact-finding meeting held on October 3, if the eighty-day injunction provided conditions for both sides to come to terms, Joseph Mayper, representing the NYSA, responded: "I don't know. We have a new factor in this situation, namely notice from the American Federation of Labor of its prospective filing for a representation election among the workers."[43]

Even though striking dockworkers returned to work under the directives of the federal injunction, the measure did not prove completely effective in preventing disruption of work on the docks. For the first month, only the ILA was cited in the injunction, leaving the ILA-AFL free to continue its "recruitment campaign." Even after the government decided to include the ILA-AFL in the Taft-Hartley measures on October 24, Federal Judge Edward Weinfeld instructed Assistant District Attorney General Warren Berger and U.S. Attorney Edward Lombard Jr. to word their citation of the ILA-AFL in a way that would not impede the ILA-AFL's organizing activity.[44] The ongoing confrontation between the two unions that disrupted port activity included ILA longshoremen refusing to work alongside dockworkers affiliated with the AFL union or Teamster truck drivers refusing to carry cargo that was loaded or unloaded by ILA longshoremen. In one such instance, the shipping company on the Breakwater (a pier controlled by Tony Anastasia) in Brooklyn replaced an ILA hiring boss with another who was supportive of the ILA-AFL.

In response, 200 longshoremen sympathetic to the ILA went to battle with police who were protecting AFL-affiliated dockworkers attempting to enter the pier for work. As a consequence of the battle, several longshoremen were hospitalized,[45] and Tony Anastasia was cited for contempt of court for violating a federal injunction. In response to the growing conflict, a second injunction was leveled against the ILA. With the support of the U.S. attorney of Brooklyn, Leonard Moore, the AFL requested that the NLRB seek an injunction against Tony Anastasia and the ILA leadership to stop the threats that ILA-AFL activists had been receiving on the port.[46] By mid-October more than 1,000 police officers patrolled the waterfront as the competing unions and the state political authorities prepared to do battle for control of the docks.[47]

The main impediment to the contract negotiations was not simply the conflict between the demands put forth by the ILA and the interests of the NYSA. Any negotiations between the ILA and the NYSA hinged on resolving the representation conflict between the ILA and the AFL. In spite of this, the ILA continued to demand that the NYSA sit down to reach an agreement. The NLRB, however, quickly resolved the conflict between Taft-Hartley's obligation to vote on the employers' final offer and the Wagner Act's restriction on bargaining due to the representation challenge. In the NLRB's view, the NYSA had made no final offer, and since no final offer was made, there could be no Taft-Hartley final offer election, thus releasing employers from their legal obligations. The shipping companies were euphoric, as an NYSA spokesman proclaimed: "[The] decision is an excellent step; now the labor board can devote full time and facilities to holding a representation election which is the crux of the whole situation."[48] The election itself would be no simple task given the competing political forces that had entered into the fray.

Foremost was the time frame in which to hold the election. Both the ILA and the NYSA favored holding the election before the Taft-Hartley deadline on December 24. The argument made by shipping employers was that resolving the representation struggle before the Taft-Hartley injunction expired would significantly lessen the threat of a port-wide strike. For the ILA, the quicker the election was held, the less time the AFL would have to campaign and lessen the strain on the dock union's already dwindling resources. In contrast, the AFL and both the state and federal governments all hoped that the election would not occur any time soon, if at all. That is, while they all favored a delay in the electoral process, at one point the AFL proclaimed that the ILA should not be included on the ballot, arguing that the ILA was a company-dominated union and that its leadership had failed to sign the Taft-Hartley anticommunist loyalty oaths.[49]

Calming the employers' fear of a strike on December 24, Dewey argued that if it was necessary, the state's commerce legislation also had the power to enjoin the ILA and thus delay the process until the representation conflict was decided.[50] Major state and federal political authorities all made public their support for the AFL's demand for a delayed representation process. Newspaper headlines agreed with the White House and Governor Dewey, who had issued a "warning" that a quick waterfront election would "help the gangsters keep their grip on the waterfront." This was followed up by declarations of support for the AFL's demand by U.S. Secretary of Labor James P. Mitchell; Bernard Stanley, special counsel to the president; Governor Dewey; Joseph Proskauer, chairman of the New York State Crime Commission; and Lawrence Walsh, executive director of the Bi-State Waterfront Commission.[51] In the struggle over when to hold the election, the interests of the shipping employers and the fear of a port-wide strike on December 24 prevailed in the NLRB's decision. At a December 17 hearing, the Labor Board decided to stage the elections quickly.[52]

The elections were to be held on December 22 and 23, 1953, giving both sides little time to prepare. Even though he predicted a victory for the AFL slate, George Meany severely criticized the NLRB's decision, calling it "a moral disgrace" and stating, "The NLRB deserves public castigation for succumbing to pressure from the NYSA in deciding conditions of the election."[53] Immediately the AFL went to the airwaves to campaign. In a radio and television broadcast on the eve of the election, Meany exhorted New York's longshoremen to support the AFL dock union: "We want you in the AFL. . . . We don't want the gangsters; we don't want the underworld characters who are exploiting you day in and day out."[54]

Strange Bedfellows

As the election deadline grew closer, the ILA also sought to expand its base of support. In a surprise move, just one day before New York's dockworkers would cast their ballots, the ILA received the financial and public support from United Mine Workers union (UMWA) president John L. Lewis. In a meeting with Lewis, Captain Bradley, newly appointed president of the ILA, announced: "We cannot be wrong. John L. Lewis is with us. The only man in history to successfully defy the AFL. This man, whose name is a byword throughout the world, has proven he is for the working man, knows we are right and is with us all the way." Lewis's underlying interest in the ILA reflected his own isolation from the ongoing merger negotiations between the AFL and the CIO and the possibility of ultimately affiliating the ILA to the UMWA. As part of the mineworkers' support, the financially strapped dock union received a loan from the UMWA for $50,000 with the promise of much more if need be.[55]

More surprising than the support the ILA received from the CIO's elder statesman was the support of the dock union's West Coast nemesis, the

ILWU, and the Communist Party. In a bulletin to New York longshoremen, the ILWU sought to explain the shift in how it viewed the ILA: "We
have long realized the rough go you fellows have had. We have been critical
of some of your past leadership, but we have always been ready to support
you in your aims to build a good union and get decent conditions and
pay."[56]

The ILWU's support for the ILA reflected the combination of local interests of the West Coast union and broader industrywide interests. It also
represented mounting inter-union conflicts that reflected a problem for
all unions that did not adhere to the Taft-Hartley anticommunist oath and
that came under siege after being expelled from the AFL. First, supporting
the ILA meant defeating the AFL, which was also involved in organizing
the "anticommunist" opposition to Bridges on the West Coast. Thus a victory for the ILA would weaken the probability of the AFL raiding the West
Coast, and since the ILA was already debilitated, it presented no real threat
of staging a raid on the West Coast itself. Second, Ryan's "retirement" had
opened positions within the ILA leadership to some who were more sympathetic to the idea of developing national bargaining strategies that could
enhance the negotiations of the unions on both coasts, such as a common
contract expiration date for the ILWU and ILA.

Increasingly, Bridges and ILA officials were developing closer relations
that had been nonexistent during Ryan's reign over the ILA. Such was the
case of Thomas "Teddy" Gleason, who had organized the Checkers Local
and was later appointed to the position of ILA general organizer. He had
supported the 1951 rank-and-file wildcat strike against Ryan. The relations
between the two dock unions included an ILWU representative, Charles
Velson, who worked closely with Gleason. He was hired by the ILA and
worked as an intermediary contact, coordinating the activities between the
two organizations.[57]

The ILWU's support for the ILA was not only verbal but financial as
well, even though limited. Tony Anastasia and Anthony Impliazzo, along
with a group of Brooklyn ILA officials, visited the West Coast, where they
received $3,675 in donations from ILWU locals, including Local 10, Bridg-
es's local.[58] Velson was ultimately subpoenaed to appear before the Waterfront Commission that was investigating the ILWU's financial support of
the ILA. When he refused to answer the Commission's questions, he was
cited for contempt, a decision that was later upheld by the New York State
Supreme Court.[59]

The CP's support for the ILA, as odd as it may appear, reflected the Party's response to McCarthyism as CP-led unions became increasingly isolated as a result of the campaign to remove left-wing activists from the trade union movement. Specifically for the CP on the Port of New York, this was not so much a change in policy as it was a strategic shift in priorities. A central aspect of the party's political analysis of the period was the need for "labor unity," that is, the unity of all unions despite their political orientation, based on the principle that all unions were fundamentally organizations of class representation. Particularly for those CP activists in conservative-led unions, this implied an understanding of the conflict between the interests of the conservative leadership and the demands of the rank-and-file workers as a long-term component of their work in trade unions.[60]

This conflict would act as the impulse for the transformation of the union, with the emergence of a leadership that better served the "interests of workers and the class struggle." With no critical mention of the past ILA leadership, the CP-led rank-and-file bulletin *Dockers News* focused its argument on defending the unity of New York's longshoremen against the actions of federal and state political authorities and the AFL. *Dockers News* stated: "It was the unity and growing strength that forced the opening of negotiations. We must maintain and increase the pressure on the ship owners in order to force them to come across. This means we must maintain our ranks more solidly than ever and stick together until we win."[61] This is not to say that the CP had no objective interests in supporting the ILA.

The predominance of the party on the West Coast waterfront and in the ILWU most certainly helped shape their decision. That is, in the context of the mounting reaction against left-led unions within the trade union movement, for the ILWU it was preferable that a weak ILA rather than a strong AFL union should be in control of the Port of New York.

To the Ballots!

Polling stations for the first election were set up in the major centers where dockworkers concentrated, in Brooklyn, at Prospect Hall; in Lower Manhattan, on Hudson Street; and in Jersey City on Grove Street. Voting eligibility was limited to those dockworkers who had worked at least 700 hours between September 1952 and September 1953, thus severely reducing the participation of those who were employed on the docks. Because of the casual nature of waterfront employment, the number of participants in the dock election was reduced to half of those who worked the waterfront. This left approximately 22,000 longshoremen eligible to participate in the election.[62]

On the first day of voting, between 14,000 and 16,000 dockworkers peacefully cast their ballots. On the second day, however, violence broke out at the Brooklyn polling place. Three AFL supporters were stabbed.[63] The AFL charged that gangsters working for the ILA had encircled the Brooklyn polling station and intimidated voters. The final results were 9,060 votes for the ILA; 7,568 votes for the ILA-AFL; 95 votes for neither union; 116 votes annulled; and 4,405 votes contested. Immediately after the results were announced, Meany declared: "We do not accept the tally as indicating the true and free choice of the longshoremen, many of whom were forced to vote under threat and actual physical assault."[64] More than just the sour grapes of someone who had lost an election, Meany's declaration signaled even further expansion of federal and state legal action. This process helped consolidate the interests of political elites with the interests of the AFL for control of the New York waterfront.

The election, however, did not resolve the immediate question of representation on the docks, nor did it permit the ILA to reopen contract negotiations, which were now six months expired. Even though the ILA pressed to restart the negotiations,[65] and the NYSA initially signaled that they would be open to renewed discussions and await the NLRB certification of the election results to sign a final agreement, legal action by state political authorities quickly dampened any expectations of a quick solution.

Reinforcing the AFL's claim that the election had been tainted by "mob violence," Governor Dewey quickly assembled an investigative commission: Merlyn Pitzle of the NYS Mediation Board, Lawrence Walsh of the Bi-State Waterfront Commission, and New York City Police Commissioner George Monaghan. As for the possibility of a port-wide strike by the ILA, Dewey responded: "What was commenced as an inter-union conflict has become a battleground to decide whether government is to be coerced or whether it is strong enough to proceed in a judicial manner and assure honest working men the right to a free, fair, orderly and deliberate choice of the union that will represent them."[66] The battle for waterfront representation had never been purely an inter-union conflict. The governor's argument was laying the groundwork for the campaign to set aside the election. A fundamental aspect of the government's strategy was to impede the counting of the 4,402 contested ballots, which they feared would consolidate the ILA's victory. Greater political pressure by the state and federal governments was necessary if they were to prevail in the NLRB's upcoming hearings.

If earlier the NLRB had bowed to the interests of the NYSA and the ILA by holding the election quickly, this time Dewey was not leaving anything to chance. First, he publicly announced that if the NLRB proceeded to open the contested ballots, it could quickly become the target of a Senate investigation, which during the time of McCarthyism was synonymous with being included in the ongoing political witch hunt. Second, for the first time in the history of the Labor Board, the governor appointed a "special assistant attorney general," Whitney Seymour, to act as the state governments' representative in the NLRB hearings.[67] In a report to Dewey, Special Counsel to the Governor George Shapiro suggested that the state seek federal legislation to expand the Taft-Hartley Act to include gangsters, since the act only excluded communists from trade union activity.[68]

The December 24 expiration of the Taft-Hartley injunction against the ILA enhanced, even if only slightly, the ILA's bargaining power, as Captain Bradley announced: "We feel that we are free now to do anything we want to. . . . If we have to strike, we strike, and if we have a strike it will be a good one."[69] Bradley and the ILA, however, were not as "free" as they imagined. The dispute whether to validate or set aside the waterfront election was heightened by the mounting threat of a strike by both the ILA and the ILA-AFL, depending on the decision of the NLRB. Bradley declared that if the election were set aside, the ILA would go on strike. In response to Bradley's statement, ILA-AFL Executive Director Ace Keeny stated that a strike by the ILA would be considered "a lockout and the result of a conspiracy between employers and the mob controlled ILA. . . . We won't go back to work under any agreement made by the ship owners and the mob." This position received the immediate support of Teamsters President Dave Beck and the SIU's Paul Hall.[70]

The possibility of a generalized waterfront strike by both unions seemed increasingly possible given the growing number of quickie wildcat strikes. For example, early in January there were two strikes on the Brooklyn waterfront, one on Pier 2, led by the ILA, and another on Pier 29 led by the AFL. In Jersey City, a dispute regarding the recognition of the AFL shop steward led dockworkers on the Holland American Freight Line to go on strike as well. As the NLRB continued to examine the dockworkers election, the growing number of strikes spurred employers to seek federal injunctions in Brooklyn Supreme Court, demanding that the ILA show cause for its actions.[71]

The mounting campaign to annul the election by federal and state political authorities also made clear the growing division among employers with regard to negotiating a contract with the ILA. Initially, ship owners seemed willing to discuss the terms of a contract and await the NLRB election certification; now with the uncertainty that the election would be considered at all, even talking seemed fruitless. The position of significant sectors of employers toward the ILA increasingly mirrored the position held by the state and federal governments. At the annual meeting of the Westside Association of Commerce (whose members included some of the larger shipping companies), many employers now echoed the notion that a port-wide strike would be less damaging "than repetition of the conditions that have brought terror to our piers; higher costs to our consumers; a gradual building up of competing ports at our expense and a lowering in the eyes of the worlds of the prestige of America's greatest waterfront."[72]

A report submitted by NLRB Regional Director Charles T. Doud to the Labor Board's general counsel in Washington, reinforced the claims of the AFL and the state and federal political authorities. That is, that coercion by ILA activists had played a significant role in the waterfront election and warranted examining the possibility of setting the election aside.[73] Dewey reacted enthusiastically to the regional director's report. If during the first election they were at odds, the NLRB's new position demonstrated that the federal and state authorities were now closing ranks. Commenting on Doud's report, Dewey, who had recently threatened the NLRB with a Senate investigation if it failed to act in the interests of the federal and state governments, now lauded the NLRB director for demonstrating "courage and thoroughness in the threats of a strike designed to intimidate him."[74] The ILA-AFL leadership took a similar position as Ace Keeny declared: "We are glad that the government of the United States, in Washington, now stands in judgment on the despoilers of the New York Waterfront."[75] Even though Dewey's claims of ILA-inspired violence during the polling process were not totally without merit, neither the actions of the ILA nor the ILA-AFL throughout the short-lived campaign were models of democratic unionism. Moreover, although Dewey publicly abhorred the coercive tactics of the ILA, the governor seemed increasingly ready to use similar methods to gain cooperation for his campaign against the ILA.

Now, with the support of the NLRB and the employers hardening their stance against negotiations with the ILA, Dewey had harnessed what he believed were the political forces necessary for the AFL to defeat the ILA. All that was missing was for the election to be set aside. This seemed increasingly possible, even though the NLRB kept advising that any decision regarding the election would take months to conclude.

Although isolated, the ILA was not entirely without alternatives. The open support of the governor for the AFL was rapidly providing the conditions for a port-wide strike. In a radio interview Bradley denounced Dewey, claiming he had become an organizer for the AFL: "We know meetings were held between Dewey, Dave Beck of the Teamsters and George Meany President of the AFL, where they worked out a program for the ILA-AFL. . . . We say deals have been made to split the longshoremen up whereby the AFL would gain."[76] By March 1954, however, the growing conflict between the AFL and the ILA was coming close to shutting down the port. The conflict erupted when ILA dockworkers on the Westside of Manhattan refused to handle cargo transported on trucks driven by teamster drivers of IBT Local 807. The job action quickly spread to New Jersey and the employers declared that the port was rapidly coming to a standstill.[77]

In response to the boycott by ILA dockworkers, teamster truck drivers set up pickets to impede other truckers from entering the port. The federal government moved quickly to stop the movement; within twenty-four hours, NLRB Regional Director Doud requested and received injunction orders from Federal Judge Edward Dimock halting the job action under the secondary boycott provisions of the Taft-Hartley Act. While the ILA contended that the job action was "spontaneous," when boycotting longshoremen refused to heed the injunction order, the NLRB then proceeded to request contempt citations against the ILA. Taking action on the NLRB contempt request, Federal Judge David N. Edelstein fined the dock union $100,000.[78] Even though the NYSA had stated within their request that the teamsters were just as responsible for the job action and should be enjoined as well, Beck and the IBT were not cited for contempt.

After one week, what had started as a boycott by ILA dockworkers had been transformed into a full-fledged strike, and the entire port was paralyzed. The striking dockworkers demanded that the NLRB certify the ILA as the victorious union in the election and that the NYSA come to terms on the long overdue contract. CP waterfront activists gave their full support to the ILA strike. The striking ILA dockworkers also received the support of the National Maritime Union, which wired the NYSA advising that their members would not board ships where "inexperienced labor" was being used, as did the ILWU, which refused to work scab ships that had been loaded in New York.[79]

In spite of mounting political and legal pressure against the union and striking longshoremen, the job action continued to gain strength. As Judge Edelstein was signing the contempt citation against the ILA, approximately fifty dockworkers manned a picket in front of the federal courthouse in Foley Square.[80] Even though authorities viewed the ILA as primarily responsible for the strike, the union kept denying it. In the second week of the job action, a strike committee appeared assuming responsibility for the port-wide work stoppage. The organization of the strike committee resembled that of the rank-and-file activists of years past that the ILA leadership had so strongly persecuted, only this time the identity of the committee members was kept secret for fear of reprisals from the Waterfront Commission. A committee spokesman summed up the tension and frustration that had been growing over the past six months: "For six months we have been working without a contract, waiting for the Labor Board to certify our union. . . . We won an election and waited out an eighty-day injunction under the Taft-Hartley Act. Now we are being told that we have to wait months and months more while the Board investigates? If the AFL is so strong, why can't it work the port now? It told the longshoremen to work, but no one is working."[81]

The AFL had been making numerous, albeit unsuccessful, attempts to break the ILA's strike; however, they were largely outnumbered by the picketing dockworkers who blocked the entrances to the piers. As the strike movement continued to consolidate its grip over the port, Checkers also walked off the docks in support of striking longshoremen, and by week's end the pickets of striking longshoremen in front of the courthouse had grown from 50 to 250.[82]

The strike was taking its toll. Ancillary industries began to lay off workers. Larger shipping companies, such as the Moore-McCormick, were considering moving their operations to Baltimore, and importers/exporters faced with bankruptcy met to consider their options if the strike continued.[83] Increasingly high levels of violence occurred almost daily, as ILA longshoremen battled the police, AFL strikebreakers, and teamsters, all of whom were attempting to reopen the port. As one longshoreman remembered: "All hell broke loose on the docks."[84]

The strike had met a stalemate; there would be no resolution to the conflict that did not include a solution to the union representation struggle. Seeking to speed up the process, New York City Mayor Wagner called the NLRB urging the board to speed up their examination of the waterfront election. Guy Farmer, NLRB chairman in Washington, responded to the mayor's request declaring that at least a month would be needed to reach a decision.[85] Even though the NLRB had projected that any decision would take thirty days to render, the long-term paralysis of the port, combined with high levels of violence, was sufficient pressure so that the NLRB rendered a decision within approximately ten days.

On April 1, 1954, the NLRB decided to set aside the December dock election and proposed new elections within six weeks. It stipulated that the ILA could participate if it ended the 29-day strike, which was considered the most costly and violent dock strike ever on the Port of New York.[86] The ILA's response to the NLRB was likewise quick. Rapidly the "strike committee" convened and decided to return to work immediately. Captain Bradley announced: "I have met with the rank-and-file strike committee and they have advised me that after meeting with their representative local members and considering the unprecedented and illegal threat by a Government agency to force the ILA off the ballot of a newly ordered election, they recommend that I as president order the men back to work."[87]

In the view of city, state, and federal political authorities, the policy of supporting the AFL while isolating and coercing the ILA appeared victorious because it brought an end to the port-wide strike and the invalidation of the December election. Dewey declared that the annulment of the December election between the ILA and the ILA-AFL was "a victory for decency," which reinforced their campaign to "drive out gangster control." He added that the ILA should be kept off the ballot in spite of having returned to work.[88]

The campaign waged by federal and state authorities was summed up best by Secretary of Labor James P. Mitchell: "The end of the illegal work stoppage on the Port of New York six days after the combined resources of the federal and state government had been coordinated, is heartening evidence of the effectiveness of team work. Without making one concession to the irresponsible leadership who paralyzed the port for 29 days, the forces of law and order, an important part of which was legitimate unionism, will succeed in restoring the port to normal operations. . . . In the future an election may be held to enable the hard working man [*sic*] on the piers to select a responsible union to represent them."[89] For Mitchell, the AFL was more than just a competing union in a port-wide representation election. The national union was part of the federal and state officials' "team" charged with restoring "law and order" to the port—it represented responsible unionism.

The strike could not be viewed as a victory for the ILA in any form. Neither of the ILA's demands for an exclusive contract with the NYSA and/or the certification of the December election was achieved. Moreover, the dockworkers were feeling the pressures of economic hardship. For the ILA, the combined actions of the state and federal governments had led to multiple subpoenas, injunctions, contempt citations, and fines adding up to over $1 million with the union under four federal grand jury investigations into its strike activities, while its leaders faced indictment.[90]

These actions had severely debilitated the dock union both financially and politically. The strike did, however, inflict serious economic damage on waterfront employers. Before the job action some employer representatives had declared that they would confront a port-wide strike rather than negotiate an agreement with the ILA, but after the strike this did not seem to be the case. The Commerce and Industry Association reported that the financial loss to foreign trade alone due to the strike was well over $25 million.[91] For example, fruit and vegetable importers reported that the simultaneous unloading of multiple ships tied up in the port during the strike created a glut in the market, forcing the prices of many perishable items to drop rapidly. As the ships began to unload their cargo, importers estimated the loss to be approximately $500,000 per day, but as one importer claimed, to calculate the financial loss imposed on employers during the strike, that amount should be multiplied many times over.[92] According to the NYSA, the combination of six months of "quickie wildcat strikes" and the 29-day work stoppage resulted in approximately 5 million man-hours of lost time.[93]

If neither the striking ILA dockworkers nor the shipping companies were victorious at the end of the strike, however, neither could the federal and state governments claim victory in their anti-ILA campaign, as Labor Secretary Mitchell and Governor Dewey had declared at the end of the strike. In spite of the strain placed on the ILA, striking dockworkers were able to bring the representation process to the forefront. A quick election was even more crucial to the ILA strategy. In many respects the strike had helped reconfigure the ILA as a trade union, lending it greater credibility. If in the past worker mobilization and strikes were not a part of the ILA's repertoire, the strike had reinvigorated the dock unions' capacity to resist the pressures of the state and federal government, forcing the ILA to assume a new role, even if only for a brief period.

In the eyes of longshoremen, the AFL, in alliance with state and federal political authorities, had pushed the ILA to assume the role of the underdog, a role well known to those who worked the waterfront. Even though the ILA commanded the strike unofficially, the strikebreaking activity of the AFL longshoremen and teamsters made the ILA-AFL union increasingly resemble the ILA of the past, when it was under the leadership of "King Joe." At the same time, Bradley was ordering the striking dockworkers to return to the piers: "We won one election and we are confident of winning the new elections. The AFL has demonstrated their inability to break the wildcat strikes with their out of town strike breakers. However, we as American citizens resent the efforts of any public official or agency to attempt to intervene on the side of one union organization against another."[94]

In spite of Bradley's claim to citizenship, as the new election date neared, support for the AFL continued to grow. This reflected mounting political pressure to draw reluctant sectors of the shipping industry that continued to favor dealing with the ILA into supporting the AFL. Austin J. Tobin, executive director of the New York–New Jersey Port Authority, was adamant in his support for the AFL dock union. Speaking at the annual meeting of the New York Chamber of Commerce, he echoed the declarations of Dewey and Meany that the ILA represented the continuity of mob rule and subsequently the diversion of commerce to other ports. More significant, however, was Tobin's strong criticism of those sectors of the shipping industry that resisted overtly supporting the ILA-AFL. He also severely criticized the NYSA's relations with the ILA as having a "shabby and servile record that does not represent the policies and principles of our shipping companies. . . . The Association deprecated the work of the NYS Crime Commission and played the game of the ILA in the last strike."[95]

On the other side of the conflict, in the days preceding the election, the ILWU and the CP rank-and-file activists became increasingly vocal in their support for the ILA. Harry Bridges wrote in the ILWU's *Dispatcher*,

"[We back the ILA] because it is the union which the majority of the long-shoremen want. . . . It led the fight against the jurisdictional raiders, the union busters, the scab herders, and the politicians—it led the fight to get a union contract from the employers."[96] The ILWU's support for the ILA provoked a reaction from both political authorities as well as the AFL. Even though the ILA continued to make rhetorical denunciations against communism, linking the ILA to left-wing activity had become the center-piece of the AFL's waterfront campaign.

The financial support that the ILA received from the ILWU immedi-ately provoked the interest of Waterfront Commission investigators, who, even though admitting that it was not against the law to donate money, said they were going to "investigate subversion on the piers." The Commis-sion spokesman reiterated that they (the Commission) had the power to deny longshore registration to anyone "who knowingly or willingly advo-cates the desirability of overthrowing or destroying the government of the United States by force of violence or who shall become a member of such group which advocates the desirability, knowing that the purpose of such group includes such advocacy."[97]

Riding the wave of anticommunist hysteria, the ILA-AFL seized on the Commission's statement and made linking the ILA to CP activity on the port a central focus of its campaign. For example, during the campaign AFL supporters appeared in front of Pier 45 on West 10th Street dressed as Cossacks. They held up signs declaring, "A Vote for the ILA Is a Vote for the Commies,"[98] indicating that voting for the AFL would help deter the spread of communism on the waterfront. AFL waterfront leader Ace Keeny argued: "They [the CP] are supporting the ILA independent hoping that a victory for the discredited organization will allow Bridges and the Communist Party to seize power when the indictment laden leaders of the ILA are tried, convicted and jailed for theft, bribery and perjury."[99] Taking advantage of the AFL's political witch hunt, U.S. Attorney Leonard Moore asked the FBI to investigate Tony Anastasia's relationship to West Coast waterfront communists.[100]

Defending himself from the accusations of seeking an alliance with the CP, Anastasia declared that the money raised on the West Coast was do-nated by rank-and-file dockworkers to help support twenty-nine Brooklyn longshoremen screened off the piers by the Waterfront Commission.[101] This resonated with the ILA leadership's vehement denial of having any understanding with the ILWU or the Communist Party. Bradley quickly responded that he "did not want or ask for help from Bridges," a sentiment that was echoed by Packy Connelly, who reiterated: "We don't want anything to do with Bridges."[102] Even Anthony Impliazzo (who had accompanied Anastasia to the West Coast) announced that no one worked on the Brooklyn waterfront without signing the Taft-Hartley anticommunist oath. Bradley even threatened that "immediate action would be taken against ILA officials trafficking with communists."[103] All of the ILA's denunciation of communism, however, would not deflect the federal government's mounting campaign.

As political pressure began to mount against the ILA, so did the federal government's action to limit the ILA's effectiveness in the upcoming election by severely limiting its access to resources. Just five days before the election was to take place, the Justice Department subpoenaed the ILA's financial records and sequestered the union's bank assets, seeking to verify its ability to pay $50,000 in criminal contempt fines that were owed as a result of the strike.[104] Three days later, the government requested that the ILA be placed in receivership to ensure that the fines would be paid. One day before the election, the ILA was placed under federal receivership, and Raymond Scully, vice president of the New York Bar Association, was appointed the union's new administrator.[105]

Coinciding with the ILA's being placed in receivership, once again George Meany hit the airwaves exhorting New York's dockworkers to vote for the AFL union. Summarizing the contest as a struggle of good versus evil, Meany argued that the choice was between "evil men, racketeers, exploiters working with crooked employers or longshoremen, working in conjunction with employers, working through a decent union."[106] Evidently, for Meany, the characteristics of shipping employers changed drastically depending on which union they were to deal with. Responding to the AFL's attack, the ILA mobilized two separate rallies, one in Brooklyn and the other in Manhattan, with the participation of 6,000 longshoremen in support of the upcoming election. Responding to Meany's statements, Bradley denounced the AFL for using the state and federal political structure as "Charlie McCarthy's in a union-busting campaign to take over the waterfront."[107] On May 26, 1954, in what was described as a "church like calm,"[108] 20,000 dockworkers lined up in polling stations set up near all major piers. The result of the second ballot was almost as close as the first election: the ILA received 9,110 votes, the ILA-AFL received 8,791, with 49 votes void, 51 votes for no union, and 1,797 votes contested by the competing unions.[109]

Initially it appeared as though the AFL and state and federal authorities would repeat the tactics used in the first election. NLRB regional director Doud announced that it could take anywhere from six weeks to two months to investigate the challenged ballots. AFL general organizer John Dwyer's statement reinforced this position: "Even if we lose we will not give up the fight to clean up the waterfront."[110] The initial move by the AFL dock union included delaying the investigation by submitting numerous protests to the electoral process. Fearing that the second election was headed in the same direction as the first, Bradley pressured to advance the certification process because he "might not keep the men at work if the NLRB keeps kicking us around like it did before." Doud responded to Bradley's threat of a strike by reminding him that any job action would be met with yet another federal injunction.[111] Bradley quickly responded: "Regardless of what the NLRB and Governor Dewey do, the rank-and-file longshoremen are going to stick to the ILA."[112] The AFL challenge had left the ILA seriously debilitated and half a million dollars in debt.[113]

As it became clear, however, that the ILA had won the second election, significant sectors of the ILA-AFL began the slow but steady return to the ranks of the ILA. For example, the chief ILA-AFL organizer in Jersey City, Willie DeNobile, announced shortly after the results were known that "98 percent of the AFL members are ready to return to the ILA. . . . They say the ILA won two elections and they want no more of this bickering. The rank-and-file longshoremen are the real sufferers from all these contests, all he wants is a strong union and a chance to work."[114] As a final solution to the electoral conflict, Doud proposed, and the NLRB general counsel in Washington accepted, that 655 of the 1,797 contested votes be counted. In the final result the ILA continued to hold the lead even if the difference between the two dock unions had diminished—the ILA received 9,407 votes and the ILA-AFL received 9,144 votes. By July the ILA was certified as the bargaining agent of New York's dockworkers.

With the election decided, the ILA turned to negotiating the contract that had expired more than a year earlier. By October 1, 1954, however, no agreement had been reached. The crux of the stalemate between the ILA and the NYSA was the question of retroactive pay.[115] The NYSA offered the ILA an 8 cent per hour wage increase and a 2 cent increase in the Welfare Fund contributions. The employers argued that the increases would include the upcoming contract year of 1954–55 while the ILA demanded that the increase cover the year past, 1953–54, leaving the upcoming contract period unresolved. By October 3, with no solution in sight, for the second time in six months, dockworkers abandoned the piers of Brooklyn, Manhattan, and New Jersey. The strike, however, was short-lived; within two days the ILA and the NYSA reached a tentative agreement that paid the wage increases retroactively but not the contributions to the Welfare Fund. The agreement also included a thirty-day truce to resolve remaining differences, at the end of which the ILA had signed a two-year collective bargaining agreement that extended to October 1, 1956.[116]

While Bradley welcomed the return of AFL-affiliated longshoremen to the ILA, he refused to allow the return of ex-ILA officials to the organization. Neither John Dwyer nor Gene Sampson had intentions of returning to the old dock union, nor was the question of representation settled as was initially believed.[117] In their national convention, held on June 28, 1954, the ILA-AFL decided to continue its battle against the ILA and adopted a new name—the International Brotherhood of Longshoremen (IBL-AFL).[118] Even though the IBL did not represent New York's dockworkers, it did hold the representation certification to some smaller, less significant units, such as Chicago and Duluth. The IBL could count on only limited support from the newly merged AFL-CIO. Meany and Beck retreated to the background of the waterfront conflict, and of the three big unions, only Paul Hall and the SIU continued to give their full support to the Brotherhood. Another significant factor that signaled the retreat of important sectors of the AFL-CIO from the dock fray was the growing approximation between the IBT and the ILA. By November 1955 the two organizations had signed a "Mutual Assistance Agreement."[119]

The IBL published a weekly newsletter, *Waterfront News*, and the focus of its campaign over the next two years continued promoting the Cold War hysteria and attempting to link the ILA to the Communist Party and the ILWU, a strategy consolidated during the May 1954 representation election. Week after week the headlines of the newsletter announced: "Bridges Opens NY Drive with Full ILA Support," "Bridges Okay's Gleason's Plan for Big New York Strike," "ILA, Bridges Sit Down to Work Out a Deal," "Velson Admits He's Here for Bridges, Mum on Commie Ties," thus hoping to draw on the national sentiment shaped by the political witch hunts of the mid-fifties.[120] The AFL leadership, however, appeared increasingly divided in relation to both waterfront labor organizations. In spite of the AFL-CIO's ambiguity, the IBL-AFL challenged the ILA to a third representation election, just two months before the 1956 ILA-NYSA contract was to expire and one day before negotiations were to begin. On August 1, 1956, the IBL filed 13,000 union pledge cards with the NLRB. Accordingly, the NLRB set the election date for October 17, 1956; it was the third representation election in a three-year period.[121]

The merged AFL-CIO leadership was clearly divided about what level of support, if any, would be given to the IBL, in spite of the fact that it was a member union of the AFL-CIO. When AFL-CIO leaders were informed of yet another waterfront election, their reactions varied. In a meeting of the executive council of the AFL-CIO, Meany announced that the IBL would receive help, but not to the same extent that they received in the 1953–54 campaign. For Meany there were "more important campaigns to support."[122] Meanwhile, Dave Beck, now AFL-CIO vice president, who had helped organize the IBL and led the 1953–54 campaign against the ILA, remained ambiguous and would not support either of the competing dock unions. He argued: "The election cannot change in the slightest degree the fundamental basic reasons why teamsters and longshoremen must work together."[123]

The most uncompromising of ILA supporters was Joseph Curran of the NMU. During the 1953–54 representation strike Curran had removed NMU members from the struck ships, alleging that he could not allow his members to work with inexperienced dockworkers. In a letter to Meany, he said, "[While] aware of the faults and shortcomings of the ILA—the labor movement should help the ILA put its affairs in order rather than replace it." In the same letter, Curran made strong attacks on Paul Hall and the SIU.[124] Even the Maritime Trades Department of the AFL-CIO refused to issue a statement of support for the IBL, preferring to remain neutral in the upcoming waterfront contest.[125] The main support for the IBL continued to come from the SIU, which donated $250,000 to the IBL election campaign.[126]

Shortly after filing the pledge cards with the NLRB, the IBL sought an agreement with the ILA that would avoid a third ballot. The demands made by the IBL, however, made it clear that they were negotiating in the interests of the SIU. The IBL demanded that the ILA adhere to the decisions of the AFL-CIO Maritime Department Grievance Board (even though the

ILA was not a member of the AFL-CIO) and cut off all ties with Harry Bridges and the ILWU. They expected full cooperation from all AFL-CIO port unions and asked that the fulfillment of the agreement be overseen by SIU president Harry Lundeberg.[127] In reality the IBL's proposal would have given the SIU and the AFL-CIO de facto control over the ILA, which for obvious reasons was not acceptable to the ILA. Rebuffing the IBL's bid, Bradley quickly answered: "If we have to fight, then fight we will, and this time we intend to make a fight that will leave no doubt who speaks for the longshoremen."[128] Early in August, IBL caravans began touring the port, even though they were much more diffident than in the previous two elections.

According to New York Police Commissioner Stephen Kennedy, the third representation election "proceeded like a Sunday School picnic." Out of 22,038 longshoremen eligible to vote, 20,597 participated in the election. In the third contest the ILA distanced itself significantly from the IBL. The ILA received 11,827 votes; the IBL received 7,428. There were 92 votes void, 143 votes for no union, and 1,107 challenged votes. Even if all of the challenged votes were counted, it would not change the outcome—the ILA had once again confirmed itself as the representative of New York's dockworkers. Informed of the results, "Teddy" Gleason declared, "The men have spoken."[129]

Although the IBL was incapable of unseating the ILA from the Port of New York, the AFL-CIO dock union continued its campaign over the next three years. After winning the election, the ILA expressed interest in returning to the AFL-CIO, but Meany initially resisted the idea. In a meeting with Bradley, Meany told the ILA president that "the organization had done nothing to rectify the conditions for which it was expelled."[130] Meany, however, would not hold this position much longer. Over the next two years, in spite of the ongoing campaign of the IBL, the ILA consolidated its control over the waterfront labor force once more. By March 1959, the AFL-CIO set up a committee to examine the return of the ILA to the national labor organization. This laid the groundwork for the special convention of the IBL, held the following October, where it was voted to return to the ILA, thus creating the conditions for the ILA to be readmitted to the AFL-CIO.

The ability of the ILA leadership to continue its control of the port reflected the politically complex alliances constructed by the distinct rank-

and-file groups and port unions. These alliances occurred within the context of expanding federal and state regulation over port employment and union activity during a period of reduced waterfront employment. The dockworkers' support for the ILA was also driven by their fear of losing their jobs to competing maritime unions such as the SIU.[131] The struggle for control of the docks would take on a new twist as the automation of waterfront cargo transportation gradually became prevalent on the docks.

Figure 1. Pete Panto, leader of the Brooklyn rank-and-file dockworkers' movement.

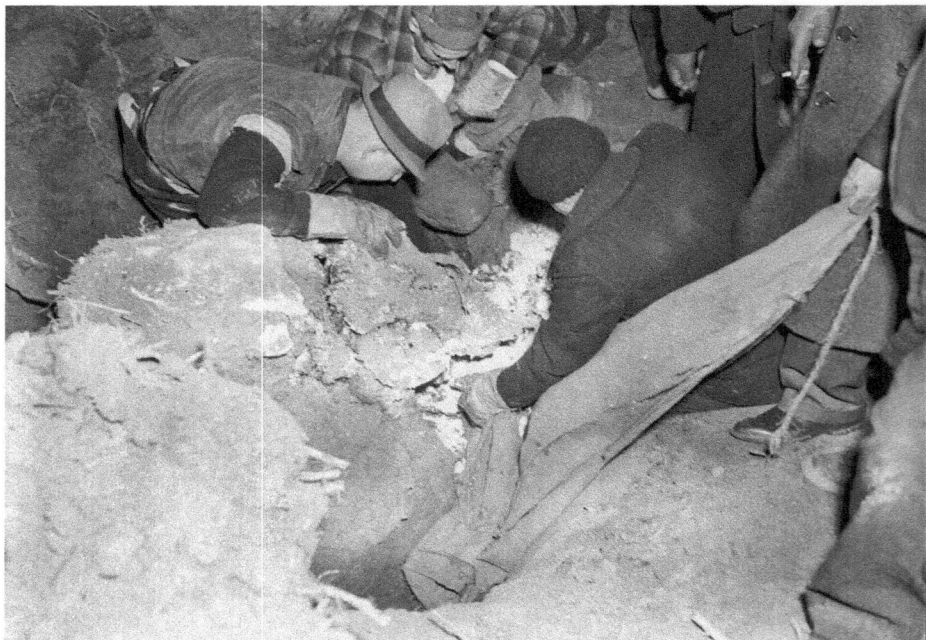

Figure 2. Panto was murdered by gangsters on January 29, 1941, and his body was discovered in a lime pit in Lyndhurst, New Jersey. Credit: New York Daily News Country.

Figure 3. In spite of the reign of terror on the Brooklyn waterfront, the slain longshore leader received a massive farewell as the funeral procession made its way down Degraw Street in Brooklyn. Credit: New York Daily News Country.

MAXIMUM
DRAFTS
2100 LBS.

Shape Up

VOICE OF THE RANK AND FILE LONGSHOREMEN

20MEN TO A GANG.
NO SPLITTING
GANGS.

Rm. 413, 186 Remsen St. Brooklyn, N.Y.   March 1, 1941

HOBOKEN MEN ENFORCE CONTRACT!!!!

The ILA contract states that no longshoreman shall work after 6PM on Saturday. On Saturday, February 23, on a Dollar Line ship being worked in Hoboken, N.J., six gangs were ordered back after 6PM. A couple of the longshoremen called the union hall, but as usual, could not find a delegate. So the men took it on themselves to enforce the contract. The 6 gangs refused to go into work in spite of everything that the boss could do. A couple of the men who led this action, after walking away from the dock, were arrested by the police for disorderly conduct and fined $10. The men in Hoboken are organizing to see that they get conditions on the job. If the ILA officials won't help them, they will do it themselves on the docks and take the ILA away from Nolan and his gang of petty racketeers. If every longshoreman was on the job to see that our contract is lived up to, we'd have a lot better conditions than we have.

SHIPOWNERS RAISE FREIGHT RATES!!!!

Shipowners raised their freight rates on cargoes going to the Orient and to the Far East by 15%. In plain words this means that the shipowners are out to make even more money than ever before. The best we can expect to get out of it is bigger drafts, longer stretchcuts, more speed up....UNLESS, every longshoreman attends his union meetings and helps to make a decent union out of his local. If the delegates we are paying $75 a week won't help us cut out the speed up then we'll fire them and elect new delegates that will listen to the membership!

ATTEND YOUR UNION MEETINGS!

LONGSHOREMEN WANT PEACE--NOT WAR!

Joseph P. Ryan and Emile Camarda say they are in favor of all aid to England who they say is fighting for democracy. We think the longshoremen should know that the longshoremen in Canada, most of them members of the ILA don't agree with Ryan and Camarda. The democracy England is fighting for is only for people like Churchill and his gang of millionaires. The Canadian longshoremen find themselves working at a terrific, dangerous speed up, worse than ever before. The officials of the ILA in Canada who tried to put up a fight for the mens' conditions, were thrown into jail. Food prices and rent have gone up sky high. Wages have not gone up. So for the Canadian longshoremen the war don't mean democracy, it means death for their sons who were forced to go overseas to fight for England. It means terrific speed up on the docks for them, and less food and comfort for their families. We should learn from what is happening to the longshoremen in Canada and try to keep our country from getting mixed up in the European war any deeper than we are. We can do this by doing everything in our favor to defeat the Lease-Lend Bill, H.R. 1776 which is now before the Senate and if passed will give Roosevelt greater power than Hitler. We Italian longshoremen remember how England sold Italy down the river in the last war. We don't intend to get burnt twice. The Irish longshoremen know from personal experience how phoney Churchill is when he speaks of "Saving Democracy".

TAKE JOB ACTION
TO END SPEED-UP!

Figure 4. Even after Panto's death, the Brooklyn Rank and File Committee continued to organize on the docks. Credit: Author's personal collection.

Figure 5. Dockworkers return to work under court order after five days on strike (1953). Credit: New York Daily News Country.

Figure 6. Over the years, striking dockworkers would regularly do battle with police. Members of the ILA-Independent confront police on Halleck and Columbia Street in Brooklyn. Credit: New York Daily News Country.

Figure 7. New York's dock strikes had a ripple effect, inspiring other maritime workers to walk out in support. Credit: New York Daily News Country.

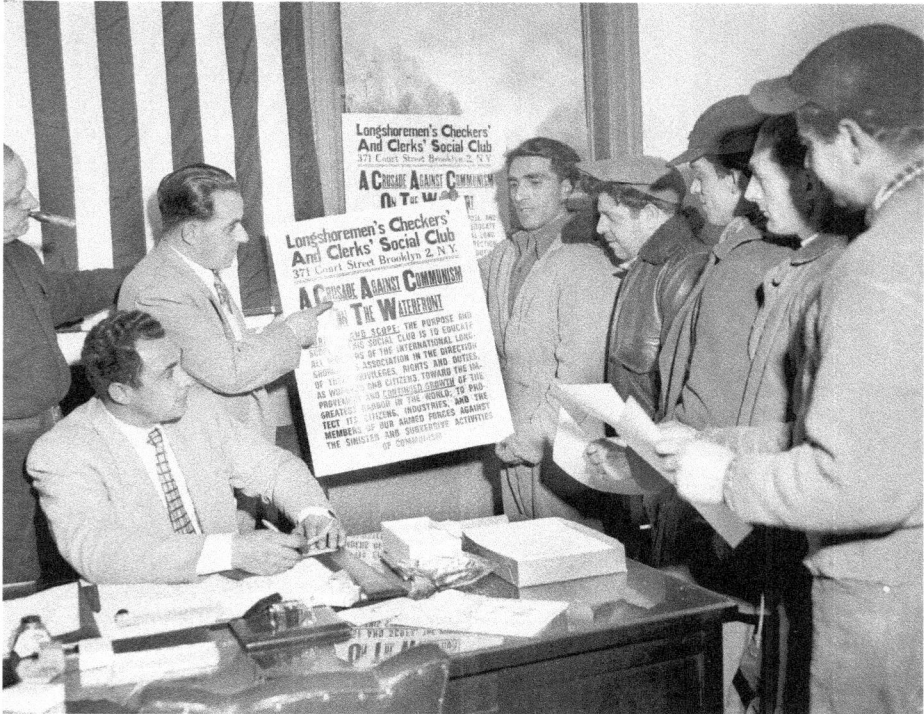

Figure 8. The ILA exerted ideological pressure on New York's longshoremen. Tony Anastasia (left, standing) and Peter Incorvia (seated) enlisted longshoremen for many union-sponsored anticommunist crusades (1952). Credit: New York Daily News Country.

Figure 9. As a result of the "crusades," the ILA regularly mobilized dockworkers for anticommunist actions, such as holding up cargo bound for socialist countries. Credit: New York Daily News Country.

DOCKERS NEWS

Issued by RANK-AND-FILE LONGSHOREMEN

The Truth
About the Waterfront

THE PEOPLE OF NEW YORK have heard everyone talk about the reasons for the present situation on our water-front. We are the men who break our backs loading and unloading the ships in this port. We think our side of the story is at least as important as any other. Read it — and then judge for yourself.

For six long months we longshoremen in the Port of New York have been fighting for a union contract with improved wages and working conditions. Any other working man would fight as we are now for the right to raise the living standards of himself and his family. But even this basic right is being denied us.

Regardless of occupation, everybody today is worried about the same things—security of our jobs, the high cost of living, the future of our children.

We dock workers earn our pay the hard way. Our work is the hardest, most back-breaking work you can find. The longshore industry has the second highest accident rate in the country. We don't have adequate safety regulations or an adequate medical, pension or welfare plan. Speed-up on the piers, discrimination in hiring, and a general decline in shipping trade keep our work irregular and our incomes low. The official figures of our employers, the New York Shipping Association, show that three out of four longshoremen earn $40 a week or less. As a result of all this we're forced to live in run-down neighborhoods and are unable to provide our children with the same opportunities others have.

We know that our fight is a justified one. That's why we're fighting so hard. Yet no other group of American workers has been subjected to the vicious smears, physical attacks and political run-arounds that we have experienced in the past six months.

The public is being deceived into thinking that anybody who works for a living on the waterfront is either a gangster or his stooge. This is not true. We resent, as any other working man would, hearing ourselves slandered and seeing our families shamed.

Down through the years we have been the only ones who have fought the racketeers carried on the payrolls of the shipping companies.

Every fair-minded New Yorker should ask himself: Why have the politicians, the press and the law enforcement agencies waited all these years to raise a hullabaloo about "crime on the waterfront"?

The truth of the matter is that the racketeers have been kept in power by the shipowners to intimidate us on the job and to try to take over our union. The truth of the matter is that the politicians in both Albany and City Hall have been "protecting" the racketeers all these years and have been getting their cut of the graft from "crime and corruption" on the waterfront.

Can it be that, under the pretext of crime-busting, a bigger crime is being committed?

What is really happening is that we longshoremen are engaged in a bitter struggle to get rid of the racketeers who have been working hand in glove with the shipowners and the politicians. Now that we are beginning to get rid of the racketeers, the politicians have come up with a new gimmick, to keep us in line for the benefit of the shipowners.

This is the trick used by Governor Dewey to saddle us with a politician-controlled Waterfront Commission that was supposed to eliminate the evils of a gangster-controlled shape-up. Instead of a solution, we have a worse deal. We not only still have gangsters on our backs, but the politicians on top of them. The Waterfront Commission's hiring halls have been used for regimentation of labor in true nazi-style and in violation of every democratic right of the American working-man. Now they are being used as official strike-breaking agencies to split and weaken the trade union movement on the New York waterfront.

The shipping companies have been taking advantage of this fake "crusade against crime" to try to outlaw the union shop on the waterfront. They are refusing to sign a union contract in the Port of New York—yet the very same companies have signed longshore contracts with the ILA in every port along the Atlantic and Gulf coasts.

Our fight for a union contract is legal and justified. It has the support of ALL longshoremen, and is not a "jurisdictional dispute". The scabs who are working piers under police protection are over-whelmingly recruited from outside industries. These strike-breakers are unskilled in the longshore industry, and are endangering lives and equipment in the port. They are not, as the newspapers state, AFL longshoremen engaged in a "jurisdictional fight" against the ILA.

This strike is not forbidden by the injunction. It isn't forbidden by anything else connected with the 80-day Taft-Hartley injunction. We are 100% in the clear in this action. We are not violating anything.

Longshoremen gave the ILA a clear majority in a fair NLRB election in December. Governor Dewey, working behind the scenes with the shipowners, prevented the certification of the ILA as the rightful bargaining agent of all longshoremen by means of a phoney charge of "coercion". Dewey's meddling in our union affairs has deprived our families of food and clothing by delaying our contract.

Residents of our city were shocked to witness Mayor Wagner's brutal use of mounted and foot police to club striking longshoremen and disperse picket lines. We certainly did not expect this kind of behavior from a man who was elected to office with the support of organized labor. It's about time that Bob Wagner stops acting like a "Republican" Mayor and starts working in the interests of the people who put him in office.

We longshoremen are leading the fight of all workers of our city against anti-labor injunctions, Taft-Hartley union-busting, state regimentation of hiring and the interference of politicians in everyday union matters.

OUR FIGHT IS YOUR FIGHT! WE NEED YOUR SUPPORT TO WIN!

- Please have your union, church or other organization go on record in support of our fight.
- Write to Mayor Wagner and protest against the use of New York City police as strike-breakers.
- Let Governor Dewey know that we demand an end to his anti-labor drive and, as New Yorkers, we resent his attempts to dictate how our city will be run.

10.a

Figure 10.a, 10.b, 10.c, 10.d. *Dockers News*, the rank-and-file newsletter, circulated on the dock for over 30 years, mobilizing longshoremen whenever there was a "beef."

Dockers News

Published of, by, and for Rank and File Longshoremen

LONGSHORE Action Now !

A STATE OF WAR HAS EXISTED ON THE DOCKS FOR THE LAST TWO YEARS! THE SHIPOWNERS HAVEN'T BOTHERED TO DECLARE WAR OFFICIALLY; BUT THE WAR IS ON! THE SHIPOWNERS' NEW OFFENSIVE AGAINST LONGSHOREMEN IS FOR MORE AND MORE PRODUCTION ... FOR MORE SPEEDUP. THEY'RE TRYING TO GET BACK NOT ONLY THE COST OF OUR INCREASE IN WAGES AND WELFARE , BUT ALSO TO MAKE US PAY FOR THE HIGHER COST OF HANDLING CARGO (AND HIGHER OVERHEAD) DUE TO HALF EMPTY SHIPS ..

Anywhere in the Port you can see signs of this war.

IN MANHATTAN ... three men killed at GRACE in one month ... accidents increasing ...on some EASTSIDE piers the men are pressured not to report injuries ... at Chelsea's U.S. LINE and GRACE piers companies threaten to move to Newark,where the gangs are cut to 14 men on container ships ,,, cutting down of extra labor all over the Port ... more screaming at gangs ... more abuse and threats ... more dividing gang against gang ... area against area ... bigger drafts ... bigger pallets!

IN BROOKLYN ... on PIER 11 dozens of old timers forced out because they can't keep up with the terrific speedup ... O'Brien,thr hiring boss on PIER 2,chases the deck men at finish time and runs TWO WINCHES BY HIMSELF ... at BREAKWATER we have a new and growing job category — "pusher" ... everyday more "pushers" and fewer longshoremen.

THIS SPEEDUP ON TOP OF A SHARP DROP OF JOBS!

The shipowners rush us and push us and shove us around and hold meetings to steam up the hatch bosses "pushers",etc ... BUT these same shipowners are in no hurry to come to an agreement on our SAFETY AND SENIORITY RIGHTS! It's TWO YEARS now that the shipowners have been stalling on a SAFETY CODE and an effective Safety machinery. Not to mention they're huggling over the still pending SENIORITY CLAUSE.

WHY DON'T THE SHIPOWNERS SPEED THEMSELVES UP!

Facts are that we have been robbed of earnings and yes,some longshoremen have lost the health and lives,because of the shipowners' TWO YEAR STALL AND SPEEDUP MADNESS. On Chelsea's GRACE PIERS for example, there's no doubt that the Company has the largest collection of Safety Posters in the Port,and it also has one of the highest accident rates in the Port. Why? THE SPEEDUP! [SEE NEXT PAGE]

EXTRA

ALL OUT! PORTWIDE MEETING!
MADISON SQUARE GARDEN!
TUESDAY-NOVEMBER 18th! 1:30PM!

10.b

Dockers' News

Published of, by, and for Rank and File Longshoremen - New York, N. Y.   APRIL, 1956

CONTRACT DEMANDS !!

It's time for some straight talk on contract demands.

IF WE GET TOGETHER ON OUR CONTRACT DEMANDS NOW and IF WE STICK TO-GETHER; and IF NO RAID DIVIDES US from our brother longshoremen we of DOCKERS NEWS feel that we will be in our strongest bargaining position in 20 years. Lots of things the rank and file has fought for, such as a Union-Management Hiring System based on seniority rotation and a Limited Slingload, CAN BE WON THIS YEAR!

On each pier there are special beefs which the Local membership will bring up. What we of DOCKERS NEWS here list are only some of the main demands which we think the whole Port can agree on.

1. UNION-MANAGEMENT HIRING SYSTEM: Hiring Halls in which all work is dispatched by a Union Dispatcher who'll be elected DEMOCRATICALLY and YEARLY by the membership. Guarantee regular gangs seniority on their piers. Dispatch extra men on rotation from the list of registered men first AND BRING IN "PERMIT MEN" ONLY AFTER ALL REGISTERED MEN HAVE WORK. (DOCKERS NEWS will discuss details on Hiring Hall System in next issue.)

2. LIMIT SLINGLOAD TO 2240 LBS.: Establish a Committee to work out limits on all slingload cargoes: cangoods, bags, etc.

3. INCREASE LIST OF EXTRA-PAY PENALTY CARGOES.

4. A SUBSTANTIAL WAGE INCREASE.

5. 10 PAID HOLIDAYS: We are one of the few remaining industries without any paid holidays. We propose: New Year's Day, Lincoln's birthday, Washington's birthday, Good Friday, Decoration Day, 4th of July, Labor Day, Armistice Day, Thanksgiving, and Christmas Day.

6. IMPROVED VACATION PLAN: Every longshoreman who works 400 hours be entitled to vacation benefits, based on one day paid vacation for every 100 hours worked.

7. IMPROVED WELFARE PLAN: Include dental benefits and eyeglasses in Welfare Plan. Also increase the maternity and sick benefits.

8. NO COMPULSORY OVERTIME.

9. ELIMINATE ALL WAGE AND OTHER DIFFERENTIALS.

10. SAFETY: A detailed "Safety Clause" in contract to be enforced by elected Union Safety Committee. We propose: (a) an ambulance and doctor for every group of piers; (b) medical office built into all new piers; (c) no work in bad weather, men to stand-by; (d) companies required to keep safety gear on every dock, etc.

11. FAIR EMPLOYMENT PRACTICES CODE: We propose a Code similar to that in West Coast Longshore Contract: "There shall be no discrimination against any registered longshoremen because of union membership and activity, race, color, creed, age, national origin, religious or political beliefs."

12. JOB PREFERENCE FOR OLD TIMERS: The old timers with long seniority ought to be given first choice for jobs requiring less physical strain.

13. 15-MINUTE COFFEE BREAK.

14. COMPANIES TO PROVIDE LOCKERS, CLEAN TOWELS, AND SOAP.

15. RELIEF FOR DRIVERS AND HOLDMEN.

We can win these contract demands and also THOSE LOCAL BEEFS every guy knows of... How? BY INSURING THAT EVERY LOCAL HOLDS DEMOCRATIC ELECTIONS TO THE PORT WAGE SCALE COMMITTEE! ATTEND your Local meeting! VOTE in the Wage Scale Committee Elections! A FIGHTING WAGE SCALE COMMITTEE IS OUR BEST GUARANTEE OF A BETTER CONTRACT!

The Price Of Dis-Unity!

What longshoremen need most in our contract talks IS UNITY! Unity on the docks, unity between the gangs, and unity with all longshoremen...

It was a good deal therefore when East Coast (ILA) and West Coast (ILWU) longshore leaders, and the Ship Owners, got together with the House Merchant Marine Committee in Washington, D. C., to agree on a common contract date. A common Longshore Contract Expiration Date is a step toward the kind of unity that would make winning our contract demands a lot easier.

But now, the NY SHIPPING CO'S HAVE RENEGED ON THE AGREED TO COMMON CONTRACT DATE, using the threatened IBL-AFL raid as their excuse. It proves once again that raids and disunity play into the hands of the Ship Owners.

WE NEED UNITY, NOT DISUNITY!

WEST COAST DOCKER

COMMON CONTRACT DATE

EAST COAST DOCKER

10.C

DOCKER'S NEWS

Published by and for
Rank & File Longshoremen

Sept. 27, 1968   labor donated

NO CONTRACT — NO WORK !!!

October 1, 1968...our 4 year contract is up. We have seen after 4 long years, that this contract was a sell-out! Dockers News, way back in 1964 said that 38 cents spread out over 4 years, was not enough! Longshoremen in the Port of New York will not let it happen again!

Dockers News said, way back in 1964, that by letting the Shipowners cut the gang 3 men, we were giving up too much. It was a giveaway for the Shipowners! They made millions and millions!

Gleason settled for the 3.2% wage guideline that the Government forced on us, and since that time we have seen other unions like the Teamsters, Steel Workers, and Machinists smash this phony wage freeze, and make wage gains that have averaged 6% to 15% of their weekly wages.

We say that the issues facing the men have to be brought up at negotiations now! NOT..after the Contract is signed, to be settled in committee!

In 1964, we thought we won a Wage Guarantee, Seniority, and a share in the Container Royalties.....but what happened??? We had to fight like hell to impliment these "victories". Men had to wait months for the wage guarantee! What happened to their families while they waited for the money??

WE WANT THE MONEY PAID WEEKLY!!

The Containers Automation Money was stolen from us, and diverted to another Fund we'll never see!   WE WANT THAT MONEY NOW!!

Seniority is all tied up in the Seniority Committee, headed by Capt. Haines of the Shipowners!

WE WANT AN HONEST SENIORITY BOARD!!

WE WANT ALL DEMANDS SETTLED BEFORE WE VOTE!!

Dockers News is written by Longshoremen, and has been published for over 25 years. It is the Voice of Rank & File Longshoremen!!

We want the same wages, working conditions, and pension bonus of $13,000 that the West Coast Longshoremen have!! The same Shipping Companies in N.Y. operate from the West Coast!

WHY CAN'T THEY COUGH UP??

Longshoremen on the West Coast have had the 6 hour day since 1936! They get time and a half after 3 in the afternoon! They got $1200 apiece in 1966 as their share of the Container Fund, and NOW they get $13,000 bonus, as a share of the Container Fund, when they retire, plus their pension!!

DOCKERS NEWS SAYS WE HAVE A LONG WAY TO GO TO CATCH UP!!

DOCKERS NEWS SAYS:

TO HELL WITH THE WAGE FREEZE!!

TO HELL WITH THOSE SHIPOWNERS WHO ARE MAKING MILLIONS OUT OF THE VIETNAM WAR !!

TO HELL WITH THOSE WHO WOULD TRY TO KEEP US FROM FIGHTING FOR THE WELFARE OF OUR FAMILIES!!

LONGSHOREMEN IN BROOKLYN, NEW YORK, STATEN ISLAND AND JERSEY SAY:

10.d

Figure 11. The Rank and File Unity Slate in ILA Local 1814—Brooklyn. From left to right: Mathew Mungin, Chatman "Smitty" Smith, Servio Mello, Pete Bel, Alfred "the Lawyer" McKenzie, and John "Coo-Coo" Guercio.

VOTATE PER UNITA

tare pe la ticketta d'Unita e un voto per quanto se$ne:

.inforzimiento severo per l'anzianita per $arantire i diritti a utti l'anziani.
Voi crediamo che tutti l'anziani dovessero avere diritti di avorare 5 $iorni alla settimana.

Jn presente automatizioni pro$rama che protetta i nostri avori $arantire un mi$liore beneficio di pensione e un ritiro i piu $iovane eta.

Mi$liore sistema per in$a$$iare i lavorante e mi$liore sistema tella sala.
Di abolire favorismo e descriminazione di razze e dare a tutti in u$uale oportunita.

Mi$liore rappresen $azioni dei dele$$i nel dock.

Di chiudere i re$ister del Waterfront Commission e di non ammettere nnovi soci nei re$ister.

Lotta continuazione per il cartellino oli presenza.

ale 1814 per elettorare L'ufficiale Lunedi Jia$no 25, 1962 da .M. to 7 P.M. nella sala d'union 343 Court Street, Brooklyn, Y. i voti saranno sorve$liati da questia ssociatione Ballotterali.

RICORDATEVI

Voi avete diritto di ricevere tempo per votare.
Siete sicuri di pressare la leva solo per i canditati D'Unita.
Votate per solo canditati.
Prendevi tutto il vostro tempo a votare.
Ballotte esemplare – Votate solo quatro.

PER POTERE VOTARE

Vio dovete provare che i pa$amenti sulvostro libretto sono state fatte fino a iano.
Dovete portare con voi il passo del Coast Guard, Waterfront Commission passo, Libretto d'unione.

VOTARE UNITA NO. 3 - 4 - 20 - 21

VOTE UNITY TICKET

A vote for the Unity Ticket is vote for the following program.

- Strict seniority enforcement to guarantee the rights of seniority men. We believe that every seniority man is on to five days work per week.
- An up to date Automation Program that will protect our Guarantee higher pension benefits and lower retirement.
- Better hiring halls and a better system of hiring, the way end favoritism, discrimination and give everyone an chance.
- Full pension after twenty years in industry regardless of
- Better delegate representation at the piers.
- Close Waterfront Commission's register to stop new from coming in the waterfront.
- Continuation of Show -Up Cards fight.

LOCAL 1814 ELECTION OF OFFICERS

Monday, June 25, from 6 a.m. to 7 p.m. at Union Voting will be supervised by the Honest Ballot Ass

12.a

Figures 12.a, 12.b. The Rank and File Unity Slate, ca. 1972, negotiating regulation and control at work.

VOTE UNITY ROW B

THESE ARE YOUR UNITY TICKET CANDIDATES

6

FOR DELEGATE

JOHN (Coo-Coo) GUERCIO from PIER 6 P.A.

8

FOR DELEGATE

ALFRED (The Lawyer) MCKENZIE

15

FOR VICE-PRESIDENT

PETE BELL from PIER 5 P.A.

24

FOR THE EXECUTIVE BOARD

SERVIO MELLO from PIER 12 P.A.

25

FOR THE EXECUTIVE BOARD

CHATMAN (Smitty) SMITH from PIER 8 P.A.

29

FOR DISTRICT COUNCIL DELEGATE

MATTHEW MUNGIN from PIER 8 P.A.

VOTE ONLY FOR THE NUMBERS ON ROW B **!**

THIS IS OUR PROGRAM:

1. DAY FOR DAY DEBITING ONLY. NO MULTIPLE DEBITING.

2. REINSTATE ALL MEN WHO HAVE BEEN DISQUALIFIED WITH 5 C DEBITS.

3. TEN DAYS SICK LEAVE WITH PAY.

4. SEVEN DAYS DEATH IN FAMILY BENEFIT WITH PAY.

5. NO SIX WEEKS WAITING PERIOD FOR GUARANTEE OR HOLIDAYS.
   ALL MONIES TO BE PAID WITHIN TWO WEEKS WAITING TIME.

ROW B

6. NO FORCED OVERTIME.

7. RE-ESTABLISH JOB CATEGORIES BASED UPON EACH MAN'S LAST FIVE YEARS OF WORK.

8. ON THE JOB DISABILITY-15 YEARS PENSION REGARDLESS OF AGE.

9. ADEQUATE FREE PARKING FACILITIES AT HIRING HALL AND PIERS.

10. NO MORE CONTRACT BOARD,
    AND BETTER UNION REPRESENTATION FOR ALL. **!**

VOTE UNITY ROW B

12.b

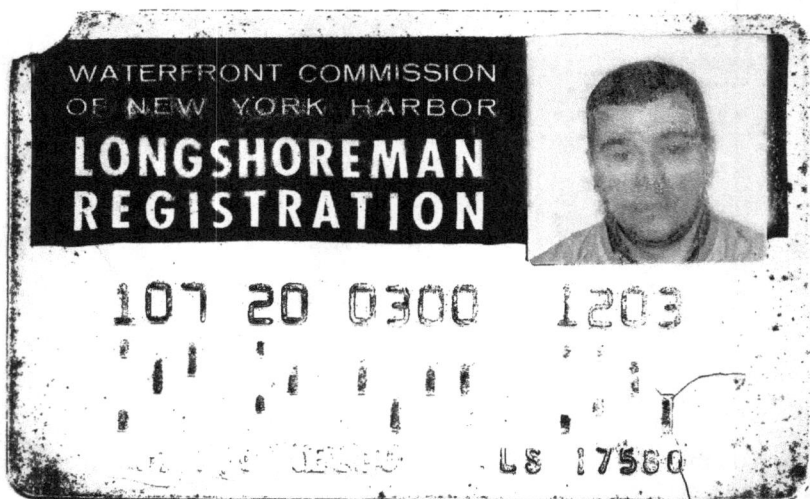

Figure 13. By the late 1950s, the Waterfront Commission would "police" the docks and dockworkers, regulating employment and exercising strict control over rank-and-file activism.

4

Port Automation and Control of the Dock Labor Process

In the latter half of the 1950s, two questions continued to frame the struggle for control of the waterfront. First, how did the ILA survive despite the mounting combination of political forces that coalesced to its demise? Second, how did workers respond to the complex political coalitions? These questions, however, take on a new significance under the shifting political alliances and the expanding automation of the dock labor process. While important sectors of the trade union movement, primarily the AFL-CIO, signaled with the slow and steady reapproximation to the dock union, state and federal authorities continued to limit the activism of waterfront workers. This was achieved by systematically using the injunctive power of Taft-Hartley as well as other legal measures in combination with the specific regulations and laws to control the waterfront labor force (e.g., by expanding the powers of the Waterfront Commission). Economic elites and political authorities sought to justify increasing the limits placed on the dockworkers' challenge for control of the waterfront labor process by defining it as a threat to national well-being.

Even though the IBL-AFL's challenge to the ILA's institutional leadership had been practically defeated after three electoral campaigns, by 1956 the internal transformations within the dock union had significantly reshaped the framework for conflict on the waterfront. As a result, the NYSA rapidly occupied the void that was created when the AFL withdrew from the front lines of the conflict. Once the dock conflict was no longer cloaked under the guise of an "inter-union conflict," shipping employers became increasingly overt in their alliance with state and federal political authorities to limit the process of waterfront reform. The effectiveness of the institutional constraints depended primarily on the capacity of shipping employers and federal and state political authorities to work increasingly in unison. This occurred not only because of the demands of the political structure but because mechanisms such as the Waterfront Commission relied on the employers' financial support for their very existence.

The liaison between political authorities and business elites was consolidated by their more immediate need to implement new automated forms of waterborne cargo transportation. For employers and political authorities alike, the perspective of automated cargo transportation, albeit incipient, presented on the horizon the possibility for expansion of U.S. foreign commercial interests and the drastic reduction of labor and operational costs. This course of action accentuated the nature of control on the port, intertwining the interests of the dock labor force with the shifting characteristics of the division of labor. Political authorities continuously sought to expand the powers of the Waterfront Commission by incorporating larger and larger sectors of the dock labor force under its restrictive jurisdiction and by intensifying their grip on the waterfront hiring process. This process enhanced the ability of business elites and state authorities to respond and curtail the mobilization of longshoremen with greater speed and precision. The added political power, however, would not have been possible without legislative support and the acquiescence of sectors within the judicial system that were working in agreement with state and federal political authorities. In some cases their actions went as far as to practically circumvent procedural measures so as to ensure favorable outcomes.

If, during the initial period, authorities cloaked their motivation in the highly moralistic crusade to expel the gangsters from the port, the existence of gangsters in the ILA leadership was less of a problem for business elites and political authorities alike. The capacity of the ILA leadership, at least temporarily, to reinvent their image and political alliances fueled their justification for greater constraint of the dock labor force. Political authorities argued that the growing mobilization of dockworkers presented an impending danger to the national well-being; it was necessary to curtail the actions of the "irresponsible union." Despite their claims that the port mobilizations presented an impending threat "to the health and safety of the nation," productivity levels on the waterfront remained steady in spite of the fact that the dock workforce was rapidly diminishing. During this period the boundaries of the conflict defined what claims the longshoremen could and could not make, such as the ILA's struggle for a master contract for all ports along the East Coast.

Even though the ILA was only partially victorious in its demand for a master contract, business elites rapidly transformed their claim for coast-wide bargaining (which had long been in existence on the West Coast waterfront) into a mechanism by which shipping employers gained even greater injunctive power. The power to legally constrain the rebellious longshoremen went far beyond that permitted by the Taft-Hartley Act. Shipping employers aggressively used the newly conceived arsenal to obligate the rebellious dockworkers to acquiesce in "collective bargaining" agreements to which they had not, in fact, agreed. In this sense, the already unequal playing field through which dockworkers and their employers interacted became even more skewed in favor of the shipping companies.

With the last representation election between the ILA and the IBL as the backdrop, the ILA focused its attentions on the 1956 contract negotiations. During this period the conservative IBL and the left-led rank-and-file group *Dockers News* continuously pressured the ILA from below. Even though the left-wing dockworkers had supported the ILA in its struggle against the IBL, they also sought to pressure the ILA by radicalizing the demands for reform through pier mobilization. From above, the ILA was consistently compelled by the ever-expanding regulatory action of the Waterfront Commission and its increasingly stringent measures. Added to this was the internal conflict among the ILA leadership, for reasons of self-interest as well as for divergent political-strategic views of the waterfront reform process. The highly contentious contract negotiations and the looming automation of the docks became the backdrop against which the struggle for control of the waterfront labor process would be played out. This process placed the economic demands of New York's longshoremen within a larger political sphere for control of the port. The interaction of diverse and competing political forces laid the framework for the radical transformation of the waterfront labor process over the next four years.

Decasualization of the Waterfront Labor Force

The growing regulation of the dock labor force underscored the conditions that set the struggle for control of the waterfront labor process in the 1950s. This process severely reduced the number of longshoremen working the port. One of the favorable effects of the regulatory process of dock labor was that it eventually stabilized and improved the work hours and wages of longshoremen. In the process, however, it also radically transformed waterfront work patterns. In this way a significant aspect of the struggle to control the waterfront reflects the underlying conflict to control the rapidly shifting characteristics of dock labor itself.

From a political standpoint, the role of the Waterfront Commission was pernicious because it systematically sought to screen radical leaders and rank-and-file longshoremen out of the industry. The Commission increasingly attempted to place itself between the shipping companies and the longshoremen, often serving as a strong arm to enforce the employers' demands. The impact of the Commission's decasualization process, however, insofar as wages and conditions were concerned, produced limited but positive results for those who remained on the waterfront. In doing so, the Waterfront Commission imposed strict regulatory mechanisms over waterfront workers while consistently seeking greater power to enhance its regulation and control of the dock labor force. The decasualization process of dock labor, combined with the longshoremen's demand for a seniority hiring system, was a far cry from the days when thousands of workers lined the piers seeking a day's work. In a little over 10 years, the number of longshoremen who worked the port was reduced to less than half of the traditional workforce, eliminating the brutal competition for work on the docks.

In the 1946–47 contract year, 54,442 longshoremen were employed on the Port of New York, working a total of 37,385,864 hours. Collectively they earned $71,983,930—with an average hourly wage of $1.93. In contrast, by the 1959–60 contract year, 23,475 longshoremen worked 31,968,147.5 hours with total earnings of $106,966,894, thus increasing the average hourly wage to $3.35. The decasualization of the waterfront labor force increased the distribution of work hours for the registered longshoremen. In the 1951–52 contract year, 57 percent of those hired worked less than 700 hours. By 1960, longshoremen working less than 700 hours declined to 19.9 percent, while those working more than 700 hours rose from 42.9 percent in 1951 to 78 percent of the workforce by 1960. The decasualization process, however, did not automatically increase wages sufficiently to improve the standard of living for significant sectors of the dock labor force.[1]

Decasualization of waterfront labor relied fundamentally on the registration process set forth by the Waterfront Commission. It included the continuous reexamination of the longshoremen's work records in order to regulate the flow of workers onto the port. Relying on the semipermanent sector of the waterfront workforce as the core for the registration process, dockworkers were divided into four groups: permanent, regular, hatch gangs, and casuals. Dockworkers were defined as permanent employees if a specific employer hired them either with a definite time limit or indefinitely. In the same way, a regular employee was considered a longshoremen if they maintained regular work with the same employer. Regular employees, however, were hired one week in advance. Also, regular employees had to have their status revalidated with the Waterfront Commission on a weekly basis.

Both of these classifications exempted longshoremen from having to appear each morning at the Commission's hiring hall; however, if their status changed, they had to report back to the hiring hall. In contrast, hatch gangs were registered with the Commission for no longer than a week and had to register by 4 P.M. the day prior to when work was to begin. Assignment to a hatch gang, however, was not a guarantee of work, and if a longshoreman were not assigned work on a specific day, he was obligated to report to the Commission's hiring center. The fourth group, casuals, filled the need for dock labor when the demand required extra hands. They were required to report daily to the Commission's information centers.[2]

The actual decasualization process began only after the registration of dock labor had been in effect for nine months, at which time the Commission's "rounds of decasualization" were set in motion.[3] This consisted of the continuous reexamination of the registered dockworkers' work records. Under the Commission's regulation, a longshoreman had to work, or show up for work, at least eight days every month for six months. Failure to do so meant that the Commission revoked his registration. This process of reexamination occurred at six-month intervals until 1965 when the dock registrar was closed to new applicants. In addition to the constant refiltering of the waterfront labor force, further reduction was achieved through attrition due to death, disability, retirement, and changes in profession, all of which allowed the Commission to reduce the number of longshoremen seeking employment on the port. At its inception in 1954, the Waterfront Commission had registered 35,117 longshoremen. By 1960, however, the number of longshoremen registered with the Commission had dropped 32 percent to 24,128.[4]

The Waterfront Commission's increasingly stringent rules for those seeking work on the docks were a moral and political examination rather than a measure of a worker's physical capacity to do heavy labor. The Commission also policed the docks for alleged "misconduct" that could cost the dockworker his livelihood with the suspension of his registration. The Commission received thousands of applications every year, but if the application was held up for investigation, there was little probability of a final approval. For example, in 1959 the Commission received 4,301 applications for registration, of which 249 were deferred pending investigation. Of the 249 applications investigated, only 46 were granted. More often than not, the investigative process consistently resulted in the denial of registration to work on the docks.[5]

The hearing that ultimately decided whether to grant or deny the longshore registration was tantamount to a trial, with charges proffered, the right to counsel, the appearances of witnesses, the presentation of evidence, and the stenographic transcription of the hearing procedure. Even more pernicious, the investigative action of the Commission could also result in more severe legal action.[6] In this way, losing one's job on the port could also result in incarceration. The Commission's ever-expanding control, however, did not go entirely uncontested, although little was achieved in the way of curbing its power. Over the first 11 years of its existence, the Waterfront Commission's decisions were challenged in court on 142 occasions; all of them were ultimately upheld.[7]

The process of decasualization and regulation of the waterfront labor process served as the basis from which the Waterfront Commission expanded its control over the workforce, first by redefining the criteria for determining who was considered a longshoreman. Initially the Commission considered longshoremen to be those workers directly involved in moving freight on and off the port. This exempted from the registration process the ancillary waterfront professions, such as carpenters, sweepers, maintenance workers, and grain ceilers. These professions involved as many as 3,000 workers on the Port of New York.[8] The Commission viewed these "uncovered" dock professions as loopholes through which workers certain that their registration would be denied could continue their employment on the port. In closing the loopholes, however, broad legislation was put into effect that radically expanded the Waterfront Commission's powers.

In July 1956, as a result of the Commission's legislative initiative, the definition of longshoremen was expanded to incorporate those professions previously exempt from dock registration, including timekeepers, checkers, and clerks. Approved by the governors and state legislatures of New York and New Jersey in December 1956, the new legislation not only redefined who was to register with the Commission but also expanded the political and legal stature of the Commission. The new legislation gave the Waterfront Commission the power to grant immunity to those testifying under oath, the Commission investigators were given legal powers equivalent to peace officers, including the power to deny and suspend the employment registration of dockworkers who refused to answer questions regarding their political loyalty.[9]

The same process occurred four years later as the Commission sought once again to expand its control over the dockworkers. In 1960, the Commission moved to include Chenangos (workers who moved cargo from ships to barges) in the definition of longshoremen and required that they also register with the Commission. In a report to the governors and state legislatures of New York and New Jersey where the inclusion of the Chenangos in the dock labor unit was proposed, the Commission also recommended legislation that imposed greater control over the ILA's welfare and pension fund.[10] In spite of strong opposition to the measure by the recently organized federation, the Maritime Port Council of Greater New York (which included the ILA), as well as the Democratic minority in the New York state legislature, the bill was passed into law. By the beginning of 1962, the Waterfront Commission held the judicial and legal control over all those who worked on any aspect of waterborne cargo in the Ports of New York and New Jersey.

The process of regulation and decasualization of the waterfront labor force had no significant impact on the cargo tonnage moved through the Port of New York between 1950 and 1960. In 1950 the total general cargo handled on the Port of New York was 13,362 long tons, while in 1960 the same general cargo tonnage was 13,736 long tons,[11] although one-third fewer longshoremen handled it. The ILA and rank and file, however, continued to merge their economic interests into a broader struggle to control the waterfront labor process, without which all economic demands seemed fruitless. While the Waterfront Commission is symbolic of the external pressures placed on New York's dockworkers and the ILA, pressures within the ILA and on the docks were also significant factors that shaped waterfront reform.

Pressure from Below and from Within

Once Ryan was finally ousted from the ILA presidency, it became evident that the leadership of the dock union was not a monolithic group, but rather an amalgamation of regional leaders, old and new, with distinct political and local interests. Throughout the contentious 1950s, the ILA leadership found itself continuously forced to placate the local interests of different ILA leaders, not only as a measure to maintain internal unity but also to ward off challenges from below. These challenges were primarily from the conservative IBL, but they also came from the left rank-and-file groups such as the *Dockers News*. Although they had supported the ILA against the IBL, left-wing dockworkers were continuously demanding greater and more democratic reforms of the waterfront labor process, which neither the NYSA nor the ILA leadership seemed interested in conceding. The ILA leadership joined such disparate elements as ILA officials reminiscent of the Ryan era, including Tony Anastasia in Brooklyn and John Bowers of Manhattan's Westside docks, with seemingly moderate figures such as Captain Bradley, previously president of the ILA's Tugboat local, and the up-and-coming leader of the ILA's Checkers Local, "Teddy" Gleason. During this period Gleason worked closely with West Coast ILWU president Harry Bridges, seeking on many occasions to draw both unions into common action.

This somewhat controversial composition helped keep at bay direct challenges to the ILA leadership as well as attempts to remove the ILA from the waterfront by attending to the interests of local leaders while distancing themselves from the past practices of "King Joe." It was also, however, the origin of contention and conflict that shaped and limited the movement for waterfront reform, such as the contentious relationship between Gleason and Bradley and ILA vice president "Tough Tony" Anastasia, president of Brooklyn's Local 1814, which quickly became the object of public scrutiny. Anastasia's "forceful" intervention in the contract negotiations of 1956–57 led a local newspaper to nickname him "the ILA's problem child" when he broke with the Wage and Scale Committee and proposed to negotiate his own contract for Brooklyn.[12] His actions increased tension in the negotiation process, especially when he expressed doubts concerning Captain Bradley's legitimacy as the president of the ILA.[13]

Anastasia's conflict with Bradley and Gleason ultimately led him to challenge Bradley for the presidency. At the onset of his campaign he threatened Bradley, trying to force him into withdrawing from the election. He warned, "If Bradley runs against me and loses, he goes back to the tugboats as a deckhand."[14] In the end, lacking votes, it was Anastasia and not Bradley who withdrew from the election.

Even more indicative of the increasingly complex relations among the dock unions' leaders was the question of the ILA rejoining the AFL-CIO. This conflict emerged just before the collective bargaining agreement with the NYSA was to expire in September 1959. The ILA leadership suffered strong internal resistance to rejoining the national labor federation. Many sectors within the ILA felt that renewing its affiliation with the AFL-CIO would allow for greater intervention into the internal affairs of the dock union. While the ILA leadership was victorious in the overall vote to re-enter the AFL-CIO, the votes in favor were far from overwhelming. The final tally registered 9,970 in favor and 7,719 against membership in the AFL-CIO. One of the rebellious leaders was John Bowers, vice president of Local 824 on Manhattan's West Side (known as the "pistol local"), where 1,520 members voted against entry and only 145 in favor.[15]

On the piers of New Jersey it was reported that some ILA locals voted 10 to 1 against reentry into the AFL-CIO. At one point Bowers even suggested that the dissenting locals abandon the ILA, even though nothing further ever came of his proposal.[16] Internal dissent by Anastasia and Bowers reminded the post-Ryan ILA leadership that their strategy also had to be continuously negotiated internally. Internal conflicts among the ILA leadership, however, were not based entirely on self-interest. To some extent, internal union conflict among the ILA leadership also reflected strategic and political views of the role of labor unionism in politics. In this way, political differences among ILA leaders also kept tensions high.

One of the most persistent conflicts revolved around the relationship and support that had been given to the ILA by radical dockworkers, the ILWU, and the Communist Party in their battle against the government-sponsored representational challenges between 1951 and 1954. The emergence of Teddy Gleason to the position of ILA general organizer signaled a somewhat uneasy approximation between the ILA and the ILWU, even though the East Coast dock union was constantly (and publicly) attempting to distance itself from the radical West Coast longshoremen's union.

For example, during the 1956 East Coast contract strike, the ILWU called a 24-hour sympathy strike in support of striking ILA longshoremen. Bradley quickly sought to disavow the ILWU's actions and sent a telegram to Harry Bridges stating, "Our organization resents the interference of you and your officers with our negotiations." Teddy Gleason later informed the press, however, that the ILA had sent a second telegram to the ILWU thanking the West Coast longshoremen for their support.[17]

In general, the ILA leadership maintained a politically ambiguous position that increased the tension in the relations among the dock union's leaders and their relationship with activists on the docks. While they continued to need the support of the left, they were highly reluctant to make it known. This "Jekyll and Hyde" relationship with left-wing dockworkers was consistently reinforced by the union's rhetorical overtures in support of the port loyalty oaths and their sporadic refusal to work on ships bound for Eastern Europe.

The radical dockworkers' earlier support for the embattled ILA did not imply their blanket approval of the ILA's policies, nor did their earlier support for the dock union weaken their legitimacy as a rank-and-file movement on the waterfront. As the ILA leadership appeared to consolidate its control over the dock union, radical longshoremen pushed fervently for greater reform, seeking to expand the mechanisms of democratic representation in the process. By consistently attempting to shift the focus of the contract negotiation process to the demands that emerged from the piers, the left-wing longshoremen focused their efforts on pressuring the leadership of the ILA to respond to the demands for greater democratic reform.

They viewed the reform of the ILA as axiomatic to the larger movement to reform the dock labor process. Significant aspects of the radical dockworkers' contract proposals were later incorporated in the ILA's Wage and Scale Committee proposals. In the early months of the 1956 process, *Dockers News* made the demands of the radical longshoremen clear: "Union-Management Hiring Hall with a union dispatcher elected annually by the membership [in contrast to the existing Waterfront Commission's hiring centers]; ten Paid Holidays; Vacation Pay (with a 400 hour work minimum to qualify); Sling-load limit of 2,240 lbs.; a Fair Employment Practice Code (antidiscrimination clause); and an increase in wages and contributions to the ILA Welfare Fund." As the *Dockers News* stated, "We can win these contract demands and also those local beefs every guy knows of . . . how?

By insuring that every local holds democratic elections to the Port Wage and Scale Committee! Attend your local meeting! Vote in the Wage and Scale Committee elections! A fighting Wage and Scale Committee is our best guarantee of a better contract."[18]

Besides making their contract proposals public, the *Dockers News* group was highly critical of both the ILA leadership and the IBL. While they criticized the ILA leadership's political red-baiting policies, stronger criticism was reserved for the IBL, which they accused of coalescing with the interests of the shipping companies. As *Dockers News* reported, "What the longshoremen need most in our contract talks is unity! Unity on the docks, unity between the gangs, and unity with all longshoremen. . . . By now the NY Shipping Co.'s have reneged on the agreed to common contract date, using the threatened IBL-AFL raid as their excuse. It proves once again that raids and disunity play into the hands of the ship owners."[19]

For their part, the IBL also continued to pressure the process of waterfront reform. They were a constant reminder of an immanent challenge and alternative, despite three electoral defeats until their dissolution in 1959. While the IBL also demanded greater democracy within the ILA structure, it continued to focus heavily on the growing relationship between the ILA and the ILWU and the supposed communist domination of the New York harbor. While both the ILA and the radical left concentrated on mobilizing the dockworkers for the upcoming contract negotiations, the IBL continued to raise the specter of communism. They centered their critique of the ILA on the ILWU's participation in the East Coast waterfront contract negotiations. The headline of the IBL's newsletter, *Waterfront News,* declared: "Bridges Opens NY Drive with Full ILA Support." As the article in the conservative dockworkers' newsletter stated: "The deal between the ILA and Harry Bridges is out in the open. *Waterfront News* reported months ago how the ILA put out the welcome mat for Bridges. . . . It is clear that the ILA has sold out completely to Bridges to block the IBL. Unless the men support IBL, Bridges Will Be the Boss of the Harbor. It means longshoremen will be pawns of the communist line. . . . They could force longshoremen to picket for Red China's cause as well as other commie political stunts."[20]

The actions and politics of the IBL reflected a notion that little or nothing had changed in the ILA, and that notwithstanding the supposed communist domination of the port, Joe Ryan was somehow still in the presidency of the dock union. Political red-baiting rather than concrete proposals for reform were an essential part of the IBL's strategy. The IBL failed to address and prioritize the most vital issues concerning New York's longshoremen at that moment, which were the upcoming contract negotiations, in spite of whatever the opinion a majority of longshoremen might have had about communism.

Even so, both left and conservative political forces maintained a constant pressure on the reform process, a pressure that the ILA leadership could neither ignore nor wish away. There was a specter haunting the waterfront, however, even though it was not the specter of communism; rather, it was the specter of automation and the containerization of waterborne cargo. Placed within the context of the highly contentious contract negotiations, automation laid the groundwork for a major transformation of the waterfront labor process and, in doing so, shifted the nature of the demands made by longshoremen and radically transformed the movement for waterfront reform.

Automation Arrives on the Waterfront

Since the mid-1950s, new forms of handling cargo were being put into practice, such as the use of conveyor belts, the construction of ships with side-port entries, "piggy-backing" (hoisting the entire truck trailer onto the ship), and containerized cargo. This last form of automated cargo handling increasingly became the dominant form of waterborne cargo transportation. Even though the amount of containerized cargo was minimal during the late 1950s, its appearance on the port signaled a radical transformation of the maritime cargo transportation industry and placed significant limits on the control exercised by dockworkers over the waterfront labor process.

The original concept of containerized cargo was conceived in the late 1930s by the Hoboken trucking company owner Malcolm McLean, who later became president of the Sea-Land Company, one of the largest shipping companies in the United States. McLean's original idea was to lift the trailers of semi-trucks directly onto the ships, thus saving the truck drivers the time usually spent waiting for cargo to be unloaded from their trucks.[21] McLean's idea, however, helped reinforce the basic goal of ship owners, which was that for maritime cargo transportation to be profitable, the ship must keep moving from one port to the next as quickly as possible.

The introduction of container technology is also important because of the impact on the international dimensions that this transformation had, not only on those who worked the docks but on the structure of the shipping industry as well. Containerization obligated the once loosely bound and competitive shipping industry into international agreements defining the standardization of containers, the remodeling of ship construction, port redesign, and ultimately the redefinition of industry practice and the large-scale reduction of the waterfront workforce. Containerization radically reduced waterfront labor costs as well as ancillary industry expenses. For example, the drastic reduction of cargo loss due to breakage and pilferage reduced insurance premiums significantly as well as the size of ship crews.

The initially slow introduction of containerized cargo occurred in large part because of the radical transformation that the new technology imposed on the shipping companies and on the port structures and ship construction required to accommodate containers. Originally, modified oil tankers were used for container transportation, but increasing demand ultimately forced ship construction to modify basic ship structures so as to safely accommodate increasingly larger quantities of containers. As Edward J. Kavney, CEO of the Metropolitan Stevedore Company, stated: "Fewer people working today handling much more cargo, it's [the docks] no longer the coastal village it used to be."

Before containerization a dock gang of 20 longshoremen could move 20 tons of cargo in eight hours. Presently, it is estimated that 10 dockworkers can move 40 tons of cargo in a matter of minutes, and container ships carry an average of 75,000 tons of cargo. To date, the shipping industry continues to be the most economically competitive form of cargo transportation available, and some have even ventured to define it as a "cornerstone of the global economy." In the 1956 contract negotiations, however, neither the diverse rank-and-file groups nor the ILA fully realized the impact that containerization would have. In spite of this, the topic of port automation quickly came to the forefront of the dockworkers' claims. By 1961, industry innovators of the new technology such as Sea-Land were earning over $3 million in profit. As shipping executive Kavney declared: "Everything we do is to do it faster and cheaper, I don't know where it is going to end."[22] In 1956, neither did New York's longshoremen.

"We Won't Be Back for a Month!"

On August 1, 1956, the ILA and the NYSA initiated negotiations for the Collective Bargaining Agreement set to expire on September 30. The demands presented by the dockworkers' union included a wage increase of 32 cents per hour, 12 paid holidays, increased welfare benefits, eight hours guaranteed wages when hired, wage differentials for dangerous work, severance pay, an employer financed workmen's compensation fund, double-time pay for work performed on holidays, and the expansion of the bargaining unit.[23] The ILA proposed a master contract for all longshoremen on the East and Gulf Coast ports, covering the docks from Portland, Maine, to Brownsville, Texas. In the union's proposal, a coast-wide contract would stipulate wages, vacation, welfare, and pensions, leaving aside port practices and rules for local ancillary agreements. In spite of the extensive economic claims proposed by the longshoremen, the negotiations and ensuing battle focused on the demand for a single coast-wide collective bargaining agreement, obfuscating all other demands made by the ILA Wage and Scale Committee.

In the past, the collective bargaining agreements between the ILA and the NYSA served as the basis for negotiations along the Eastern and Gulf ports. Unlike the ILWU on the West Coast, which had a master contract with the Pacific Maritime Association, East Coast ports negotiated separate contracts. The demand for a master contract was more than just a negotiating expediency; it reflected the continuity of the long-standing contentious conflict for control of the docks. The ILA argued that the shipping companies that operated in the various ports along the East and Gulf Coasts were the same as those that comprised the NYSA, and in this sense, the other ports would be represented in their negotiations with the New York shipping employers. A coast-wide agreement would expand the capacity of the ILA to influence the waterfront labor process along the entire East Coast. Since the Port of New York was the most organized and was far more readily mobilized compared with the Southern and Gulf ports, it would remain the center from which the ILA could intercede in all of the Atlantic and Gulf Coast ports. Thus a master contract would allow the ILA, through its bargaining process on the Port of New York (where conditions were more favorable for the union), to exercise influence on ports where the union's mobilization and organization were limited. Moreover, a coast-wide agreement would safeguard the ILA leadership against future challenges to their representation rights. By expanding the bargaining unit to all ports on the East and Gulf Coasts, it would be much more difficult for competing rank-and-file groups to mount opposition because they would have to include the dockworkers of those ports in the bargaining unit.

On the first day, negotiations were reportedly harmonious; on the second day, however, negotiations between the ILA and the NYSA came to a quick halt when the union put forth its claim for a coast-wide contract. The NYSA positioned itself adamantly against any form of coast-wide collective bargaining agreement and refused to discuss the topic. The shipping employers argued that they were only authorized to negotiate for the 170 members of the NYSA constituted around the Port of New York. In response, ILA Vice President "Packy" Connelly argued: "They [the NYSA] have member companies operating in all the ports we want to include. We believe they can speak for the others."[24]

The demand for a master contract quickly overshadowed any and all other claims made by the ILA, economic and otherwise, bringing the negotiation process to a standstill. While the ILA insisted on representing the dockworkers of the Atlantic Seaboard and the Gulf, the NYSA demanded that the longshore union present its proposals for the dockworkers on the Port of New York. In an attempt to pressure the NYSA, the ILA Wage and Scale Committee members representing the South Atlantic and Gulf Coast broke off negotiations with local shipping employers, stating that they, too, demanded a coast-wide agreement.

The ILWU and Harry Bridges immediately came out in support of the ILA's demands. In the union's newspaper, the *Dispatcher*, the West Coast union applauded the ILA's position, noting that the claim for a coast-wide agreement would strengthen the bargaining power of West Coast longshoremen. Bridges viewed the movement for an East Coast master contract as a means of advancing his own claim toward achieving a single contract expiration date for both the ILA and the ILWU. The demand for a single contract expiration date was the result of a mutual commitment made by both unions during congressional hearings held by the House Merchant Marine and Fisheries Committee headed by Congressman Herbert Bonner (D-NC). The Committee examined the proposal of national bargaining among the maritime trades and suggested that it would in fact contribute to the stabilization of the industry.[25]

As the contract expiration date drew closer, the ILA sought to mobilize the membership for the upcoming deadline and to reinforce the idea that a master contract was worth the battle. At a meeting of delegates of the Atlantic and Gulf Coast ILA Wage and Scale Committee, held in Washington, which employers refused to attend, Captain Bradley stated: "[The employers] didn't see fit to come here and meet with us, the responsibility of what happens on October 1, lies with them . . . go back and tell your ports that we are going to stick with coast-wide bargaining. . . . We don't want to strike but we will strike if necessary. The responsibility is with the employers." Reiterating Bradley's comments, Teddy Gleason, ILA general organizer, added: "After today the employers will know that we are not kidding about coast-wide bargaining."[26]

In spite of the union leadership's declarations, however, the ILA was not in a rush to go on strike. With the jurisdictional election against the IBL approaching on October 24 in New York, a strike at that moment could jeopardize their position and create the conditions for further representational challenges. With less than a week to the October 1 deadline, the ILA made a proposal to the shipping employers stipulating a 30-day extension on the current contract with the guarantee that any wage and benefit increases would be retroactive to the original October 1 deadline. The ILA demanded that the agreement be accepted by shipping employers on all ports for it to be valid.[27] All employer associations quickly accepted the new deadline, which allowed the ILA to resolve the IBL challenge and reopen the stalled contract negotiations.

ILA vice president Tony Anastasia, however, undercut the show of unity at the ILA meeting in Washington. Feeling the movement for a master contract was overshadowing his local interests in the ILA bargaining process, he advised Brooklyn dockworkers after the meeting to "disregard the propaganda of Captain Bradley and Teddy Gleason."[28] Anastasia's position reflected an ongoing conflict between the leadership of Local 1814 in Brooklyn and the ILA national leadership for influence in the negotiation process with employers. Anastasia's claim to power was not unreal, as approximately 10,000 of the 30,000 dockworkers on the Port of New York were members of his Brooklyn local. The conflict between the Brooklyn ILA leader and the leadership of Bradley and Gleason would deteriorate even further. After storming out in the middle of contract negotiations in New York on October 22, he reportedly threatened Gleason, "Stay out of Brooklyn or you don't come back alive," after which he telegraphed the NYSA declaring that the ILA Wage and Scale Committee "was not negotiating any contract for the men in Brooklyn."[29] As the ILA leadership sought to resolve the conflict with the Brooklyn local and win the election against the IBL, the NYSA moved swiftly in a series of legal challenges that seriously restricted the dock union's capacity to bargain.

By mid-October Captain Bradley had notified all ILA locals on the East Coast that the demand for coast-wide bargaining was a strike issue and that if employers wished to avert a strike they would have to address the matter.[30] The following day, the ILWU informed officials of the federal government that if the ILA went on strike, similar action could be expected on the West Coast. The circumstances were heading rapidly toward a situation that the federal government and employers alike had long sought to avert, a national dock strike. The NYSA moved to coerce the ILA into bargaining on their terms and limit the demands that the dock union could raise. Central to their strategy was their ability to transform the issue of a master contract and coast-wide bargaining into a nonnegotiable issue. On October 24, the NYSA entered a complaint of unfair labor practices against the ILA to the NLRB charging that by demanding a coast-wide negotiation the ILA was refusing to bargain a contract for New York's longshoremen.[31] In this way, if the NLRB ruled in favor of the employers' charge, the ILA could once again be enjoined in federal court, thus making it illegal for the ILA to raise the demand for a coast-wide contract.

As the new contract deadline loomed closer, the ILA began to gain control of the internal conflicts that were diverting its efforts from the contract negotiation process. It won the representation election against the IBL, and the national leadership reached an agreement with Tony Anastasia, who returned to the ILA Wage and Scale Committee.[32] Insofar as the economic demands of the dockworkers were concerned, the NYSA had presented the ILA with a substantial wage and benefit proposal, which included a 32 cent increase in hourly wages over a three-year period, an increase in the welfare benefit contribution from 9 to 12 cents per hour per employee, two paid holidays, Labor Day and Christmas (up until then longshoremen had no paid holidays), and an increase in the vacation benefit.[33] This led federal mediators to suggest that the contract expiration deadline be set back once again in the hope that both sides might reach a final accord.

Even though both sides agreed to the new expiration date of November 15, the employers refused to consider the dockworkers' claim for coast-wide contract negotiations. This left the ILA little alternative because, as it had stated earlier, the demand for a master contract was a strike issue, and on November 16, approximately 70,000 dockworkers from Portland, Maine, to Brownsville, Texas, walked off the piers, paralyzing all East Coast maritime cargo transportation.

In a public statement at the outset of the strike, Bradley declared that the employers' adamant refusal was at the heart of the work stoppage and that "united and with the help of God we shall win." In a show of force in response to the appearance of ILA pickets along the Port of New York, the New York Police Department assigned 3,000 police officers to the task of harbor patrol. The striking dockworkers immediately received the support of the National Maritime Union which, hours earlier on the November 15 deadline, ordered all deck crews off the strike-bound ships. Similarly, ILA officials in Montreal announced that Canadian longshoremen would not work on ships diverted from the East Coast. The ILA also received the support of the ILWU and Harry Bridges, who advised all West Coast ILWU locals to schedule "stop-work meetings" to discuss the ILA strike.[34]

The largest dock strike in the history of the U.S. waterfront had begun, paralyzing all of the Atlantic and Gulf Coast ports and with the mounting possibility of the West Coast longshoremen entering into the conflict. In addition to their claim for a master contract, the striking longshoremen demanded eight hours guaranteed pay when hired and a limited sling load weight. During the negotiations, employers had demanded a reduction in the gang size from 20 to 16 dockworkers on palletized cargo, a demand that was quickly rejected by the union's Wage and Scale Committee.[35] The fundamental issues of the strike were not those involving economic claims but questions regarding the control of the waterfront labor process.

Tensions between the NYSA and the ILA grew rapidly at the onset of the work stoppage, and hopes for a quick resolution to the conflict were immediately dashed. NYSA spokesman Louis Waldman grimly stated, "As of this moment, the employers and the union are farther apart than they ever were."[36] This led the New York Board of Trade to immediately appeal to President Eisenhower to invoke the Taft-Hartley emergency measures, a demand that was reinforced by the New York Commerce and Industry Association's assessment that a prolonged work stoppage could cost the port $1 million per day. Also, the American Railroad Association prepared to embargo cargo headed for the New York waterfront.[37] Captain Hewlett Bishop, the Atlantic Coast director of the Maritime Administration, reported that 196 ships were strikebound in the ports from Maine to Florida and five more in the Gulf ports, totaling over 200 ships. In addition to the economic cost of strike, Secretary of Labor James Mitchell argued that the strike could deepen an already growing international shipping crisis created by the Suez Canal blockade.[38]

On the West Coast, shipping employers tried to limit the effects of the ILWU's growing solidarity movement. Arguing that the work stoppage meetings called for by the ILWU were in fact a breach of the unions' no-strike pledge, West Coast shipping employers broke off wage negotiations. The West Coast dockworkers responded by approving a 24-hour sympathy strike in support of striking East Coast longshoremen.[39] On November 19, the fourth day of the strike, West Coast dockworkers joined the Atlantic and Gulf Coast longshoremen, thus paralyzing every port in the United States. Even though it was only 24 hours, the biggest fear of American shipping employers had become reality: work on all U.S. ports had come to a standstill.

The federal government quickly warned striking dockworkers on both coasts that the job actions were creating "repercussions that spread far beyond the maritime industry." The one-day national work stoppage, combining the East and West Coasts, increased the financial losses caused by the strike by approximately $20 million.[40] By the fifth day of the strike, the accumulated total losses were estimated at more than $100 million.[41]

The solid support for the ILA longshoremen from other unions in the maritime industry and the receptivity the strike received from the longshoremen in the South Atlantic and Gulf Ports, where ILA mobilization was traditionally weaker, pressed the federal government into action. The federal government and the shipping employers combined efforts to halt the ongoing strike and to reconfigure any future contract discussions. Responding to an NLRB decision that the ILA's claim for a master contract was in fact refusing to bargain for New York dockworkers, Federal Judge Frederick Van Pelt Bryan forbade the striking dockworkers to demand a coast-wide agreement in their negotiations with the NYSA.[42] Even though this decision alone would not end the strike, it allowed the shipping employers to limit and reshape the terms and conditions of the contract negotiation process. Within 24 hours of Bryan's decision, President Eisenhower requested that the emergency provisions of the Taft-Hartley Act be set in motion, claiming that a continued dock strike "would imperil the national health and safety."[43]

The government's wish to put an end to the strike was evident by the speed with which the Taft-Hartley injunction was approved. Just two days after Eisenhower's initial announcement, the emergency measures were put into effect. The federal government circumvented the procedures outlined in the Taft-Hartley Act by moving for an injunction in a federal court without first holding the necessary hearing to approve the measures. Judge Bryan granted the government an immediate 10-day temporary injunction during which time the Taft-Hartley hearing was scheduled and held.[44] In this way, when the hearing to decide the validity of the government's actions was held, striking dockworkers had already been forced back to work.

In sequence with government measures, the NYSA cancelled upcoming contract negotiations. ILA attorney Louis Waldman warned: "In our opinion the employers have been doing precisely this for the last four weeks. They have been hoping to use the weapon of the injunction to gain for them what conciliation and negotiation cannot do. This is a throwback of 30 years. . . . If there is the same adamant attitude there will not be a contract in 80 days because there must be a will to contract."[45]

After nine days on strike and under the force of two federal injunctions, East Coast dockworkers returned to the ports along the Atlantic and Gulf Coasts. The total cost of the strike was estimated at $180 million.[46] Tons of perishable goods, such as 11,250,000 pounds of bananas, had been held up in the cargo holds of strikebound ships, approximately one-quarter of which would be sold at a loss.[47] Even though the Taft-Hartley injunction barred any future strike before February 12, 1957, the dockworkers continued to press their demands for a coast-wide collective bargaining agreement.

As soon as the longshoremen returned to the cargo-laden docks, employers began reporting that a work slowdown was spreading throughout the Port of New York. They claimed that longshoremen were taking up to four times the usual amount of time necessary to perform their work. The shipping companies declared that the movement had reached "serious proportions" and that many workers were refusing to show up for work on a daily basis. One lower Manhattan pier reported that 100 trucks had to be turned away so that the ships could keep their schedule, another ship left 6,000 bags of mail behind so that it could sail on time, and the *Queen Mary* reported that it left the port with only 20 of the 300 tons it was supposed to carry. Even though the ILA denied any "direct involvement" in the movement, they voiced support for the actions. Teddy Gleason stated: "It's a natural thing for the men to resent the way the union has been treated. What did they expect these guys to do—kiss them? . . . All the law did was enjoin us from striking—it did not say how many tons an hour the men must give the employers."[48]

The employers responded to the slowdown by equating the job action to a "partial strike." In a letter to ILA President Captain Bradley, NYSA spokesman Alexander Chopin demanded that the ILA "take every appropriate action to prevent any disregard of the specific language and spirit of the national emergency injunction."[49] In spite of their demands, the work slowdown continued, prompting the NYSA to return to federal court and request of Judge Bryan that the word *slowdown* be included in his injunction order.[50] As the slowdown continued into its second week, Captain Bradley promised employers he would try to persuade the men to keep shipping schedules, but he reminded the employers that if no agreement was reached by February 12, the union would not think twice about going back on strike.[51]

Minor disputes on the port continuously disrupted the work process and subsequently the contract negotiation process. For example, a dispute erupted between local ILA representatives and the John W. McGrath Shipping Company on Pier 10, located on the lower end of the Hudson River. Forklift operators refused to handle 28 bags of potatoes, each weighing 100 pounds, on a single lift. They argued that only 24 bags could be lifted safely, to which the company supervisor responded that if they did not do as they were told, they could "check out." Within two hours the entire pier was idle. The NYSA accused the ILA leadership of calling a strike on Pier 10 and in retaliation cancelled all further contract negotiations until the longshoremen had returned to the pier.[52] Contract talks only resumed after both sides agreed to remit the case to the Labor Relations Committee.

On January 4, 1957, negotiations between the ILA and the NYSA resumed, although the discussions remained perfunctory over the following month. The upcoming vote on the NYSA's final offer divided the ILA in some regions. The leadership of the dockworkers' union defended the rejection of the employers' proposal. On the South Atlantic and Gulf ports, however, where the ILA organization was weaker, the continued contract negotiations led to a settlement between the local ILA organizations and the shipping companies.[53] It came as little surprise when, on January 30, New Orleans dockworkers reached an agreement with local shipping companies. The contract included an overall wage and benefit increase of 31 cents per hour, 8 cents of which would go toward wages while 23 cents was applied toward welfare, pension, and vacation benefits.[54] Similar agreements were subsequently reached in all ports along the South Atlantic and Gulf Coasts, thus weakening the ILA's claim for coast-wide bargaining.

The new collective bargaining agreements in the South, however, did not have the effect on the negotiations process that the NYSA hoped for. According to Alexander Chopin, the discussions between the union and the employers "did not warrant optimism."[55] Chopin's pessimism proved to be accurate. As the Taft-Hartley injunction deadline neared, the remaining North Atlantic longshoremen overwhelmingly rejected the NYSA's final offer. In New York, more longshoremen turned out to reject the employer's offer than the ILA had received votes in the IBL's representation challenge three months earlier. The final tally registered 14,458 against the employers' offer and only 1,185 in favor.[56]

Strategically, since the ILA was legally impeded from demanding a coast-wide contract, the union focused on other demands that sought to give longshoremen greater control over the waterfront labor process, such as a one-ton sling load limit, seniority hiring, and the eight-hour pay guarantee, none of which were included in the employers' final offer, nor were they disposed to accept. Despite the intervention of federal mediators in the negotiation process, the stalemate continued.

One day before the Taft-Hartley injunction expired, ILA attorney Louis Waldman stated: "They [the NYSA] not only refused to grant us the demands which the mediators found our members to be entitled to, they refused to abandoned their own demands which the mediators found they were not entitled to." In turn, shipping employers remained unwavering, stating that they had reached their limit. On the eve of the strike deadline, Alexander Chopin declared: "We made what we believed to be a considerable movement in granting the union a number of things they wanted. Evidently the union believes they are not enough."[57] The stalemate, however, was not over economic demands, as the employers wished to portray it. The struggle continued over control of the labor process, and even though the dockworkers could not make the demand public, the claim for a coast-wide contract undermined any possible solution to the conflict.

As soon as the 80-day injunction expired, dockworkers on the North Atlantic ports returned to the picket lines, as they had done so many times before. From Portland, Maine, to Hamptons Road, Virginia, an estimated 45,000 dockworkers abandoned the ports. In Chelsea, it was reported that many longshoremen anticipated the 5:00 P.M. deadline, calling out to pier supervisors, "We won't be back for a month," leaving 790 passengers on an American Export Line luxury ship stranded to carry their own luggage.[58]

Immediately, 150 cargo ships lay paralyzed, and the American Railroad Association renewed its embargo on all cargo trains headed for the strike-bound ports.[59] The enduring contentious reform movement on the port imposed financial losses that were greater than just the cost of lost cargo, because passenger ship companies had to create alternatives for ships seeking to land in New York. For example, some passenger ships were diverted to Halifax, which obligated the shipping companies to charter planes to transport U.S. Customs inspectors and health officials to the Canadian port to process the arriving passengers. After arriving in Halifax, passengers were transported to New York by train.[60] As the strike entered its fourth day, the New York Commerce and Industry Association once again tallied the financial losses imposed by the work stoppage. The Association estimated that, "should the strike continue for any great length of time, the familiar patterns of losses can be expected to develop."[61] Implicit in the declaration was the concern that the strike would develop into a long drawn-out movement.

The NYSA had little choice but to acquiesce to the demand for a coast-wide collective bargaining agreement for the longshoremen who worked on the North Atlantic ports. In spite of last-minute dissent from the three major Manhattan ILA locals at the Wage and Scale Committee meeting, after almost seven months of negotiations, two strikes, two federal injunctions, and a 24-hour national strike that paralyzed all U.S. ports on February 18, the NYSA and the ILA reached an agreement.[62] The agreement, however, did not signify a quick return to work by striking longshoremen.

The terms of the new collective bargaining agreement between the ILA and the NYSA stipulated that they were based on a master contract that included all ports of the North Atlantic coast, regulating wages, hours, and pension and welfare contributions. Local working conditions and the administration of pension and welfare benefits, however, would continue to be negotiated locally. In addition, the dockworkers would receive a 32 cent per hour wage increase, retroactive to October 1, 1956, paid holidays, an additional week's paid vacation, a seniority hiring system, and automatic dues check-off of all ILA members working the port.[63]

The strike, however, did not end as quickly as the NYSA desired. Shipping companies in Baltimore, Norfolk, and Philadelphia resisted the master contract and delayed the return to work. In response, longshoremen in all North Atlantic ports refused to return until all employers became signatories to the agreement, arguing that the return to work would only occur after all longshoremen had voted on the agreement. Oddly enough, at one point the Baltimore Steamship Association broke off negotiations with the local ILA representatives, refusing to agree to the coast-wide contract, even though the association comprised branch offices of New York shipping companies.[64] Their action led many to believe that the last-minute "rebellion" on the part of these employers was in fact a last-ditch effort on the part of New York employers to recant on the master contract. Even though the strike ended on February 17, the return to work only occurred on February 23, almost a week later, when all ports became signatories to the coast-wide agreement. The victorious strike reinvigorated the debilitated waterfront union both politically and financially.

The master contract, representing all ports of the North Atlantic Coast, expanded the representational claims of the ILA leadership while devices such as automatic dues check-off helped to quickly restructure the financially strapped labor union. The long and drawn-out process of contract negotiations, however, also served to meld together distinct moments in the process of waterfront reform. That is, instead of the three years of labor peace that a contract would normally buy, because of the lengthy contract negotiations, in just a little more than two years the Port of New York once again became the stage for rebellious dockworkers and their highly contentious movement.

Redefining the Value of Work

A little less than a year before the 1956 ILA collective bargaining agreement was to expire, the increasing use of automated methods of stowage set the framework for upcoming contract negotiations and remained the center of port-wide conflict in the years to come. On November 18, 1958, the ILA organized a massive "stop work" rally at Madison Square Garden to discuss the growing process of port mechanization and the subsequent loss of employment.[65] At noon, 17,500 dockworkers descended from the ships along the port and marched through the streets of Manhattan.[66]

At the meeting, local newspapers reported, the longshoremen "cheered when the shipping industry was warned that they would have to 'share the benefits' of automation with those who would be displaced." Even though Tony Anastasia declared at the meeting that ultimately the dockworkers could not stop port mechanization, the main thrust of the ILA at the meeting alerted longshoremen to the threat that port mechanization posed to waterfront employment. Reading a statement by Teddy Gleason, ILA District Council President Fred Field warned that the impact of automation was already being felt. Over the previous two years, dockworkers had lost approximately 4 million work-hours, and container operations could manage 12 tons of freight in four minutes, "15 times faster than the normal stowage."[67]

The rally was also an indication of the growing contention between shipping employers and dockworkers concerning automation, which was the topic of an upcoming discussion between the ILA and the NYSA. The following week at a meeting between the ILA and the NYSA, the dockworkers presented their decision to the employer group: they would not handle any form of cargo that was not in use before the signing of their present contract. After delivering what some considered an ultimatum, the ILA left the meeting when the employers threatened to take legal action against what they considered to be an illegal boycott.[68]

The conflict reflected competing strategies with regard to port mechanization. On one hand, the ILA sought to decelerate the introduction of new technology, if only momentarily, so as to gain more information on its subsequent impact on the longshore industry and allow for greater mobilization of the workers. In contrast, the strategy of the shipping association, according to Alexander Chopin, was to introduce the changes first and discuss them with the union at some later date.[69]

By September 1, 1959, contract negotiations between the ILA and the NYSA were once again in high gear. After a little over two years since the signing of the master contract for the North Atlantic ports, rapid technological transformation of maritime cargo transportation and its implications in redefining the very nature of the waterfront labor process served as a fast-acting catalyst for renewed revolt on the Port of New York. For longshoremen, the increasing mechanization of waterborne cargo transportation not only raised questions regarding the intrinsic value of dock labor, reflected in their wages. It also caused concern about how to continue to influence the waterfront labor process. By 1959 the ongoing battle for control of the waterfront reemerged on the port, now exacerbated by the rapidly shifting nature of the dock labor process.

Immediately, at the opening of the contract discussions, the ILA demanded a reduction of the regular workday from eight to six hours with no reduction in wages. The effect would have been to automatically increase the wage rate from its actual $2.80 per hour to $3.73 per hour. The reduction in work hours, however, would also have guaranteed the continued employment of a significant number of waterfront workers on the port. Their numbers had dwindled over the years due to the introduction of regulatory hiring practices and the incipient automated changes in waterfront work, such as palletized cargo and mechanized conveyor belts. As containerized cargo also began to appear with greater frequency on the port, the longshoremen's fear of a radical reduction in the workforce was not so far-fetched.

In addition to the growing fear of automation, the ever expanding power of the Waterfront Commission and its interference in the struggle for control of the dock labor process exacerbated and complicated negotiations between employers and the ILA. At the opening of contract discussions between the union and the NYSA in 1959, the Waterfront Commission served 60 members of the ILA leadership with summonses, alleging that criminals had "re-infiltrated" the dock union.[70] Serving the summonses at that moment clearly indicated the employers' intention to pressure and weaken the role of the dock union in the contract negotiations by raising the specter of criminal activity at the outset of port-wide mobilization. This is not to say that there was no criminal activity in the ILA, but the criminals did not re-infiltrate the organization: it is doubtful they had ever been removed. The desire of state authorities to regulate the waterfront labor process was the political motivation behind their attempts to reopen the investigations and not a deeper interest in securing democratic unionism on the docks.

Even the AFL-CIO, which had long condemned the high levels of criminal activity in the dock union, strongly indicted the actions of the Waterfront Commission. In a resolution calling for the abolition of the Waterfront Commission, the Maritime Trades Department of the AFL-CIO argued that "the Commission has denied dockworkers the right to free democratic bargaining and deprived them and their employers of the power of self-administration over the hiring halls."[71] Responding to the pressures, the ILA leadership threatened to break off negotiations with the NYSA if the Commission continued to serve the summonses, leading the Waterfront Commission to delay the investigation.

As the September 30 contract deadline drew closer, the NYSA proposed wage increases of 8, 3, and 4 cents over the hourly wage rate, respectively, over the following three years between 1959 and 1962. The employers estimated that at the current number of man-hours, the proposed wage increase would raise shipping costs by $14.5 million over the next three years. In exchange for the wage increases, the employers demanded a reduction in the gang size on ships that worked with containerized cargo.[72] The NYSA's contract proposals were in effect demands that sought to drastically reduce and deregulate past practices and employment on the docks. Given the very nature of their proposals, it is evident that they were well aware of the drastic transformations in course in the waterfront labor process with the growing adoption of containerized cargo.[73]

Needless to say, the employers' proposals fell far short of the demands made by the dockworkers. In contrast, the ILA leadership demanded an increase in wages and benefits that added up to approximately $1.40 over the hourly rate for the upcoming three-year contract period.[74] The growing stalemate in their discussions of wages and benefits, however, was accentuated by the struggle for control of the docks. The rapidly automating waterfront labor process reshaped and rearranged the priorities and demands of New York's dockworkers.

Four days before the contract was to expire, longshoremen on the Port of New York began refusing to check cargo off the piers during the weekend. The longshore union maintained that this was a normal practice, even though by doing so most cargo that was unloaded in the days preceding the strike would wind up staying on the port. This led the NYSA to break off contract negotiations, declaring that the unions' action was tantamount to declaring a strike before the expiration of the collective bargaining agreement. Chopin stated: "There is no point in negotiating a new contract when they are so irresponsible they won't live up to the old one." The ILA argued that weekend delivery of cargo was never part of their regular work schedule. According to Patrick "Packy" Connelly: "We have offered to do our normal work and we do not work on delivering cargo over the weekend, we have not done so for the life of the contract."[75]

In spite of the growing contention, the NYSA made a final offer. The employers proposed a wage increase of 20 cents for the first year and 5 cents for the following two years in the hourly wages of longshoremen. But the employers conditioned their proposal: the wage increase would be valid only if the ILA allowed "us to determine certain work rules." Among

the rules the NYSA demanded was the "right of the employer to operate his operation in a manner deemed desirable."[76] In fact, the NYSA was
demanding that workers relinquish any claim for control of the waterfront labor process. This was a fundamental necessity if the NYSA were
to implement new technology that would ultimately result in the drastic
reduction of the waterfront labor force.

In proposing flexible regulations over the waterfront labor process, the
NYSA sought to introduce the mechanization of maritime cargo transportation without assuming responsibility for the loss of jobs that the new
technology would create. In 1959 containerization was still in its infancy
and only slowly being implemented. Neither the ILA nor the dockworkers
themselves demonstrated a full understanding of just how fast the process
of port mechanization would occur. Shipping employers, however, had a
full understanding of the impact automation would have on the port. Even
though the NYSA appeared reluctant to recognize the growing impact of
containerization in the longshore industry, the truth is that early on employers realized that the future of waterborne cargo transportation was
linked to expanding container technology, and their plans for such had
long been set in motion.

In a meeting of 300 New York shipping executives and government
officials held in January 1959 specifically to discuss port mechanization,
industry leaders referred to containerized cargo as a "must" if they were
to stay ahead of the rising handling costs. Lewis A. Rapham, president of
the Grace Line, argued that 55 percent of the company's operating cost
went to handling. Responding to the complaints of the anxious shippers,
Francis Ebel, assistant chief of the Division of Ship Design of the Maritime
Administration, informed the meeting that the growing use of containerized cargo would imply modifying ship design and constructing larger and
more mechanized ships to "reduce handling costs and fasten turnarounds
in ports."[77]

Contentious Politics and Automation

In what had since become a pattern, on October 1, 1959, dockworkers from
Maine to Texas walked off the piers. This time, however, the strike was
initiated by the dockworkers of New Orleans and spread rapidly along
the entire Eastern Seaboard. More surprising was the fact that the ILA
had already signed a 15-day extension to the existing contract only two

days before it was to expire, even though it had faced significant internal resistance to signing the agreement. Local 791 declared that they would not accept the contract extension and threatened to call a wildcat strike. This position was also supported by the rank-and-file left.[78] The quick resolve with which New York's longshoremen paralyzed the port in spite of the ILA having signed a 15-day extension was also a reflection of the inability of ILA's top leadership to control competing factions that dominated individual piers.[79] Southern shipping employers refused to agree to retroactivity of wages and benefits based on any future agreement.

The ILA viewed the southern shipping companies as regional representatives of New York shipping concerns and perceived that by refusing to agree with retroactivity on the southern ports the NYSA was attempting to weaken the coast-wide bargaining process, which did not include the South. The ILA leadership quickly claimed that the New York job action was their own doing, even though the Manhattan locals that initially called for the walkout put significant pressure on them to do so. Captain Bradley understood the shippers' strategy: "They know our men in the South would not work without retroactivity, but they figured with the extension in the North Atlantic District we would have to work on ships diverted from the South. . . . But we won't do it—we won't put our organization on a competitive basis."[80] In total, approximately 70,000 dockworkers participated in the strike.

Businesses mobilized rapidly. They attempted to minimize the effects of the strike and force the intervention of federal authorities, just as they had done on previous occasions. The American Railroad Association quickly embargoed all cargo destined to the paralyzed ports as the New York Board of Trade pressured President Eisenhower to once more invoke the Taft-Hartley emergency measures. In a telegram to Eisenhower, the trade association defined the situation as a "national emergency" and urged him to "invoke all laws and take such action he deemed appropriate to end the strike and avoid irreparable loss to the individuals and businesses and to the City and the Port of New York."[81]

The strike immediately paralyzed 200 passenger and cargo ships—87 of which were docked in the Port of New York. Approximately 3,000 passengers on six ships were forced to sort through 12,000 pieces of luggage and make their way across the picket lines of striking dockworkers.[82] Employers estimated that the strike was imposing losses of $20 million per day to the U.S. economy—$50,000 per day in lost wages and benefits on the Port of New York alone.[83] The dockworkers' job action also had an impact on the defense industry. The eastern ports handled 81 percent of the U.S. cargo and more than 75 percent of the total national imports of manganese, chrome, cobalt, rubber, and other primary resources that helped sustain the production of war materiel for NATO forces in Europe.[84] Other maritime unions supported the strike; particularly vocal in their support for the dockworkers were the NMU, SIU, and IBT, all of which promised to "take every legal step possible to support the efforts of the longshoremen to obtain a fair and equitable contract."[85]

In retaliation to the ILA's general work stoppage, the NYSA broke off negotiations, stating that they would only restart the talks after October 15, the date when the contract extension would expire. The employers argued that the strike was illegal. Once again the federal government moved to invoke the Taft-Hartley emergency measures,[86] which had been invoked against unions 16 times in 12 years, including four longshore strikes, which made the ILA the union that had been the object of the most Taft-Hartley injunctions. In less than 24 hours after his decision, President Eisenhower instructed Attorney General William P. Rogers to seek an injunction and end the strike.[87]

The presidential fact-finding report once again argued that if the longshoreman's East and Gulf Coast strike were to continue, it would "imperil the national health and safety." The report pointed out that a long-term work stoppage on the East and Gulf Coast would paralyze the distribution of perishable products and the distribution of food to major urban centers.[88] On the evening of October 8, 1959, Federal Judge Irving Kaufman ordered all longshoremen along the Eastern Seaboard to halt the strike and return to work. The injunction pushed the contract deadline to December 27, 1959. One week later Eisenhower would invoke the Taft-Hartley measures once more, enjoining workers to end a weeklong strike in the steel industry.

The employers estimated the total losses of the strike at approximately $160 million.[89] In spite of the enduring conflict on the docks, the Port of New York continued to be the center through which most domestic and foreign commerce was processed, making it the most lucrative port in the United States. According to a report published by the Army Corps of Engineers, in 1958 the Port of New York handled 41,474,764 tons of foreign commerce valued at approximately $8.5 billion. In addition, during the same year it handled 104.1 million tons of domestic cargo. It was the highest cargo tonnage handled in the port's history.[90]

The main conflict of the strike was not simply about wages but rather the NYSA's demand to implement automation technology "at will" and its implications for defining who controlled the waterfront labor process. At the onset of the strike, when the ILA and the NYSA returned to the bargaining table, they rapidly reached agreement on the economic questions, but continued to wrangle over the implementation of technology. Questions concerning automation continued to mobilize both dockworkers and employers. In the proposed agreement, longshoremen would receive an overall increase in wages and benefits of 41 cents per hour, divided accordingly: 22 cents to wages; 7 cents to pensions; 4 cents to welfare contributions; 3 cents to the ILA/NYSA medical clinics; and 5 cents toward vacation and holiday pay.[91]

The longshoremen's concerns about automation were only partially assuaged when the NYSA agreed not to reduce the gang size of those working containerized cargo and thus to continue hiring 20 longshoremen per work gang. To offset the loss of employment due to the introduction of mechanization, the employers offered a severance package. Given the casual nature of waterfront employment, that proposal was quickly rejected by the ILA.[92] The ILA reasoned that not only would automation reduce the waterfront workforce but it would also reduce the number of hours worked for those who remained.[93]

The ILA proposed that the employers contribute to a fund based on the tonnage of containerized cargo handled by dockworkers. The employers eventually dropped their proposal for severance pay in favor of the union's container royalty scheme, but the amount to be paid remained unresolved. The NYSA offered 25 cents per ton of containerized cargo, while the union demanded 75 cents per ton. The formula for calculating the premium pay for handling containerized cargo was remitted to binding arbitration, and later an award was made to the dockworkers. Called the Container Bonus Fund, the NYSA agreed to pay a premium wage rate that was calculated by the amount of containerized cargo that was handled and deposited into a fund.[94]

The dock arbitration board's decision, however, reflected the continuing uncertainty created by the uneven introduction of container technology into the shipping industry and the inability to predict how quickly it would become the dominant form of maritime cargo transportation. The standard for devising the payment of the container royalty was broken into three classifications: 35 cents per ton for containers unloaded from traditional freighters, 70 cents per ton for cargo unloaded in partially automated ships, and $1.00 per ton for work done on completely containerized ships.[95] Even so, the Container Bonus Fund set the precedent for expanding the longshoremen's claim that the shipping companies should assume the onus for the loss of employment due to automation.

By December 1959, with the Port of New York making record gains primarily in international commerce, it is easy to see why the economic demands of the dockworkers were easily resolved and why those that revolved around the question of automation persisted. According to reports published by the Port Authority of New York and New Jersey, New York's docks handled 4,261,972 tons more than in 1958. Compared with the same period during the previous year, the volume of bulk and general cargo handled on the Port of New York had increased by 23.5 percent. Some of the main products that passed through the port were vehicles, sulfur, liquor, wood pulp, bananas, coffee, cocoa, lumber, and rubber.[96]

On December 10, 1959, dockworkers from Maine to Virginia overwhelmingly approved the proposed agreement. In New York, longshoremen voted four to one in favor of the new master contract for the North Atlantic ports. On the southern and Gulf ports, employers held out, but with the threat of a renewed walkout on December 27, by Christmas, first Gulf and subsequently southern shipping employers agreed to terms similar to those signed in the North Atlantic master contract.

By the end of the year, Captain Bradley and Alexander Chopin of the NYSA stood side by side, gold-plated shovels in hand, in the groundbreaking ceremony for the new Manhattan medical clinic of the ILA.[97] In spite of appearances, however, it was not a return to "business as usual" on the highly contentious docks of New York. If originally the shipping employers had imagined that by resolving the question of representation and the master contract, labor peace would prevail on the port, they were very mistaken. Rapidly expanding port automation would increasingly reintroduce the struggle for control of the labor process in the most basic terms. The question of who controlled the waterfront would continue to prime the contentious process of rank-and-file activism on the docks.

5

"The Health and Safety of the Nation"

After 1960, constraints set in place against the dockworkers' reform movement consolidated a series of procedural measures narrowing even further the boundaries of interaction between business elites, political authorities, and longshoremen in the struggle for control of the waterfront. This process was driven by the conflict between dockworkers and ship owners as a consequence of the implementation of automated work procedures and technology such as, but not limited to, containerized ship cargo. The transformation of waterborne cargo technology redefined the very nature of the struggle for control of the port and melded with the mounting concerns of authorities seeking greater measures to contain the rebellious waterfront movement. The limits to working-class collective action gained national prominence as a result of the "arsenal of weapons" put forth by the Kennedy administration, the expansion of federal intervention into the dock labor conflict, and the growing public debate concerning the waterfront conflict.

The strategy of elites and state authorities to respond to the mounting dock labor conflict was shaped in large part by a growing strike wave experienced in the United States during the 1950s. In this context, the arsenal-of-weapons strategy was an attempt to develop a response to mounting labor conflict that was adaptable to the unpredictable situations that arose with the strike movement. That is, in spite of the increasingly stringent labor legislation put in place between 1947 and 1959, such as the Taft-Hartley and Landrum-Griffin Acts, waterfront unions had been able, at least partially, to incorporate some of the restrictive legislative measures into their repertoire of contestation, illustrating organized labor's flexibility and staying power. Particularly on the waterfront, the Taft-Hartley injunctions had proven ineffective at maintaining "labor peace." Harry Bridges, it was said, normally used the 80-day cooling-off period to whip up stronger support for work stoppages, and the recent history of labor relations on the Port of New York had demonstrated, with one exception, that injunctions alone were fruitless in establishing long-term tranquility between employers and unions. Not everyone involved, however, accepted the adoption of this strategy toward labor. Recent legislative history confirms that, left to their own devices, both Democrats and Republicans responded to labor conflict by enacting more stringent and structured regulatory measures, which many in the Kennedy administration believed were ineffective. Those in favor of the strategy, however, seemed to believe that the miscellany of industries holding variable levels of importance and distinct local and regional political structures demanded a flexible strategy that could meet each conflict in the specific context in which it was presented.

In this sense, a strike in the auto industry was not the same as a strike on the waterfront and as such should be treated differently. Even some significant sectors of the labor movement, such as Walter Reuther, were favorable to the arsenal-of-weapons strategy. First, they favored it because they feared that Congress was ready, willing, and able to pass even stricter national regulatory measures that would further limit their negotiating power. For unions with strong local political presence, such as the UAW, the flexibility of the proposed strategy continued to provide breathing room for negotiated outcomes. In this sense it was less deterministic than steadfast measures that could be applied indiscriminately. This logic, however, proved misleading when it was put into practice on the Port of New York.

The arsenal-of-weapons strategy significantly enhanced the power of shipping elites and the authorities to respond quickly and effectively to the growing work stoppages on the Port of New York. Issuing a 10-day federal restraining order at the onset of a dock strike allowed shipping employers to bypass waiting for the approval of Taft-Hartley measures, permitting them to force longshoremen to return to work almost immediately. By the time Taft-Hartley injunctions were approved, longshoremen were already back on the job. Shipping elites and political authorities worked closely within multiple spheres of the federal judicial system to guarantee favorable outcomes to their demands, even if it was necessary to practically circumvent the rule of due process. A perfect example is a case where the federal courthouse was reopened at night so the judge could serve striking dockworkers with an injunction. The judge later admitted that he did not read the proceedings and that the union was advised of the measures with almost no time to prepare a defense. The increasing use of "unfair labor practice" regulation, once labor's device to contain employer abuses, was progressively redefined and used to constrain the actions of rebellious dockworkers. A device originally used to diminish the inequalities of social location in the collective bargaining process was transformed into a mechanism to further the constraint of working-class collective action. During this period, political authorities and shipping elites vigorously asserted that the continuous work stoppages on the port were a threat to "the health and safety of the nation" and argued that the alternative to using the arsenal-of-weapons approach would be for Congress to approve stricter labor legislation, such as compulsory arbitration among others. If all else failed, federal political authorities easily reverted back to red-baiting, raising the specter that the rebellious movement was part of a communist plot. Democratic mechanisms of control and regulation, such as those existing on the West Coast, were never an option.

The contentious politics of the 1960s in American society were no less conflictive on the Port of New York. The struggle between dockworkers, the shipping companies, and federal and state political authorities to reorganize the waterfront labor process continued to mount. At the crux of the controversy lay a process that melded the rapidly changing characteristics of dock labor. Longshoremen were pressured by an ever-increasing waterfront automation process, and their claim to safeguard their employment stood in direct conflict with the employers' demand for faster and less expensive labor. The demands of the shipping companies were accompanied by the action of federal authorities to gain greater control of the port workforce. They argued that the persistent waterfront job actions posed an immediate threat to the national economy and the political order.

Since the expansion of the ILA bargaining unit and the institution of the master contract, New York waterfront strikes increasingly involved all ports along the East and Gulf Coast in some way. The unified action of dockworkers along the Eastern seaboard combined with the limited effectiveness of the Taft-Hartley Act drew the participation of federal authorities in the conflict in an unprecedented manner. Increasingly, the dock labor conflict involved not only federal mediators but also the secretary of labor and the president. Working closely with federal judicial authorities, the actions of the federal government reflect a deeper search for alternative responses that would limit the dockworkers' strike repertoire. Activist presidents had increasingly expanded the federal government's role in the labor conflicts over the years. Richard Nixon's initial attitude of nonintervention seemed to depart from this tendency. While the Nixon presidency seemed to bode well for allowing the dockworkers' movement greater autonomy, it in fact signaled a broader conflict between labor and his administration that was emerging on the political horizon. For the shipping companies and the federal government alike, the longshoremen's economic demands were more readily attenuated than their claims for control of the docks and democratic unionism.

Equally important, because its leadership no longer saw its immediate authority challenged, the ILA sought to reposition itself within the mainstream trade union movement and adopted a repertoire that accommodated the demands of the NYSA for greater control of the dock labor process. Given the nature of the conflict and its political actors, complete union acquiescence was never really an option. The dock unions' efforts toward cooperation with the NYSA were blocked by the increasing independence of local ILA leaders and the emboldened actions of a limited, albeit growing, rank-and-file movement particularly, but not exclusively, from left-wing dockworkers. Strikes continued to grip the waterfront throughout the 1960s and grew longer and costlier. Recognizing that the Taft-Hartley measures alone were ineffective, political authorities, with the support of the NLRB and the judiciary, continuously reinterpreted the law and invented new mechanisms to force striking dockworkers to return to work. As the waterfront strikes of the 1960s grew longer and costlier, life on the waterfront was by no means business as usual for the ILA or the dockworkers.

Radicals and Racketeers

Even though left-wing dockworkers were never capable of presenting a viable electoral challenge for control of the ILA, they did mount opposition slates, especially targeting "Tough Tony's" Local 1814. Union elections, however, seemed to remain secondary in the general scheme of the activists' work on the docks. By 1960, the CP-inspired *Dockers News* group was the most vocal and vibrant on the Port of New York. In spite of a numerically small contingent, after a little over 10 years of activism on the port, the group had developed strong ties to local pier leaders based primarily on issue-driven mobilizations, such as pier wildcat strikes, slowdowns, and the struggle against race discrimination.

In spite of the limits, the *Dockers News* group enjoyed the necessary prestige that reinforced their ability to (in many instances) challenge the ILA on the essential issues of waterfront reform. Their methods of pier mobilization put them in direct conflict with local ILA leaders. "Wildcat strikes are outlawed in Brooklyn," declared ILA Local 1814 president Anthony Scotto. "They are not necessary. They are not permitted. No one will touch this beef until you go back to work. Then, but only then, your officers will negotiate for you."[1] In spite of this ILA policy, over time dockworkers continued to resort to independent action as a way to push their demands forward.

The ILA leaders also resorted to red-baiting.[2] The October/November 1962 issue of the *Brooklyn Longshoremen*, newsletter of Local 1814, declared: "There has never been any mystery about the purpose of the real loyalty of *Dockers News*. Since its very first issue its only interest has been to stir dissension, to manufacture grievances, to attack the ILA leadership. No one was fooled. . . . The made in Moscow label was too transparent." If the ILA leadership really thought that the longshoremen were ignoring the proposals of *Dockers News*, however, there would not have been a need to deride its influence.

Over the years, radical dockworkers organized "Unity Slates" that joined black and white dockworkers to push forward their claims for reform, focusing on the demand for greater union democracy. The ILA leaders' initial response to the electoral challenge mirrored the past experience of activists confronted under Ryan's stranglehold on the union.[3] Over the years, repeated complaints to the ILA national leadership concerning the local's electoral improprieties fell on deaf ears. This is not to say, however, that all electoral challenges were entirely without result.

In the 1961 election, both the radical Unity Slate as well as anti-Anastasia independents made substantial gains. The September 1961 issue of *Dockers News* reported on the results of the election held in June:

> 5340 longshoremen voted and cast almost 20,000 ballots in the June election for Local 1814 officers. Eleven incumbents ran for reelection and nine independents livened the contest for eight open union delegate positions. . . . A combination of four men ran as a Unity Ticket. Two were black and two were white. . . . Of the eight delegates elected

only three could be identified with Tony Anastasia's machine, the five who won running as independents were:

1) Frank Matera, 36 Street Pier
2) Tony (Mom) DiNicola, Pier 7, (Bush)
3) Benny Terranova, 23 Street (Mooremac)
4) Louis (the Pipe) Amalfatone (Mooremac)
5) Freddy Smalls (past delegate), Breakwater

The men in Brooklyn voted for change in the way the men are treated by the delegates, in the way beefs are handled, a change in the "brush" policy of the local towards the shipping companies and the stevedores. . . . The men in Brooklyn "have written on the wall" it's time for change!

Commenting on the results, one radical activist said:

What happened in the 1814 elections was that Tony Anastasia was running the local. You can't blame Tony himself. There were a whole lot of Italian families with different interests, and they wanted their own men. One guy wanted the Bush Pier, the other guy wanted the downtown pier, and there was a division within the families caused by the process of consolidation of the Brooklyn locals. We got a group together that ran in opposition, aimed at different sectors of the leadership. Freddy Smalls was from the Breakwater, Tony's pier, and a good section of the families wanted Tony to dump him, to favor Italian guys. We incorporated Freddy within the rank-and-file opposition, and we were pretty successful. Freddy got elected; some progressive Italian workers got elected as well. We elected Freddy Smalls and Frank Matera. We were able to dump the worst elements from the union, some of the crooked hats. This reflected a better composition for the union.[4]

Another activist recalled:

These were truly democratic elections. Tony Anastasia had to run it on the up-and-up. The 20 guys that were there represented different pieces of the machine, so the only way he could make peace with them was to say, "Here, you guys run. That's it. Whoever wins, wins." The front of the union looked like Times Square on New Year's Eve. You had thousands of leaflets, hundreds of guys standing on corners.

I never saw a scene like it before, when you brought some kind of democracy to the place. Before, the delegates were all handpicked.[5]

A third *Dockers News* activist remembered:

Anastasia said, "We'll never hold elections like this again." He said it right out. He lost a lot of his guys.[6]

For the left-wing activists, the elections were a format through which they could place the issues of reforming the waterfront labor process before the broadest possible public. As one activist, Gus Johnson, argued: "The main reason for participating in the election was to push our program, to fight for better working conditions for the men. . . . The only thing we were immediately interested in was direct benefits for the men from automation, safety sling loads, and democracy in the local. We weren't looking to overthrow the leadership of the local."

Their desire not to "overthrow the leadership of the local" is indicative of the complex relationship that developed between radicals and the local ILA leadership over the years and a reflection of the activists' ability to work simultaneously inside and outside the formal structures of waterfront unionism. Their relationship with the local union leadership was based on their ability to mobilize for direct action in ways that called attention to the workers' demands. Neither the large-scale corruption in the union nor the ILA leadership's proximity to the ship owners was viewed as an impediment to their interaction, as Johnson explained: "We had a pretty good relationship with the union leadership, even though we would criticize them in union meetings. We were always principled about outside intromission [*sic*] like the FBI or the Waterfront Commission. We did not want anything to do with them. We felt it was the men who had to change the situation in the union."[7]

Life on the docks for the radical activists was not easy, and the politics of direct action continued to be a dangerous task, as Frank DiLorenzo remembers: "The local leadership tried to intimidate us. They would put stooges on the piers to try and find out who was leading the movement. I remember one time a union leader came down with one of these mob guys and called the leaders on the pier to find out who were the guys causing the work stoppage."[8] In spite of their weaknesses, the rank-and-file leftists were a permanent force to be reckoned with in the upcoming battles for control of the waterfront labor process.

"Plugging in the Holes"

At a meeting of the National Safety Council in April 1962, Teddy Gleason, soon to be elected president of the ILA, sounded highly optimistic and accommodating with regard to the upcoming contract negotiations with the NYSA. "I am for a contract before October 1," he stated, "and no strike in this industry if possible." The shipping employers responded to Gleason's declaration in a similar manner, stating that his comments were "sound," "sensible," and "sincere," and NYSA chairman Alexander Chopin called for a "mutual approach to a mutual goal."[9] Wishing not to repeat what both sides called "deadline bargaining," the ILA and the NYSA agreed to initiate contract negotiations two months earlier than usual.[10] The limited bargaining period, however, had never been the problem, as both sides would soon find out. Rather, the demands of the shipping companies to reorganize the waterfront labor process and at the same time gain greater control of the dock labor force was the real crux of the matter.

The upcoming contract negotiations were far from amicable. Even before discussions were under way, employers began making claims regarding the tenuous financial situation of the shipping industry. Speaking to 1,000 industry executives in a meeting of the Frozen Commerce Club, Chopin declared that the "shipping industry was in a struggle for survival" and that the industry could not withstand "meeting impossible demands or facing an equally ruinous strike."[11] Similarly, a report by the president of the NYSA, Vincent Barnett, questioned whether the ILA should expect higher wages automatically with every contract renewal and urged the ILA leadership not to present demands "which both sides know are unattainable."[12]

Responding to the early pressures placed on the negotiation process by the NYSA, the ILA leadership declared that the growing mechanization of waterborne cargo transportation was posing an immediate threat to longshoremen and that this was a central issue to be discussed during the renegotiation of the collective bargaining agreement. Shipping companies were increasingly using such devices as pre-palletized cargo and portside loaders, among other forms of labor-saving processes that drastically reduced the number of man-hours required for loading and unloading ships. A study of dock labor practices prepared for the ILA by the economist Walter L. Eisenberg noted that the growing mechanization of waterfront work, such as portside loaders, "had cut four to six hours spent in loading and unloading a ship by conventional means."[13] The problem of automation would shape the context and demands presented by the ILA, which linked the introduction of new labor practices and control of the waterfront labor process to economic claims, such as the establishment of the Guaranteed Annual Income, improvement in pension and welfare benefits, expansion of the Container Royalty Fund, and the establishment of a six-hour work day.[14]

In spite of their declarations of mutual cooperation and accommodation, the employers' virulent reaction to longshoremen's demands presented at the first negotiation meeting on June 13, 1962, was an indication that neither cooperation nor accommodation was high on the list of priorities for either side. The ILA demanded the reduction of the workday from eight to six hours (with no reduction in wages), 12 paid holidays (they received 8), double-time pay for all overtime work, penalty pay for palletized work, an increase in the pension rate from $85 to $125 per month, and increased contributions to the union's medical clinics in Brooklyn and Manhattan. The ILA argued that the ship owners were already using labor-saving devices and imposing changes on the waterfront without considering the impact it had on the dockworkers. Justifying the list of demands, Teddy Gleason argued that the demands were "beefs or complaints that had developed since the present contract began in 1959. . . . Now we will plug in the holes."[15]

The NYSA's reaction to the dockworkers demands came immediately. Shipping Association chairman Alexander Chopin declared: "Unless they change their tactics we are faced with either meeting impossible demands which would be economically suicidal for the industry or take an equally ruinous strike." Arguing that the longshoremen's demands would increase the cost of cargo transportation by $200 million a year, Chopin described the ILA's claims as "utterly irresponsible" and predicted an early stalemate in the negotiation process.[16] In reality, the NYSA estimated that the longshoremen's demands would increase shipping costs by less than $54 million. Gleason responded that the longshoremen would "hold out indefinitely to get what should have been given to us years ago."[17]

Even though shipping employers balked at the economic demands presented by the ILA, their main interest lay elsewhere. The counterdemands presented by the NYSA to the ILA focused primarily on port practices and rules. The thrust of the employers' demands centered on reducing the dock labor force while simultaneously gaining control of the waterfront labor process, as Chopin stated: "First, most important step in our current negotiations, labor join with us in a reevaluation of the present 20-man gang concept and a revision of the work rules to provide increased flexibility in the use of the labor force to bring about a more efficient operation and increased productivity."[18] The economic aspects of the employers' counterproposal were also far from the dockworkers' claims and were conditioned on the longshoremen's acceptance of a reduced workforce and revised work practices. The employers proposed an increase in wages and benefits of 27 cents per hour over the actual rate divided over a three-year contract, and a reduction of the waterfront gang size from 20 longshoremen to varying sizes, ranging from 8 to 16, depending on the type of cargo that was handled.

The ILA projected that the employers' proposal would increase shipping costs by $22 million over the life of the contract.[19] Adding to the conflict, the rank-and-file activists pushed forth their own demands, which in part coincided with those of the Wage and Scale Committee but which the union had little interest in pursuing. Among their demands were portwide seniority, lower pension age eligibility, an end to the waterfront register, and automation benefits paid directly to the workers.[20] The terms of the conflict were set.

ILA vice president Tony Anastasia also disagreed with the ILA's contract proposals and publicly criticized them as "unrealistic," leading him to file a petition with the NLRB to exclude Local 1814 (the largest ILA local) from the bargaining unit. In fact, Anastasia's arguments gave encouragement to the shipping employers' complaints. "All of their demands," Anastasia stated, "add up to an explanation of why costs on this port are five times over what they were in 1957."[21] One month later, Anastasia withdrew his petition from the labor board. The conflict remained, however, and his withdrawal of the petition proved to be too little, too late. The ILA leadership subsequently removed Anastasia from the Wage and Scale Committee and replaced him with ILA District Council president Fred J. Field. It was also proposed that he be removed from the ILA vice presidency for "supporting the aims of the employers by statements that ridiculed the demands of the Wage and Scale Committee."[22] Gleason described Anastasia's actions as "sabotage."[23]

The crux of the shipping companies' argument was that despite the Waterfront Commission's efforts to reduce the dock labor force through decasualization, there were still too many workers. Alexander Chopin claimed that the increasing use of automated work processes made the ILA's resistance to changes in worker utilization tantamount to "featherbedding." The employers justified their claim of featherbedding by arguing that the steady decrease in port productivity lay in the overemployment and stringent labor practices that continued despite the introduction of mechanization and decasualization of the dock workforce. They based their claims on a comparative study of the workforce developed by the Department of Labor that examined the waterfront labor process between 1950 and 1960. The government study stated that in 1950 the Port of New York moved 16.8 million tons of cargo using 25.6 million work hours and that by 1960 the port moved a total of 17.4 million tons of cargo using 31.9 million work hours. Thus the increase in work hours was far greater than the increase in tonnage that moved through the port.[24]

As the NYSA had predicted, contract negotiations quickly stalled. According to Chopin, "The ILA had deliberately misinterpreted our proposals of which is to reverse the downward trend in productivity since 1950 and thereby provide economic gains for the regular longshore workforce." The employers claimed that data provided by the Waterfront Commission reinforced their position. With 22,070 registered longshoremen in 1962, daily hiring was approximately 18,000. Thus there was an average daily unemployment rate of 4,000 longshoremen.[25]

For the ILA, however, the problem of the excess labor force and change of work practices could not be resolved independently of the problem of automation and control of the dock labor force. The pejorative term *featherbedding* used by employers was in fact the longshoremen's demand for participation in the benefits of automation and not some hidden desire for unearned income, as employers argued. The ILA's insistence on maintaining the 20-man gang size was reinforced by the underlying conflict over who controlled the dock register. Employment levels on the waterfront were controlled by the Waterfront Commission. This was a power that both employers and the union claimed for themselves. The union remained adamant about the size of the workforce. "We worked for 35 years to get a 20-man gang," Gleason declared, "and we are not going to break it. It is inviolate."[26] The ILA charged that the calculations that the NYSA used to devise its proposals were based on an average of 25 million work hours per year instead of the 41 million hours that were actually worked.[27]

The shipping employers were already tailoring the contract to allow for a subsequent reduction of work hours that would be lost by automation. As Gleason stated: "If we accept their [the steamship and stevedore companies'] proposal we lose 16 million man hours of work. It is a phony offer."[28] The stalemate, with little more than 30 days until the contract expiration date, led the federal government to usher in the participation of mediators Robert H. Moore, Thomas Dougherty, and Daniel Fitzpatrick. Assistant Secretary of Labor James J. Reynolds soon joined the mediators and advised the ILA and the NYSA to "get down to hard bargaining."[29]

Reynolds's advice went unheeded, and instead of negotiating, both sides geared up for the ensuing conflict; negotiations at this point would probably not have helped. By mid-September, freight forwarders had increased their tonnage requests substantially, and NMU president Joseph Curran advised the president of the International Transport Workers Union to inform employers of the possibility of a strike so as to withhold ships bound for the Port of New York.[30] Within a week of their entrance into the port conflict, federal mediators suddenly withdrew from the negotiations, and the discussions between the ILA and the NYSA broke off completely. As mediator Robert Moore stated: "Continued mediation conferences not only serve no useful purpose, but can do a disservice by leading the public and both parties to think that progress might be made, but cannot be made."[31]

The ILA leadership began mobilizing for the upcoming battle. On September 20, 1962, the union held meetings along the port in social clubs and halls to "get out the word." At a meeting held at the Palm Gardens, it was reported that over 2,000 longshoremen cheered when Teddy Gleason outlined the union's strategy: "We will not call a strike. We will force the steamship operators and stevedore companies to lock us out. No contract—No work, that is our slogan"[32] Following the pattern of past contract negotiations, at 12:01 A.M. on October 1, 1962, approximately 75,000 dockworkers on ports from Maine to Texas filed off the ships. The strike was on.

On the PBS television program *Search Light*, which aired the first day of the strike, Gleason and Chopin argued their positions. Gleason declared, "The federal mediators inferred that this was a vital industry and couldn't at the present time, because of the international situation [the Cuban Missile Crisis], continue to let these ships be idle. This is the way it has always been. The operators have always taken advantage of coming down to the line, figuring the government was going to bail them out. The only time we become vital to the country is when we're going on strike." Chopin's response confirmed the union's claim that employers consistently awaited the intervention of the federal government. He argued that, under the existing conditions, only "complete capitulation" to the union's demands would produce a contract. He added that "unless the union moves off its mountain of demands we are in trouble. Once the ILA gets the strike out of its system, that perhaps with the saving factor of the Taft-Hartley, then sooner or later we'll have to talk about productivity."[33] The predictions of the ILA leader proved correct, and the federal government moved swiftly to force striking dockworkers back to the port.

Less than 12 hours after the strike had begun, President Kennedy took the initial steps toward imposing a Taft-Hartley injunction. Kennedy asked his fact-finding commission to return with its report within 48 hours. "If this strike is allowed to continue for any length of time," he stated, "its effects will have grave and far-reaching repercussions on our total domestic economy and upon our ability to meet urgent commitments around the world, that the national interests would be gravely jeopardized."[34] As promised, within two days the commission presented its findings, and Judge John F. X. McGohey ordered everyone back to work.[35] It was the fifth time that the Taft-Hartley measures were invoked against East Coast longshoremen. In contrast to previous injunctions, however, the ILA did not contest the court order. Arguing that they wanted to demonstrate their support for the president because of the growing conflict between the United States and Cuba, the union essentially agreed with the court's decision. This made little difference, however, as past experience had proven; dockworkers were restrained from any further action until December 23.

The union's acquiescence to the injunction, however, did set off strong criticism from rank-and-file groups. Particularly, *Dockers News* did not let Gleason's capitulation go unnoticed and linked the ILA's position to its growing indifference to resolving the most basic problems on the docks. Under the headline "Super Patriots or Super Contract Sell Out?" the radical newsletter related a recent fatal accident as proof of the union's increasing accommodation to the interests of the ship owners: "Just this past Monday, October 22, at the Grace Lines, Pier 57 in the North River, a longshoreman was crushed to death and a couple others were sent to the hospital with serious injuries as a result of the UNSAFE conditions on Grace's banana operation. . . . We rank-file [*sic*] longshoremen think the appointed wage scale committee, which Gleason heads should center its attention against the ship owners, if we are to win a decent contract."[36]

As the "cooling-off" period came closer to its expiration date, little change had occurred in the port labor conflict, in spite of renewed efforts by federal mediators. The ILA subsequently voted to reject the employers' final offer because it had no significant modifications from past discussions, and as expected, on Christmas Eve longshoremen paralyzed the ports all along the East Coast.[37] Appeals from President Kennedy and Mayor Robert F. Wagner Jr. to delay the job action for 90 days had no effect in holding off the longshore strike. Gleason's response to Kennedy was that "the employers had not bargained in good faith . . . [and] any additional extension would only prolong the situation and in our opinion would be fruitless." Secretary of Labor Willard Wirtz, who had assumed the role of mediator in the days leading up to the strike, made veiled threats when the ILA refused to heed the presidential appeal. Arguing that a strike on the Gulf and East Coast could cripple the national economy, he stated that there was a "critical weakness" in the Taft-Hartley Act, and that the union's rejection of the president's request could shift the balance in Congress in favor of those who were pushing for more far-reaching legislation regulating labor-management conflict. Publicly the NYSA agreed with Kennedy's request because their acquiescence would not change the situation. The *New York Times* reported, however, that "off the record" they were inclined to let the strike occur, obviously in the hopes of eventually starving striking longshoremen back to work.[38]

In what had by now become a routine, the NMU immediately notified its members not to cross any of the ILA picket lines that emerged at pier entrances. The willingness of both the ILA and the NYSA to commit to a prolonged struggle seemed apparent. Stating that the strike had 100 percent support of longshoremen, Teddy Gleason announced that all ILA officials were taken off the union's payroll, since the union was still in a tenuous financial situation and had no strike fund. Shipping employers also prepared for battle. They began raising contributions among employer members for an advertising fund with the intention of swaying public opinion away from the union.[39] In this way the strike moved quickly into the public debate. In "An Open Letter to Striking Longshoremen, Their Families and the Public," the NYSA claimed that New York's "longshoremen and their families have one of the best welfare plans of any industrial groups in the nation." They advised the dockworkers that by striking they were acting against the national interests and that public patience with the strike was wearing thin.[40]

Rank-and-file dockworkers responded to the employers' attempt to portray the strike as self-serving by asserting that their demands were in the best interests of the city's population. In a pamphlet signed by the Dockworkers Rank and File Committee and distributed throughout the city, the longshoremen argued that in fact there was no conflict between the interests of the striking longshoremen and the public at large. The dockworkers declared: "We for our part think that the national and public interests can only be served when the companies give their workers a share of the benefits of automation, which in turn will raise our purchasing power and boost the city's and country's economy."[41]

In spite of the predisposition of both factions for a long battle, Secretary Wirtz kept pushing for the resumption of negotiations, stating: "It is imperative to the national interests that negotiations be resumed."[42] Adding to the pressure, business elites and regional political authorities began to demand that the federal government take measures. Foreseeing large financial losses with a prolonged dock strike, Georgia governor Ernest Vandiver reportedly urged President Kennedy to intervene in the strike, predicting "economic disaster" for the 20,000 Georgians employed in the jute industry. Equally, the Brooklyn Chamber of Commerce predicted that if the job action surpassed two weeks, 250,000 workers employed in 8,000 businesses would lose their jobs.[43] Customs House officials stated that on January 2, 11 passenger ships with 6,000 passengers and 30,000 pieces of luggage arrived on the port, adding to the highly frenzied situation.[44] As ships began to pile up along the port, Alexander Chopin estimated the financial losses at $20 million a day.[45] By January 7, the estimated financial loss had reached almost $300 million, prompting the assistant secretary of labor to add that the strike was also threatening U.S. foreign aid programs.[46]

Repeated attempts by federal mediators to resolve the issues were deemed "fruitless." The deadlocked negotiations spurred Kennedy to appoint a panel with greater powers beyond simple mediation to attempt a settlement. They were instructed that if no mutual solution could be reached they were to "recommend a procedure" to end the walkout, which had already lasted 24 days. On the panel were Senator Wayne Morse (D-OR), Theodore Kheel, a labor attorney, and Professor James Healy of Harvard University. In Kennedy's statement it became apparent that tensions were running high. "This shutdown is doing intolerable injury to the national welfare. Hundreds of ships are immobilized. Over 100,000 longshore and maritime workers are idle. Economic losses to the nation are running at the rate of millions of dollars a day. Serious damage is being done to the United States dollar balance. Vital foreign aid and relief shipments are blocked. The lifeline between Puerto Rico and the mainland has been cut; and commerce imperative to the economic well-being of the free world is disrupted."[47] It was reported that over 600 ships were immobilized by the strike.[48]

The recurring dock strikes were also reinforcing the demands by Democrats and Republicans alike for stricter labor legislation. They were critical of Kennedy's initial reluctance to intervene more forcefully by imposing compulsory arbitration. Kennedy's unwillingness to impose stronger measures was twofold. First, at that moment he did not wish to divert congressional attention away from his pending tax legislation. Second, Kennedy proposed an "arsenal of measures" to deal with the dock conflict. His concept implied the establishment of a series of measures that the federal government would have at its disposal to systematically force the process of collective bargaining to produce results. This notion diverged from Congress's "strong measures" approach, such as compulsory arbitration, that would ultimately have had an impact on the framework of U.S. labor legislation.[49]

One day after his appointment, Senator Morse offered both sides a "final opportunity to settle before the president acts."[50] After three days of discussions, the presidential panel made a settlement proposal to the ILA and the NYSA. The government's offer included a 15 cent per hour wage increase (retroactive to October 1, 1962) and a 9 cent increase the following year; a 14 cent increase in the contribution to the pension fund; and an increase in the pension payment to $100 per month.[51] In spite of the fact that the wage proposals surpassed the federal government's wage guidelines, it was deemed necessary to reach an agreement.[52] The main causes of the strike—proposed changes in the waterfront labor process and reduction of the workforce—remained unresolved. The government proposed that the discussion of these questions be held over, pending a study to examine the waterfront manpower scheme.

The ILA readily agreed to the offer, primarily because it kept the waterfront labor process and workforce unchanged for two more years. The NYSA initially resisted but then accepted the proposal grudgingly. Admiral John M. Will, chairman of the America Export Line, declared that the federal panel had "deprived the industry of the right to bargain," calling it "compulsory arbitration of the worst form." Other industry leaders complained that the panel had accepted most of the ILA's demands and "forced them down our throat."[53] The employers declared their acceptance of the government-sponsored agreement "in national interests and in cooperation with the president." Chopin demanded, however, that in the future there was a need for safeguards against "union power plays."[54] The total estimated financial loss imposed by the 34-day strike of East and Gulf Coast dockworkers was $800 million.[55]

If the ship owners did not like the agreement, the rank-and-file left was also wary of the federal accord. The *Dockers News* group accused the ILA leadership of succumbing to the NYSA's demands. The newsletter affirmed: "The Rank-and-File Wants Action on Demands!" The group argued that by agreeing to the federal study without gaining any guarantee of job security, the ILA was "caving in" to the ship owners' interests. "This study business will allow cuts just as other study groups have allowed job cuts in railroad, telegrapher, tug boats, scow captains, etc."[56] The radical dockworkers reiterated their argument that greater control and regulation of the waterfront workforce required closing the Waterfront Commission's "dock register" in order to stop new hiring. These predictions were not far off the mark, because given the increasing resistance to workforce reduction schemes, reducing the port labor force would be no easy task.

Economic losses aside, the strike also had an impact on redefining the ILA leadership in its upcoming convention in July 1963. The Wage and Scale Committee's chief negotiator, Teddy Gleason, had assumed the leadership of the strike and had become the ILA's spokesman. Bradley's absence from leadership of the strike signaled a growing divergence about strategy and tactics within the dock unions' leadership. How to confront the rapidly changing labor process? Accepting full responsibility for the strike, Gleason stated: "There were some in the ILA leadership who had panicked during the negotiations and were ready to settle for a bit of porridge."[57]

Bradley, however, remained adamant in his critique of Gleason's actions during the job action. "At last Teddy Gleason admitted responsibility for what I consider an unnecessary strike." Gleason's logic reflected the growing fear that longshoremen confronted with the process of automation, which for the most part was out of their control. "If we had given in," Gleason answered, "on the matter of job security last year, there would have been many longshoremen on the public relief roll today."[58] In this sense, large increases in wages and benefits alone would not suffice, since many longshoremen would have become permanently displaced by the process of automation had the ILA conceded to the NYSA's manpower scheme. The convention delegates ultimately sided with Gleason, who assumed the presidency of the ILA.

Not Even a Raft Moved Downriver

The government-sponsored agreement only delayed the inevitable discussion of the wide-scale overhaul of the waterfront labor process. The government study was published a week before the NYSA and the ILA renewed their contract negotiations and just 18 months after the last strike had ended. The study examined all major conflicts along the East Coast ports and argued that the introduction of new technology (which was considered incipient) would rapidly increase and that the hiring of excess labor was a central problem. One of the measures that the document proposed was the complete elimination of hiring casuals and the restructuring of the port seniority system, which it deemed inadequate. The report substantiated the employers' demand for reduction and flexibility; however, the study also recognized the ILA's demand for job security. Teddy Gleason responded that "the time was ripe for a guaranteed annual wage for dockworkers."[59] The demand for what became known as the Guaranteed Annual Income (GAI) set the tone for negotiations. The GAI fundamentally contested the nature of U.S. employment relations and had a far-reaching impact on the port labor process, including seniority and work assignments. It defined work as a right of citizenship that could not be eliminated by changing conditions of employment.

At the opening meeting between the ILA and the NYSA to discuss the renewal of the collective bargaining agreement, Alexander Chopin asked Teddy Gleason to comment on the government study.[60] Gleason refused, stating that he would rather examine the employers' counterproposals, since the ILA had submitted their demands almost 20 days before the meeting.[61] Gleason's refusal to comment indicated that the issue of automation would figure prominently in any future labor accord. Among the demands the ILA submitted were a 12 percent wage increase, longer vacations, shorter work hours, and a $75 increase to the monthly pension benefit.[62] The employers responded that they would consider these demands only if the ILA agreed to end the Container Royalty Fund and to reduce the gang size from 20 to 16 longshoremen for general cargo and only 13 dockworkers per gang when handling automated cargo, either palletized or in containers.

Supporting the shipping employers' claims of featherbedding, the Port Authority quickly sided with the NYSA. In a letter to both the ILA and the NYSA, Port Authority executive director Austin Tobin urged them to consider making the port costs of New York equal to the costs of other East Coast ports, adding that in New York "there were frequently more longshoremen employed in work gangs than are required on the job to be handled."[63] Gleason responded, "I resent this interference in our negotiation by this type of pressure. . . . Actually the reason for any higher costs of handling cargo in this port can be attributed to pier rentals and payroll taxes on steamship lines for the Waterfront Commission which cost more than $2 million a year."[64]

Conflicting reports of the hiring of dock labor over the years did not sustain the employers' claims. The Waterfront Commission reported that the hiring of dock labor had reached a five-year high with 394,314 workers hired in the month of July 1964, compared with 372,293 in the same month the previous year, a 7 percent increase mainly on the Port of Brooklyn.[65] In spite of record hiring, the report claimed a shortage of workers, since 2,210 calls for employment went unanswered, compared with an average of 680 unanswered calls over the past five years.[66] Even though the ILA agreed to study the question of workforce reduction and to participate in a joint work group, the union restated its position that it was committed to maintaining the gang size to 20 longshoremen.[67] Negotiations deadlocked shortly thereafter and remained that way because the ILA remained steadfast in insisting that the union control the levels of labor usage on the port.

With a little less than 60 days to the contract expiration date, and no foreseeable solution to the conflict in sight, the ILA and the NYSA informed President Johnson of the situation and requested the intervention of the same presidential panel, led by Senator Morse, that had devised the existing waterfront labor agreement less than two years earlier. Secretary of Labor Wirtz quickly agreed to the request, hoping to avert another strike.[68] The presidential panel, however, had little impact on breaking the deadlocked pier negotiations. For the ILA, axiomatic to any change in or reduction of the dock labor force was the discussion of job and wage guarantees and control of the dock labor process. As one ILA negotiator stated, the union would agree to manpower reduction "only when we see concrete evidence of job guarantees and a guaranteed annual wage. . . . We see automation as the worst threat to our jobs, before we can make concessions we want guarantees."[69]

Since the NYSA conditioned the discussion of the guaranteed wage on the concession of broad and sweeping powers to reduce and control the waterfront workforce, there was little the presidential panel could do, and on October 1, 1964, all ports from Maine to Texas were paralyzed.[70] Defying Gleason's order for an "orderly walkout at midnight," dockworkers halted their activities hours before the deadline. This was not only a sign of the longshoremen's strike disposition but also an indication of their growing weariness with the role of the ILA leadership during negotiations. Some sectors of the rank and file feared that the ILA was ready to accept the offer proposed by the presidential panel; it had already been accepted by the NYSA.[71]

In the proposal, longshoremen would receive a 54 cent per hour wage increase over four years, increased vacation and pension benefits, and a guaranteed wage scheme starting in April 1966 equivalent to 75 percent of the average dockworkers' annual income over the past two years. In exchange, however, the panel's proposal granted employers the right to large-scale reduction of the waterfront labor force and the flexibility to move and shift longshoremen, as they deemed necessary.[72]

The ILA rejected the proposal because "hidden in the terms was the blanket authorization of employers to reduce jobs unilaterally."[73] In this sense, it was not just the guaranteed wage but also the control of the waterfront work process that remained at the center of the dockworkers' claims. The Department of Labor vented its frustration and anger at the dockworkers' rejection of the offer. "Every possible tool was at their command," Assistant Secretary of Labor James Reynolds declared, and "to anyone interested in the preservation of collective bargaining this is a matter of grave concern." The federal government, however, did not waste time. Informed of the job action, President Johnson immediately put the Taft-Hartley mechanisms into motion.[74]

Within 24 hours, the Department of Justice received a 10-day temporary restraining order issued by Federal Judge Frederick Van Pelt Bryan, thus forcing dockworkers to return to work the very next day.[75] To ensure the quick return to work, shortly after receiving President Johnson's request for the Taft-Hartley measures, Judge Bryan reopened his court at

7 P.M. and granted the injunction, declaring he already had knowledge of the documents of the case. The collusive action of the federal and judicial powers prompted a strong denunciation by the ILA attorney Louis Waldman. "The way it was rushed through," he stated, "the way it was scheduled after business hours comes close to violating due process. . . . How can we represent our clients adequately under such circumstances?"[76]

Essentially, the strike was a continuation of the 1963 job action where automation, job security, and its ramifications for the waterfront labor process remained unresolved. The *Dockers News* pointed out at the onset of the strike movement that unlike the West Coast, which had a union-controlled hiring hall that regulated dock employment with a "one job—one man" policy, the Waterfront Commission controlled East Coast hiring. As long as this was the case, overemployment would continue because it was beneficial to employers to reduce benefit costs. Radical dockworkers proposed instead that a program that included closing the dock register and providing incentives for early retirement through the funds collected from automation penalties would more easily reduce employment levels without provoking large-scale unemployment on the docks.[77]

Even though contract negotiations resumed in the latter part of October, they continued at an impasse until early December. During the period that they were enjoined from striking, dockworkers continued to pressure employers and defy the Taft-Hartley no-strike injunction on a local level. For example, while still under the force of the injunction, longshoremen on Pier 14 refused to only partially unload a ship, causing a brief work stoppage.[78] As the deadline drew closer, federal mediators proposed a one-year agreement in an effort to avert a renewed strike by the end of December. This proposal, however, met strong employer resistance because it failed to address the issue of manpower utilization on the port. In early December, the special panel informed President Johnson that they had failed to reach an agreement.[79]

Two considerations forced the ILA leadership to resist any contract that agreed to a reduction of the waterfront workforce. First, mounting pier-wide mobilization by rank-and-file activists against workforce reduction hampered any desire the ILA leadership might have had to sign on to such a clause. Second, among ILA leaders, some argued that the work procedures that the employers were proposing to eliminate were in fact being transferred to non-union employers. Recently elected president of Brooklyn Local 1814, Anthony Scotto, who assumed the presidency after

Tony Anastasia (his father-in-law) had retired, declared, "The longshore-man is not willing to give away his own work, especially when this work—pre-palletized cargo—is performed not only by non-waterfront, non-ILA members, but often by people belonging to no union at all."[80]

Given the context and past history of the waterfront negotiation pro-cess, it was a surprise when three days before the Taft-Hartley injunction was to expire, the NYSA and the ILA announced a tentative agreement. The main points of the proposed four-year agreement included a guaran-teed annual income (based on 1,600 hours of work); a 36 cent hourly wage increase; monthly pension increase to $125; and one additional week of paid vacation after 20 years of service. In exchange, the ILA agreed to the NYSA's major demand for a reduction of the workforce and flexibility in port work practices. Sitting side by side at the head of the negotiation table with Teddy Gleason, Alexander Chopin declared: "The union had realized that something had to be done to get better utilization of our manpower," after which Gleason added he would inform all port leaders of the agree-ment.[81] The ILA leadership declared the new accord was "the best contract we ever made."[82] Both the NYSA and the ILA, however, failed to take into consideration the opinion of the rank-and-file dockworkers, which proved to be a major error.

Immediately after being informed of the new agreement, all longshore-men along the East Coast began raising opposition to the contract because the ILA leaders had agreed to the workforce reduction and flexibility de-mands of the NYSA. Workers on two piers along the Hudson River walked off the job in protest and were followed by dockworkers in Brooklyn and Hoboken. In ports as far away as South Carolina, shipping companies noted that strike preparations were under way. Immediately the ILA lead-ership assured the shipping employers that the rebellious dockworkers would return to work as soon as the contract was explained to them, as if the problem were a simple lack of communication.[83]

Fearing that the contract would not be ratified in the plebiscite sched-uled for January 8, the union leadership set out to campaign for its ap-proval. Added to the conflict, the dock union still had to negotiate con-tracts in the Southern and Gulf ports (which were not signatories to the master contract), and when the strike deadline passed, Gleason's assurance that the paralyzed piers would soon be back to work proved wrong. Four days after the ILA had announced the proposed accord with the NYSA, the Port of New York became the stage of a major wildcat strike, which had not been witnessed since 1945. Initiated by ILA Local 791 on the Hudson River, the movement quickly spread, paralyzing 55 piers throughout Brooklyn, Manhattan, and New Jersey.[84]

The central contention of the rebellious longshoremen was the ILA's acquiescence to the employers' proposal to reduce gang size from 20 to 17 dockworkers per gang and the change in long-established work practices. Gleason declared the job action "unauthorized" and pressed local union leaders to hold meetings to explain the terms of the new agreement. The strike against the ILA leadership resembled in form the movement to remove Ryan from the ILA presidency. In spite of Gleason's repeated attempts to convince the dockworkers of the contracts' benefits, the strike movement continued to spread, and by the second day local union officials recognized that 50 percent of the Port of New York was paralyzed and the movement had spread to Baltimore.[85]

After three days on strike, dockworkers returned to the port, but Gleason's problems were far from over. Rebellious dockworkers began campaigning for the rejection of the contract in the upcoming ratification vote. Furthermore, the conflict moved quickly to Galveston, Texas, where contract negotiations continued deadlocked. Resistance to the contract also grew in Baltimore, where dockworkers shouted down ILA officials who attempted to "clarify" the terms of the new agreement.[86] The possibility of a new East Coast dock strike forced the ILA and the NYSA back into negotiations in an attempt to change the terms of the agreement. This, however, also proved fruitless, because the NYSA was just as adamant about reducing the level of waterfront employment, as ILA vice president Fred Field declared: "They offered us the same deal that our members already rejected a week ago."[87] The crux of the conflict remained, in spite of the highly advantageous economic package: the longshoremen rejected any proposal that empowered the NYSA to reduce waterfront employment and change the conditions of dock work at will.

Even though at the last minute the NYSA withdrew its demand for "flexibility" to reorganize the waterfront labor force, dockworkers continued to reject the proposed accord. Despite the strong campaign by the ILA leadership in favor of its approval, the final vote tallied 8,508 votes against and 7,561 in favor of the new contract. After learning of the results, Gleason stated that he was "a little disappointed but guided by the vote of the majority," while Alexander Chopin declared that the longshoremen did not "understand the financial gains and advantages offered them" and urged that a new vote on the proposed contract be held.[88] Undersecretary Reynolds met with ILA leaders in hopes of averting a new strike, but shortly afterward he announced that it was impossible to halt the strike. With the strike imminent, shipping employers warned the rebellious dockworkers that if the port were paralyzed, they would "request the president for congressional action on compulsory arbitration."[89]

Rejecting appeals from the government and threats by the employers, on January 11 dockworkers renewed their strike movement, paralyzing all East Coast ports. In contrast, the ILA leadership renewed its campaign to "sell" the accord to the membership. After one week, the financial impact of the job action could already be felt, particularly in exports and imports of fruits and vegetables held in the strike-bound ships. Economists estimated the financial losses of the strike at $25 million a day, with 300 ships paralyzed. Gleason and the ILA Executive Board moved for a new ratification vote, certain that a week of heavy campaigning, which included letters and telegrams to the homes of all longshoremen in favor of the contract, had swayed enough votes for its approval.[90] In a four-page letter sent to all longshoremen on the Port of New York, the ILA leadership defended its proposed contract, exhorting longshoremen "to get the facts, ignore rumors; know the truth about the contract and what it will do for you."[91]

On the day before the second ratification vote, the ILA leadership held meetings along the Port of New York to "educate" longshoremen as to the benefits of the new contract. At the meeting of Local 1814 in Brooklyn, one dockworker demanded: "What I want to know before I vote tomorrow is why do older men have to die? Why can't we pension them, then they can smell the flowers while they're still alive."[92] The union leadership had failed to respond to a wide array of dockworkers' demands, and this had finally come to a boiling point during the contract negotiations. In spite of strong opposition to the contract, however, the campaign provided the advantage that the ILA leadership needed, and in the second vote the new contract was ratified in New York. The strike, however, was far from over. Following a long-standing tradition, New York's dockworkers refused to return to work until contract negotiations were resolved on all the South Atlantic and Gulf ports.

Even though Teddy Gleason promised to resolve all pending contract negotiations within 24 hours, after one week the East Coast ports continued paralyzed.[93] As the strike entered its sixteenth day, shipping employers renewed their threats of legal sanctions against the rebellious longshoremen and the ILA. Alexander Chopin demanded the immediate return of New York's dockworkers to the port. "We have a contract," he stated. "It is senseless to continue damaging the port and the national economy." Chopin's demands were accompanied by renewed threats to appeal to President Johnson and to reissue the injunction that impeded New York's dockworkers from using the coast-wide bargaining issue in contract negotiations. The federal government echoed the threats made by shipping employers: Assistant Secretary of Labor James Reynolds warned of the growing possibility of White House intervention into the conflict. "There is a sick man in Washington," he stated, "who is beginning to get very worried about this."[94]

Longshoremen, however, continued to demonstrate their dissatisfaction with the new accord, despite its approval in New York. In Baltimore, dockworkers voted to reject the ILA-NYSA accord, which inflamed even further the federal government's representatives. In response to the negative vote by Baltimore dockworkers to the proposed contract terms, Reynolds accused the movement in New York and Baltimore of being communist-inspired, and he asked the FBI to investigate the Baltimore job action.[95] Reynolds said there was proof of "communist allied subversive influences in New York outside the labor movement and also in Baltimore."[96]

The ILA leadership kept pleading for more time and promised that a solution was near at hand, but shipping officials requested immediate federal intervention. In a telegram to Johnson, they demanded that he "terminate this senseless, suicidal and unjustified strike and reopen the port, pending congressional action towards compulsory arbitration." Over the course of 20 days the Maritime Administration estimated the financial losses of the strike at $1 billion.[97] Despite the intense pressure and the wavering union leadership in favor of a return to work, New York's dockworkers remained steadfast in their strike. The three main centers of the conflict were Baltimore, Philadelphia, and Galveston. Even as the strike moved into its second month, and Baltimore and Philadelphia finally approved the contract proposal, the inability to reach an agreement on the Gulf ports kept all East Coast ports paralyzed.

Speaking for President Johnson, Secretary of Labor Wirtz urged all longshoremen who had ratified contracts to return to work; however, this also had little or no effect. Shipping employers then renewed their pressure on the federal government for more decisive action. In a strongly worded telegram to President Johnson, the NYSA demanded action "either through congress or any other measure at your command. . . . Our bitter disappointment at the flaunting of your high office prompts us to again appeal for your personal intervention."[98]

The strike was beginning to impose overwhelming financial losses in industries around the country and in the international market as well. Citing financial problems imposed by the strike, fruit and vegetable importers declared that some businesses were already "facing bankruptcy. The Brazilian Coffee Institute reported that American coffee imports had declined by 600,000 bags since the beginning of the strike." The president of Cargill Inc., a leading grain exporter, declared that "the farm economy had received a severe blow, and that some lost sales would not be recaptured," and Memphis cotton exporters complained that the strike "was crippling the cotton export business." The A. E. Staley Manufacturing Company announced that they would have to lay off 3,000 workers who would only be called back at the end of the strike.[99]

Demonstrating increasing anxiousness to end the strike, ILA vice president Anthony Scotto declared that with the agreement in Philadelphia, North Atlantic dockworkers would return to work. Even so, Baltimore and subsequently Philadelphia dockworkers' ratification of the contract failed to prompt a return to work, and the NYSA with the support of the NLRB moved against striking longshoremen. The shipping employers charged the ILA with unfair labor practices for using coast-wide bargaining in contract negotiations and with the practice of secondary boycott, since North Atlantic dockworkers refused to return to work without contract agreements on the South Atlantic and Gulf ports. Coinciding with the shipping employers' legal measures, President Johnson charged a three-member panel with the task of making recommendations to end the strike immediately.[100] Serving on this panel were Secretary of Labor Willard Wirtz, Secretary of Commerce John Connor, and Senator Morse; they were instructed by the president to resolve the issues of the South Atlantic and Gulf ports within 24 hours.[101]

Echoing the employers' demands, Johnson called the maintenance of the strike "unjustified" and said that the "injury to the national economy had reached staggering proportions."[102] After accepting the charges leveled by the NYSA, the NLRB proceeded to federal court to enjoin striking dockworkers. Pending future hearings to issue permanent injunctions against striking longshoremen, Federal Judge Sidney Sugarman issued five-day restraining orders against the rebellious dockworkers in New York. Similar orders were issued in New Orleans, Baltimore, and Mobile, Alabama, thus ending the 33-day strike on the ports where collective bargaining agreements had been reached.

The injunctions, however, had little effect on other ports. On the Southern and Gulf ports, the heated battle continued for another 22 days, primarily on the ports of Miami and Galveston. The striking dockworkers cited the increasingly harsh intervention of federal authorities as one of the major reasons why they continued on strike. As a Miami ILA official declared, "As long as the southern employers feel that the federal court is on their side and using its vast power to force the ILA to knuckle down they will not budge." Employers denied the Southern dockworkers' claims, stating: "If they think the only thing holding us on our feet is Uncle Sam they vastly underestimate us."[103] The forced return to work on the North Atlantic ports, however, severely reduced any possibility of Southern dockworkers remaining on strike for too much longer.

By the first week of March, Miami longshoremen had reached an agreement, following the move by dockworkers in Galveston the week before. After 55 days on strike and an estimated financial loss of $3 billion, East and Gulf Coast dockworkers returned to work victorious.[104] First, they were able to break with traditional forms of employment relations where workers usually bore the brunt of economic and technological transformations by being subjected to large-scale unemployment. The GAI demonstrated that other forms of employment transition measures were possible. Second, despite employers gaining greater regulatory clauses written into the agreement, East Coast dockworkers continued to resist the enforcement of the new rules devised to regulate the waterfront labor process and reduce their employment possibilities. Third, implementation of the GAI forced the reexamination of control of the waterfront at the most basic level, such as hiring practices and waterfront seniority. Labor peace on the Port of New York was still short-lived. As the ILA leadership increasingly spoke of "partnership and cooperation" with the shipping employers, independent rank-and-file action, particularly from the left, would push the process of waterfront reform forward.

Who Controls Dock Employment?

The struggle for control of the waterfront did not always place dockworkers in direct conflict with their employers. That is, the expanding powers of the Waterfront Commission in everyday life on the docks often joined the interests of employers and the union in opposition to the Commission's control of the dock labor process. The longshoremen's demands for a union-management hiring hall and to close the dock register went unanswered. As early as 1961 radical longshoremen had made closing the Waterfront Commission's "dock register" a major aspect of their struggle for waterfront reform because they perceived that the growing problem of automation with its attendant weakening of job security would eventually lead to the reduction of the workforce. In the September 1961 issue the *Dockers News* group asked, "You want to protect your job, don't you? Whether you're a 'steady' or a 'floating extra.' You want to insure your chance to keep working, not only on your pier, or section, but in the whole port in case something happens where you now work! Or will you settle for another raise, more fancy words about seniority, a few extra cents for welfare, pension, or even hospital funds which won't benefit you if you're not working enough to qualify?"

In January 1964, the ILA sought unsuccessfully to pass legislation in the state assembly to abolish the Waterfront Commission.[105] By 1966, the movement to close the dock register had gained momentum, and the ILA promoted a one-day port-wide work stoppage supporting legislation that sought to remove the hiring power from the Waterfront Commission. The two central demands, a union-management hiring hall and the end of the dock register, enjoyed broad support from the ILA, the NYSA, and even waterfront arbitrators such as Theodore Kheel. The first objective was to wrestle the power of waterfront employment from the commission. But these demands had a broader impact on the dock labor process that went far beyond the demand for control of the hiring process. Anthony Scotto announced: "We will stage a massive all-day demonstration to prove to Governor Nelson Rockefeller and to every assemblyman and senator that the ILA rank and file has unanimous labor support in its efforts to democratize the Waterfront Commission."[106]

In opposition, Rockefeller supported legislation that would only temporarily close the dock register for 80 days after which the Waterfront Commission would decide when to open and close the register, thus retaining the power of regulating the levels of dock employment under the purview of state political authorities.[107]

The power to control the levels of waterfront employment became even more important and its effects even more far-reaching with the inception of the GAI. Eligibility for the GAI required that longshoremen be considered "regulars" (only those who worked at least 1,600 hours). Under the new agreement, however, the union had conceded to a smaller gang size. A continued flow of new dockworkers onto the port would create an overabundance of longshoremen for a limited number of openings, thus creating the possibility of invalidating or severely limiting the number of longshoreman eligible for the guaranteed wage scheme.[108] The struggle to close the dock register melded with claims of port seniority and a rebellion against the recently adopted work rules. Even though the ILA did little beyond the legislative pressure of the one-day work stoppage, rank-and-file dockworkers had other plans, as the battle to control the docks mobilized the ports once again.

On Friday, April 1, 1966, when the new work rules and port structure reducing the actual gang size from 20 to 18 were set to go into effect, longshoremen on the ports of Newark, Elizabeth, Staten Island, and Brooklyn walked off the job in protest.[109] By Monday, the strike had spread to Manhattan. Alexander Chopin said the rebellious movement was "extortion" and that the NYSA had "paid a high price in the form of a guaranteed Annual Income to longshoremen, and higher more liberal pension as well as other fringe benefit improvements in order to secure greater man power efficiency."[110] The underlying demands of the rebels contested the work rules that had been accepted by the ILA leadership in the last contract negotiation, which was only approved after a strong campaign by the union leadership. Their demands focused on the distribution of work assignments, which employed two instead of four dockworkers on the pier to receive sling loads, and the problematic seniority system, which did not allow seniority hiring to be carried from one port to another.

Longtime longshoremen who worked as deckmen in Manhattan could be forced to work in the hold of a ship on the Port of Brooklyn. The conflict over the reorganization of the dock labor process was also a reflection of the changing economic structure of New York City. As early as 1964, the New York City Board of Estimate and the City Planning Commission had proposed removing cargo handling from the East and Hudson rivers and shifting all cargo operations to Brooklyn, Newark, and Elizabeth. Under the Planning Commission's proposal, Manhattan's waterfront areas were to be transformed into residential and recreational areas.[111] Thus the rapid deactivation of the river ports forced Manhattan's longshoremen to seek work on other piers.

In spite of pressure by the union leadership and employers, the strike continued to gain support. In its fourth day, Staten Island remained completely paralyzed, and in Port Newark only 7 of the 55 gangs appeared for work.[112] An estimated 28 ships remained idle primarily on the ports of Newark, Brooklyn, Staten Island, and even the Brooklyn Army Pier—where operations had never been paralyzed, even during union-sanctioned strikes. While applauding those ILA locals that were working, Chopin threatened the rebellious longshoremen: "Management will not tolerate attempts by certain groups in the union to force realignment of assignments within the general cargo that would nullify the economies called for in our contract designed to increase efficiency on the piers."[113]

The dockworkers were unwavering in their resistance to the threats of employers, and the demands of the union leadership that they return to work provoked a meeting of the Joint Board of the ILA and the NYSA. Led by port arbitrator Burton Turkus, the meeting declared the strike "illegal" and once again ordered the dockworkers to return to work. This, however, had little effect on the movement. Realizing the ILA leadership had no control over the striking dockworkers, the NYSA moved quickly into the New York State Supreme Court and the Superior Court of New Jersey, which issued restraining orders against striking longshoremen.[114] The dock-hiring agents served the restraining orders on individual longshoremen when they refused to accept work assignments, and New York State Supreme Court Justice George M. Carney threatened others with imprisonment if they did not return to work immediately.[115]

Forced to return to work, longshoremen began to slow down their activities, and "brush fire" strikes plagued the port. Workers continued to press the issue of reorganization of the dock labor process by tying up the work process. One employer declared that he would withdraw from the NYSA if the movement continued, and another employer stated that the job actions were "the biggest mess since I have been on the waterfront and that's been a long time."[116] The ILA leadership continuously "cruised" the piers, pressuring the longshoremen to work, but the job action ended only after longshoremen were promised that the issue would be taken to arbitration. Even so, many employers had decided early on not to enforce the new work rules and quickly reverted back to the traditional port practices. As one employer declared, "If this keeps up, the union gains will remain and our quid pro quo will flow down the river and out to sea."[117]

The expansion of the automated work process continuously renewed and reconfigured the parameters for conflict. In particular, the uneven growth of containerized cargo ultimately placed the Port of Brooklyn at a disadvantage. Because there was relatively little physical space for container storage and movement near the Brooklyn docks, the cargo handled in Brooklyn was primarily in "break-bulk" form (loose cargo), while increasing numbers of container ships were being sent to Port Elizabeth and Newark. This trend reflected the interests of the shipping companies in expanding the use of the New Jersey ports. In one year cargo tonnage handled on the ports of Newark and Elizabeth increased 34.6 percent, reaching a total of 2.6 million tons.[118] The conflict caused by the growing shift in pier usage was enhanced by the disparate number of dockworkers registered to work on each port.

Despite the growing use of the New Jersey ports, there were only 2,200 registered longshoremen in New Jersey, while in Brooklyn there were approximately 10,000 registered dockworkers. Sensing that ultimately a large part of the waterfront work would be transferred to New Jersey, Brooklyn's Local 1814 president Anthony Scotto announced that Brooklyn dockworkers would no longer handle containerized or pre-palletized cargo; he hoped this would force an increase in the contributions to the Container Royalty Fund.[119] Scotto based his boycott on a recent Supreme Court decision that the boycott of prefabricated construction material was not included under the "hot cargo" provisions of the Taft-Hartley and Landrum-Griffin acts.[120] Speaking at a dinner at the Rudder Club, Scotto stated: "If work now being done on the docks is to be done away from the dock then I believe it must also entail the shifting of that area of longshoremen, checkers, and other craftsmen now doing the work on the docks. Very simply, we want to do it ourselves, whether on the docks or away from the docks."[121]

Scotto's demands for revision of the container work process and increased royalty fees coincided with the Waterfront Commission's attempt to reopen the dock register. Responding to a request by the New Jersey governor, who claimed that employment levels were insufficient, the Commission planned to hire 750 new longshoremen for Ports Elizabeth and Newark. The Commission's reopening of the register immediately brought the port to a standstill as approximately 500 longshoremen converged on the offices of the dock agency protesting the measure. Gleason condemned the Commission's actions, stating that in fact there was "an oversupply of longshore personnel due to the advent of containerization, palletization, and automated cargo handling." For the union the main problem was labor mobility within the port system and not a shortage. The NYSA supported the union's claims, and together they filed a suit against the reopening of the dock register in the New York State Supreme Court.[122]

While the employers supported the union's demand, they vehemently condemned the work stoppage. Calling the movement "illegal," Alexander Chopin also filed an action in New York State Supreme Court to stop the strike.[123] As one employer declared, "Although we are partners in this objective we are the ones being hurt by the union's methods."[124] Dockworkers defied the court order and continued the strike, while continuing with the daily mobilizations in front of the Waterfront Commission's office. Ultimately, the union won in federal court and had the restraining order lifted. The financial losses imposed by the strike were estimated at $1.5 million a day, and after the ports had been idle for nine days, the American Railroad Association embargoed all cargo trains headed for the Port of New York.[125] After 11 days on strike and with a backlog of half a million tons of cargo on the ports, the ILA agreed to return to work after Turkus proposed the formation of a joint labor-management seniority board with the power to create mobile gangs to fill labor shortages while maintaining seniority and job classification rights.[126]

This initial step toward port-wide seniority allowed dock labor greater mobility and thus provided the 1,600 work hours necessary to guarantee eligibility for the GAI. The measure also provided the employers and the union with the device necessary to sidestep the commission's power to open the register. With port-wide seniority and mobile gangs, the employers and the ILA leadership retained for themselves the power to limit the hiring of dock labor by eliminating labor shortages caused by oversupply on some ports and undersupply on others. At the same time this weakened the Waterfront Commission's control of the dock register because there was no justification to reopen the register if there were no labor shortages. The Port Authority criticized the agreement because it weakened the effective control of political authorities over the waterfront labor force. In a letter to the governor of New Jersey, Port Authority executive director Austin Tobin declared that the ILA/NYSA seniority agreement was "a pact contrived to subvert the statutes, the courts, and the legal responsibilities of the waterfront commission."[127] The 11-day strike, however, was just a warm-up for the contract negotiations set to start in just three months.

At the opening of the 1968 contract negotiations, the ILA proposed major increments to the longshore wage and benefit package. The union's demands included $6 per hour wage rate and double time for overtime work, four additional paid holidays, increase in the GAI hours to 2,040 per year, and a pension rate of $400 per month with retirement after 20 years of service regardless of age. The union proposed a two-year contract after which time the economic clauses would be renegotiated. The NYSA counterproposed a reexamination of the port-wide seniority and mobility agreement, freedom to control work assignments, speedy arbitrations to end "quickie strikes," no restrictions to the introduction of new machinery, free use of containers, and a 48 cent increase in wages and benefits.[128]

The ILA's claims at the opening of negotiations, however, did not obfuscate the deeper tension between the dockworkers and the NYSA regarding the introduction of automation and the utilization of the waterfront workforce. After one month of discussions, little progress in the way of a new contract had been made, even after the NYSA increased their economic offer and the ILA reduced their expectations. The control of container operations and the reorganization of the dock labor force obstructed any progress the negotiations may have made, as one employer announced after a meeting: "The pension issue is completely subsidiary to the container traffic question."[129] Much of the negotiation process remained fruitless despite the NYSA's increasingly attractive economic offers to the ILA; the central issues of the negotiations were not economic but rather the employers' demand for control of the waterfront work process. Fearing that a strike was looming, six days before the October 1, 1968, contract expired, President Johnson appointed Undersecretary of Labor James Reynolds to intervene in the negotiation process, even though no federal assistance was requested. Joseph Califano, special assistant to President Johnson, defended the intervention: "It was a fully appropriate act" because "this is a dispute of major national importance."[130]

Despite federal intervention in the negotiation process, the talks remained deadlocked on the eve of October 1. Employers kept insisting on their willingness to agree to the union's job security scheme (GAI) and to their expansive pension and benefits demands if the union would agree to "provide a steady workforce and end the abuses." The "abuses" that shipping employers referred to were the dockworkers' long-standing resistance to the NYSA's demand for workforce flexibility and the longshoremen's limited control of the container transportation process, such as the packing and unpacking of containers on the port. The union was not apprehensive about the economic aspects of the negotiations; as Gleason argued,

"The money problem can be quickly solved."[131] While in 1968 container ships composed 20 percent of the port's activity, it was projected that by 1975 it would account for 75 percent of all cargo transportation on the Port of New York.[132]

Added to the growing strike sentiment was the rank and file's discontent with the previous contract negotiations and distrust of the union leadership. The radical dockworkers argued that Gleason had "settled for the 3.2 percent wage guideline that the government had forced on us." Workers in other industries, such as steelworkers, teamsters, and machinists, had successfully broken the government's wage freeze. The growing distrust of the ILA leadership's negotiating capacity was tied to claims of weak enforcement of seniority rights and the union's withholding of the container royalty funds awarded to longshoremen. Under the banner "No Contract—No Work," *Dockers News* demanded that the ILA Wage and Scale Committee disregard the government's wage freeze in the upcoming negotiations and that the Container Royalty Fund be distributed to longshoremen. "To hell with the wage freeze!" the newsletter declared. "To hell with the ship owners who are making millions out of the Vietnam War! To hell with those who would try to keep us from fighting for the welfare of our families! No Contract—No Work! All Out October 1."[133]

Following what appeared to be a well-organized ritual that had developed over the years, several hours before the October 1 deadline, work on ports from Maine to Texas came to a standstill. Following the same routine as presidents before him, President Johnson invoked the Taft-Hartley Act. The act had been applied in every dock strike since its approval in Congress in 1947. In a White House statement, President Johnson argued: "In terms of the impact of the strike government economists estimate that the strike would cost about $70 million a day in terms of exports and imports; that wage losses for longshoremen and seamen would be about $2 million a day." Furthermore, the federal government argued that "the strike would have severe implications for our balance of payments."[134] At the Board of Inquiry hearing, employers estimated their direct financial losses at $1.3 million a day and said that 2.8 percent of the nation's jobs depended on the waterfront activity in one way or another.[135]

The main issue of the job action, employers argued, was a response to their demand to assign dockworkers to any port in New York or New Jersey, which they said would end the abuses to the GAI. Because of the limits to where a longshoreman was obligated to work, they continued, some longshoremen were receiving a full year's salary without working a single day.[136] Teddy Gleason responded that the central issue was the process of automation. Hoping to divide container carriers and the break-bulk shipping carriers, he offered to offset the losses of the break-bulk carriers by subsidizing their employment costs with money from the Container Royalty Fund.[137] Gleason's proposal did little to avert the judicial restraining order and subsequent injunction forcing dockworkers back to work once more, just three days after the strike had begun. His offer to subsidize the break-bulk shipping carriers with money intended for longshoremen sparked a major revolt. New York's dockworkers were not restrained for very long.

As negotiations resumed, Gleason expressed optimism that a new contract could be reached by November 8, his birthday, and more than a month before the Taft-Hartley injunction was set to expire. Beyond unjustifiable confidence, Gleason's expectation that a new accord would soon be reached demonstrated the increasing distance between the actions of the ILA leadership and the demands of rank-and-file dockworkers. He did not expect the birthday present New York's longshoremen would give him.

Disobeying the court injunction, on October 31 a wildcat strike quickly spread throughout Port Elizabeth, Newark, and Brooklyn. Activists denounced Gleason's proposal as "a steal" and called for a "container bonus holiday." *Dockers News* announced: "We longshoremen who bust our asses climbing all over those containers stacked two and three high and who take all the chances when they buckle. We want the money! We have waited, we have listened to all the speeches, we are fed up!!! Now—Mr. Gleason we are telling you . . . we want the container money; we want it as a Christmas bonus. As a step to show that we mean business we are calling on all rank-and-file longshoremen to stay home on October 31, 1968. . . . It is time we went on strike for ourselves!"[138] The radical dockworkers argued that a similar fund on the West Coast distributed $1,200 annually to each longshoreman and $13,000 upon retirement.

The ILA leadership was surprised by the speed with which the job action spread. On the first day of the strike, half the ships in New York harbor remained idle.[139] "I can't comment," Gleason stated, "since I don't know anything about it. But they'll be back at work tomorrow."[140] In spite of his assurances, the movement spread, and by the second day the piers of Jersey City and Hoboken were also paralyzed. According to the Waterfront Commission, 3,500 longshoremen were involved in the work stoppage. Unable to control the wildcat strike, the assistant U.S. attorney general for the Southern District demanded that the FBI begin an immediate investigation into the strike.[141]

The employers also expressed surprise. A NYSA spokesman declared that he could not remember another instance in which a strike had occurred while a Taft-Hartley injunction was in effect.[142] The NYSA demanded that Attorney General Ramsey Clark take immediate action against the rebellious dockworkers in what they called a "flagrant violation of the existing Taft-Hartley injunction."[143] The strike also demonstrated the willingness of the ILA leadership to revert to methods of coercion and violence that were commonly used during the presidency of Joe Ryan, and fighting erupted between striking dockworkers and ILA loyalists. For example, at the Grace Line terminal in Port Newark, struggles broke out after 200 striking dockworkers attempted to stop banana handlers from working.[144]

The Waterfront Commission quickly warned that it would act "swiftly," suspending the registration of any dockworker "engaged in acts of violence, intimidation, or coercion."[145] This warning, however, did not seem to apply to the ILA leadership's campaign against the rebellious longshoremen. *Dockers News* activist Gus Johnson remembers: "In Brooklyn the union used strong-arm tactics by locking the men on to the piers, like on Pier 5. On the 37th Street pier they pulled up the gangplank and wouldn't let the men off the ship. Whatever the men's participation was, there was no work done for five days."[146] After a weeklong strike, the longshoremen returned to work, and shortly thereafter the ILA distributed $6 million to dockworkers as a Christmas bonus.[147] The strike had two immediate results. First, striking dockworkers were able to block Gleason's attempt to entice break-bulk shipping employers with funds that were destined for the longshoremen as compensation. Second, it sent a message to the ILA leadership that the rank-and-file left was also a force that had to be considered.

By early December, the presidential board of inquiry informed President Johnson that the cooling-off period had done little to resolve the issues still pending in the contract negotiations. The NYSA made its final offer to the ILA, but even the presidential board overseeing the negotiations did not think the ILA would accept it. The shipping employers offered two choices in the final proposal: a two-year contract with a 63 cent wage and benefit increase, or a three-year contract with $1.01 increase in wages and benefits, and an increase in the GAI income hours from 1,600 to 2,040.[148]

For dockworkers, neither proposal was acceptable, and they chose a third option: to reject the employers' final offer. In New York, 8,796 longshoremen voted to reject the NYSA's final proposal, while only 871 voted in favor.[149] In ballots over the entire East Coast, dockworkers voted 15 to 1 to reject the shipping companies' final offer.[150]

With three days remaining for the expiration of the Taft-Hartley injunction, the ILA and the NYSA emerged from negotiations with a tentative agreement. The terms of the agreement proposed a $1.60 increase in wages and benefits, expanding the coverage of the GAI from 40 to 52 weeks, or 2,080 hours annually. In exchange, the ILA promised employers greater flexibility in waterfront work practices, such as loading and unloading containers on the port, and Teddy Gleason promised that if the wording was acceptable, he and the other ILA vice presidents would campaign for the contract's ratification.[151]

The dockworkers, however, had another strategy in mind. At a meeting of the ILA's Wage and Scale Committee, Gleason was "shouted down" by local ILA leaders when he proposed that the contract be approved without its being "finished." The local dock leaders demanded that the contract be rejected.[152]

Two major concerns emerged from the meeting. First, the workers didn't believe the ILA leadership would rewrite the container clause, and second, many of the benefits of the proposed agreement were only for dockworkers on the Port of New York, which quickly unified the dockworkers of the "outer ports" such as Baltimore and Philadelphia against the new accord. By the time a vote was taken at the meeting, even New York ILA locals voted a resounding "no" to the new agreement. Few of those involved in the negotiation process expected the dockworkers' reaction. Just before they voted to reject the offer, an assistant to President Johnson, David Cole, had made a "victory speech" congratulating dockworkers for winning a "generous and far ranging contract."[153]

The two essential points of contention were the dockworkers' continued participation in the container packing process and the extension of all provisions of the contract to all ports along the East Coast. As expected, the strike resumed on December 20, 1968; dockworkers all along the East Coast abandoned the ports once again. President Johnson reacted strongly, declaring that "the country could not pay the high price involved in a long-term strike" and that "it was the responsibility of the parties to resolve this matter and do so immediately."[154] His appeal fell on deaf ears. The

Maritime Association reported that 163 ships were paralyzed from Maine to Texas as a result of the strike, 49 of which were berthed in the Port of New York.[155]

The central contention of the shipping employers was that the master contract only regulated wage, pension, and welfare increases, not benefits in general, and thus all other terms and conditions of employment were to be negotiated locally.[156] Longshoremen, however, had a long-standing policy: "if one port is down, all out," meaning New York's dockworkers would not return to work until all ports had reached an agreement. Johnson threatened to send a message to Congress when it reconvened in January as the financial impact of the strike began to multiply. By the end of the year, 200 freighters were paralyzed and employers were beginning to threaten to close plants if the strike was not resolved shortly.[157] Financial losses were calculated at $2 million a day; added to that were lost wages calculated at $15 million during the first 15 days of the strike.[158] Passenger cruise lines began canceling scheduled trips, leaving thousands of passengers stranded.[159] The strike's domino effect on port-related industries and services was almost immediate, leaving 5,000 trucks and 1,100 railroad cars idle.[160]

Although Richard Nixon would soon succeed Johnson, business elites continued to pressure the outgoing president to act against striking longshoremen. In a telegram to Johnson, G. G. Tegnell, executive vice president of the New York Chamber of Commerce, urged that the "full powers of the presidency be brought to bear." He also requested congressional legislation against striking longshoremen.[161]

Echoing the claims of the Chamber of Commerce, a few days later retired Admiral John M. Will, president of the NYSA, demanded that President Johnson promote legislation in Congress that would force the ILA into compulsory arbitration, pledging the industry's acquiescence to a "responsible tribunal provided by statute." "This demonstration of abuse of union power," he stated, "should not be permitted to continue at the expense of the nation's security of our position in competitive world markets and our delicate balance of payments positions."[162] The New York State Motor Truck Association sent similar messages to both Johnson and Nixon.[163]

By mid-January, even though the major issues of contention on the Port of New York had been settled, employer resistance in the outer ports continued high. The NYSA agreed to extend the ILA's jurisdiction to include the packing and unpacking of containers that were less than complete or that held multiple shipments (more than one cargo load). In addition to the proposed settlement of the work rules, the three-year contract provided proposed wage and benefit increases of $1.60.[164]

Even though the ILA announced that an agreement had been reached in New York, the union leadership did not ask the dockworkers whether they would agree to the new contract. The proposal was not well received by dockworkers in other ports, primarily because of the disparate work hours of the different ports and because benefit rates were calculated based on the total amount of work hours. In ports with fewer longshoremen than New York (which were most, if not all, of them), the stipulated monetary increase provided for in the agreement allowed for lesser benefits. In Philadelphia, shipping employers agreed to the $1.60 wage and benefit increase. In large part they agreed because fewer work hours were done on the port and the increase would not provide the two extra weeks of vacation that it provided for New York's dockworkers.[165] Similar problems arose in Baltimore.

In contrast, on the Southern and Gulf ports, employers not only resisted the economic terms of the agreement, but primarily the longshoremen's demands for control of the waterfront labor process. In New Orleans, while economic aspects of the agreement were subsequently deemed acceptable, issues of the port labor process continued to block any chance of a settlement.[166]

Past experience of New York's dockworkers had shown that if they ratified the contract before agreements were reached on all ports, the NYSA would charge them with unfair labor practices and subsequently forbid the strike, forcing them to return to work and weakening the bargaining power of other ports. For all practical purposes, the strike remained unsettled until all ports had reached an agreement. The deadlocked negotiation process increased the pressure of business elites demanding federal action to end the strike. In a telegram to Senator Jacob Javits, small business owners Arthur Bushman and Paul Minkoff complained: "It is incredible that not one member of the New York delegation either in the House or the Senate has spoken forcefully regarding the pier strike travesty that is causing irreparable harm and threatening many small businesses."[167]

Pressure on the federal government to take action against the striking dockworkers was also renewed shortly after Nixon's inauguration. In a joint statement, Governor Rockefeller and New York senators Jacob Javits and Charles Goodell declared that the strike "now poses a critical danger to the health and safety of the entire nation."[168] By day 33 of the strike, the Maritime Administration announced that 408 ships were immobile along the East Coast, and some businesses began laying off workers. Syrup and Sugar Inc. announced that it would begin dismissing 400 employees for lack of work.[169] Moreover, lost wages had reached an estimated $30 million and financial losses almost $1 billion.[170]

The New York dockworkers' "unofficial concurrence" with the new accord shifted the negotiation process and subsequently the power to decide the duration of the strike to the outer ports of the North Atlantic and the Southern and Gulf ports. The ILA leadership turned its attention to resolving the conflicts outside of the New York area. Attempting to intervene in the Philadelphia contract negotiations, the dock union sent ILA general organizer Fred Field to the city in the hopes of removing any existing impasse. Distrust of the ILA leadership, however, was strong in the City of Brotherly Love, and local union leaders promptly barred Field from negotiations, stating that "he had not been invited to participate and there would positively be no joint meeting with management if he were present."[171] Field returned to New York. Hoping to break the stalemate on other ports, the ILA leadership also appealed to President Nixon to influence Southern and Atlantic Coast employer groups to come to terms with striking dockworkers. It was reported that in a telegram to Nixon, Werner Brock, counsel for the ILA Gulf Coast District Council, urged the president to "insist that the Maritime Association in the South and Gulf Coast areas be fair in their dealings with the ILA and urge them to forget that longshoremen in the South can be bought more cheaply than longshoremen in the North."[172]

In spite of mounting pressure from congressional leaders, employer and business groups, and even factions of the ILA to intervene in the dock strike, Nixon broke with a growing tradition of both Democratic and Republican presidents and repeatedly refused to intercede in the East Coast dock crisis. Even though government economists had estimated that in its seventh week economic damage had reached $2 billion, Nixon's labor secretary, George Shultz, minimized the impact that the strike was causing the economy. When exporters questioned him about the strike, Shultz replied: "It is easy to exaggerate these things," and "it is almost impossible to determine the exact impact of the strike at this point."[173] The Nixon administration sought to minimize the effects of the strike and not declare a national emergency,[174] as many political authorities and business groups demanded, ignoring public and political pressure.[175]

Nixon's policy toward labor was in large part driven by his deeper interest in driving a wedge between the two largest support bases of the Democratic majority, labor and the civil rights movement, and to draw their support or at least weaken their political capacity to contest his administration's policies.[176] While Nixon refrained from intervening directly in the dock strike, this did not mean that all federal political authorities followed suit. Specifically, congressional Republicans and the NLRB picked up the banner of federal intervention in the dock conflict. After meeting with Nixon, Senator Everett Dirksen and Congressman Gerald Ford declared "that Congress would act if the strike was not resolved promptly."[177] The strike, however, from all appearances was far from over.

One stumbling block was that the ILA leadership appeared increasingly bogged down attempting to carry on multiple negotiations on various ports simultaneously, thus prolonging the strike.[178] The endurance of business and federal political authorities finally reached its brink. The NYSA, fearing the strike would endure for a second month, charged the ILA with unfair labor practice for "failing to hold a ratification election on the Port of New York." Similar to the charges in past job actions, this time when the longshoremen refused to ratify the proposed agreement, employers used the threat of first forcing a plebiscite under the auspices of the NLRB, which would then enable them to seek an injunction if the contract was ratified. Gleason's first response to the threat of a forced ratification election was to rhetorically declare that he would urge the rejection of the agreement, even though "it was the best contract ever."[179]

Divergences concerning the future of the strike also began to emerge among the ILA leadership. Fearing that dockworkers might reject the accord in spite of appeals from the union leadership as they had done in the past, Anthony Scotto decided to call a meeting as part of an "educational campaign" to reinforce the drive toward ratification. To a standing-room-only crowd of 2,500 dockworkers at the St. George Hotel in Brooklyn, Scotto announced, "It's about time we figure out what we are going to do. After 46 days it is hard for me to say that we got what we wanted, but it is the best contract we've ever negotiated." It was reported that the dockworkers responded with resounding rejection, booing and disparaging the union leader, leaving his face "blanched and flushed." Scotto continued to appeal to the crowd: "If you are going to feel that way you won't have any trouble with me. If you want to stay out another 46 days or 96, you can count on me, but let's look at the document."[180]

As the longshoremen rose to speak, the dissatisfaction with the results after almost two months on strike was evident. "Why didn't we get the six-hour day?" demanded one dockworker. "Why no double time on Saturdays, Sundays, and holidays?" said another. The generalized revolt forced Scotto to make one more appeal: "You know I have a double responsibility. I've got to get everything I can get for the membership. Yes, I've got to draw blood from management—I've got to be a good cutter, but I also have to know when to stop cutting and to avoid the jugular. We don't want to kill the companies that employ us, we are hoping to keep them in business and still get our fair share."[181]

The union leaders proposed a vote to ratify the contract proposal, which was also met with shouts of disapproval from the crowd. Pointing his finger at a group in the crowd, Scotto responded: "I know some of you up there, you're not members of Local 1814."[182] Others, however, endorsed the union's proposal. "Why did we elect them in the first place if we don't want to follow their leadership?" one dockworker asked.[183] Slowly Scotto was able to move a significant part of the dissatisfied dockworkers to approve the proposed agreement, although it was apparent that resistance remained strong.

Responding to a petition by the NLRB for an immediate back-to-work order, Federal Judge John F. X. McGohey subsequently scolded the striking dock union for failing to hold a ratification election.[184] In response, the ILA leadership set out to persuade members to approve the new agreement. Even Teddy Gleason, who had initially threatened to urge dockworkers to reject the accord if a ratification election was forced upon them, campaigned for the contract's ratification.[185] In the subsequent NLRB-sponsored election, New York dockworkers voted 3 to 1 in favor of the new collective bargaining agreement. In the final tally, 9,328 approved and 3,213 opposed the new contract. The longest and costliest strike in the history of the Port of New York had ended, with 56 days on strike; the job action was estimated to have imposed losses of $2 billion on the national economy, immobilizing 651 ships of which one-third were berthed in the Port of New York. Even though shipping executives complained that the new rates and conditions "were murder," they found quick solace "that the only salvation rests in seizing all benefits of the new trend—carrying most of our general cargo in the big box containers."[186]

As was expected with the end of the strike in New York, the remaining East Coast ports quickly resolved their pending negotiations, and by February 24 all East Coast ports were humming with activity, removing backlogged cargo from the piers. One federal mediator noted: "Dockers' pay ranks among the highest of any industry, and the Guarantee feature is not matched in any industry."[187] *Dockers News*, which had been circulating on the port for almost 25 years, continued pressuring the ILA leadership. The radical dockworkers demanded greater safeguards for waterfront employment and linked the lack of union militancy to Gleason's personal interests in a container company. The radical longshoremen charged that his use of pro-Vietnam War rhetoric was obfuscating the longshoremen's deeper interests. As the headline declared, "Gleason, Stick to the Issues!"[188]

In a little over two years, New York's dockworkers would paralyze the port still again, and they continued over the years, through various devices, to demand control of the waterfront labor process. Shipping employers continued to confront the rebellious dockworkers, as in 1971 when they unsuccessfully pushed to repeal the longshoremen's victory over automation.[189] The question posed by dockworkers beginning with the 1930s rebellion led by Pete Panto—"Who controls the waterfront?"—continued to be posed by longshoremen in various ways and different contexts. Contention on the waterfront, however, was not resolved through contractual agreements or collective bargaining. Conflict on the docks ended with the demise of the Port of New York as an economically viable operation. The growing trend toward containerized cargo shifted most waterfront activity to Port Elizabeth and Newark along with an ever-diminishing labor force that was consistently being redefined.

Conclusion

Class and Power

A View from the Docks

Despite the dockworkers' increasing capacity over the years to impose heavy financial losses on shipping elites and political pressure on state and federal authorities, the waterfront rank-and-file movement proved unsuccessful at achieving its most fundamental demand for greater control of the dock labor process and their union. A close examination of almost thirty years of continuous conflict and revolt on the Port of New York indicates that the capacity of New York's longshoremen to impose financial and political pressure far outweighed their ability to translate their revolt into effective political power. Similar to most American workers, for dockworkers power remained insubstantial. The limited ability of the longshoremen's movement to reform the waterfront, however, was not solely a reflection of their own weaknesses or simply the result of limited resources.

Over time, waterfront workers saw their demands for greater control of the workplace systemically constrained, as their movement became the object of increasingly high levels of physical, political, social, and economic coercion. As the dockworkers' movement expanded its capacity to mobilize longshoremen and impose increasingly larger financial losses, concurrently so did the wherewithal of shipping elites and political authorities to devise mechanisms, formal and informal, to contain the rebellious movement.

The limits imposed on the dockworkers' reform movement had two distinct phases. Each phase reflects discrete political alliances that redefined both the short- and long-term objectives of rank-and-file activists and, subsequently, the way in which longshoremen intervened in the process of reform. During the first phase, immediately following World War II, dockworkers responded to high levels of domination, defined by highly perverse informal relations between the ILA leadership, state and local political authorities, and the shipping companies, with massive wildcat strikes. The early alliances of those in favor of reform mirrored a popular-front formation, which had been carried over since the late 1930s. This phase, however, was short-lived, as Ryan's incapacity to control the dock labor force became more and more evident. Under the mounting pressure of the wildcat strikes and the ideological pressures of McCarthyism, political authorities and business elites devised alternative policies and procedures to control the increasingly rebellious dockworkers. By 1947, the passage of the Taft-Hartley Act represented the centerpiece of a loosely demarcated shift from the first to the second phase, where, increasingly, formal relations between employers and shipping companies sought to control the dock labor force through a set of complex legal and regulatory devices that were further refined in the passage of the Bi-State Waterfront Compact and the organization of the Waterfront Commission in 1953.

During the first stage of phase two, political authorities in alliance with sectors of the shipping companies and the AFL leadership joined forces to challenge the institutional leadership of the ILA. The importance of this stage for the reform process was twofold. First, the formation of a conservative political alternative that emerged at this point effectively diminished the possibility of a united rank-and-file movement to reform the docks, dividing major political forces of the waterfront labor movement between those in favor of and those against expanding federal and state regulation of the dock labor process. Second, albeit unsuccessful in their attempt to replace the ILA on the Port of New York, the alliance succeeded in consolidating the political framework through industry-wide regulatory measures that limited the power of longshoremen. The government-sponsored partnership was a force with elevated political influence capable of providing the basis for expanding the regulatory devices of reform. With the question of institutional representation decided, the second stage of phase two became apparent. Business elites and political authorities, with the support of acquiescent sectors of the judiciary, sought, through the political structure, to contain the process for waterfront reform by systematically applying and redefining laws and creating regulatory measures in response to the continued revolt of dockworkers. The overall effect of this process was to severely limit the power of New York's longshoremen in the ever-changing waterfront labor process.

After 1945, under the mounting pressure of strikes and pier mobilizations, control of the dock labor process moved slowly from the control of King Joe Ryan's dictatorial control of the ILA, where gangsters ruled the docks largely with the consent of local political authorities and shipping elites, to an increasingly institutionalized structure that incorporated high levels of coercion and control. After World War II, the dispute for control of the docks moved from a model that relied on high levels of elite domination to a paradigm in which institutional barriers prevailed. In this process, dockworkers were able to do little more than respond to the immediate effects of long-term strategic policies that were set in place over time.[1] This process melded the implementation of restrictive national labor legislation, such as the Taft-Hartley Act, with industry-wide mechanisms, such as the Bi-State Waterfront Compact and the Waterfront Commission. The process was construed through a series of industry-specific regulations (with the qualifications and task of an internal police force), in combination with national labor legislation to curtail labor protests, providing the framework through which the interests of business and state and federal authorities merged. Political authorities and business elites emerged from this process with an arsenal of devices devised to curtail and coerce the rebellious movement.

The creation of the Waterfront Commission, notwithstanding its regulatory function, indicates the political disposition and desire of state and federal authorities to respond quickly to the internalization of Taft-Hartley's injunctive power by rebellious dockworkers. The Commission argued that the dock registration and decasualization process would ultimately reduce the overabundance of workers on the waterfront and eliminate the infamous "shape-up." As we have seen, however, this process had only a limited effect on regulating the dock labor process, which continued to be the center of conflict, and it was used to intimidate rebellious longshoremen and purge many radical activists from the docks. Increasingly, as the contentious movement grew, so did the political ability of elites and authorities, often with the acquiescence of the union leadership. Systemic limits to the dockworkers' mobilization was in effect the growing power of political and business elites to place obstructions that contained and redirected the movement for waterfront reform. This occurred by limiting the nature of demands that were considered the object of negotiations, such as the struggle for coast-wide bargaining, or, ultimately, by imposing collective bargaining agreements that the longshoremen had not agreed to at all.

It is important to point out that a significant segment of this process occurred under the growing political influence of McCarthyism, and as such, anticommunism had a considerable long-term impact, by providing the legal-institutional constraints and, more importantly, by reconfiguring political alliances among those sectors seeking reform. The fragmentation of the reform movement was in large part a direct result of the intervention of state and federal authorities and the leadership of the AFL on the Port of New York. Undoubtedly, without the pressures of McCarthyite policies and purges, the alternatives available and alliances for those groups working to transform the Port of New York would have been significantly different. Throughout the 1950s, the capacity of the ILA leadership to withstand the political pummeling they received from their erstwhile allies was in large part a reflection of the dockworkers' ability to reinvent their organization. Along the way, the centralized iron-fisted rule of King Joe fragmented, allowing regional and local dock leaders to gain greater, albeit limited, control of the union. Besides providing much needed political legitimacy and resources to the battered dock union, the support given to the ILA by left-wing and progressive labor activists during this period was a strategic position with the intent of inhibiting the actions of elites and political authorities that sought to influence and gain greater direction of the longshoremen's reform movement and the transformations of the dock labor process.

The slow return of the ILA leadership to the mainstream of organized labor by the 1960s, however, did not signify the complete acquiescence of the longshore union leadership to elite business interests. Even if at some moments during the recurrent dock conflicts there appeared to be more than a budding desire for the waterfront union leadership to do so, rank-and-file action and independent mobilization had long become a permanent aspect of waterfront labor politics. Even though longshoremen saw their political mobilization limited, shipping elites could not entirely impose regulations at will. The power of the longshore rank and file proved most effectual in its ability to construct a movement that offered multiple responses. Alternating through formal and informal spheres of waterfront life, the struggle of New York's dockworkers interposed their claims for control of the contentious waterfront labor process and structure with the employers' growing demands for automated waterborne cargo transportation, thus creating the political conditions that allowed dockworkers to move beyond traditional employment relations driven by commercial interests. For longshoremen, employment and income had become an acquired right after long years of working the docks, and conflict, not consensus, continued to drive the waterfront labor process until its slow deactivation. They forced ship owners to take social responsibility for structural changes in the shipping industry, a feat which has never been duplicated.

The history of the rank-and-file dockworkers' movement on the Port of New York is not simply an exercise to evoke important moments in labor history, itself a worthy endeavor. More importantly, the tumultuous history of New York's longshoremen provides important insight and subsidy to further the ongoing debate regarding the future and revival of the American labor movement. The longshore rebellion, if nothing else, conjures from the not-so-distant past important notions of employment and permanent income as a right of all workers and contests prevailing notions that limit the rights of workers in society. The current economic crisis and long-term effects of economic inequality, driven by neoliberal notions of work and employment, have led many (including some sectors within organized labor) to severely limit the scale and scope of labor's battles. At the same time, the long-term struggles of the longshore rebellion remind us of the important role that the organized left has in the struggle for labor's revival. If organized labor is to grow in spite of the current constraints, undoubtedly a significant part of labor's rebirth will occur outside of the union halls and meetings, demanding of present-day activists the same level of audacity and commitment demonstrated by New York's dock activists

Currently the waterfront represents the global battleground of American labor. Considering the expansive and increasingly global nature of the economy, maritime transportation continues to be the principal and most cost-effective means of transportation of goods, and it plays an important role in the world economy. Drawing on highly advanced information technology, the docks and dockworkers are essentially unwilling participants of "lean and mean" production schemes, such as "just in time" commercial structures that move significant quantities of manufactured goods across the globe. In the context of labor's political power, waterfront unions continue to be the center stage of important working-class battles, and they have added important victories to recent struggles.

In 2003, West Coast longshoremen, in the midst of contract negotiations, defeated the threats of President George W. Bush to invoke the Taft-Hartley Act, when with the support of Teamsters the ILWU formed the "Unity on the Ports" movement. Fearing the complete standstill of the West Coast port and ground transportation of goods coming from the Pacific Rim, the federal government quickly stopped threatening to intervene in the dock conflict. On the East Coast, the activities of the Charleston, South Carolina, ILA Local 1422 have similarly led significant struggles, in spite of threats and amid legal charges levied against union president Ken Riley and four union leaders. The fight to free the "Charleston Five" clearly illustrates the expansive implications and power of the longshore unions. In contrast, the Bi-State Waterfront Commission's promises to rid the docks and its unions of corruption and gangster influence have had dubious results. To date, the New York ILA continues to be accused of criminal activity. If there is to be a revival of organized labor in American society, dockworkers and their unions will play an essential role that will impact the conditions of workers and unions in all sectors of society.

Notes

Introduction

1. Nelson, *Divided We Stand*, 50. Nelson notes that the ILA's experience in New York reflected four "overlapping stages of development."

2. Eley and Nield, "Farewell to the Working Class?" 9. They argue that previously nonpolitical locations (the workplace, the neighborhood, the subculture, the family, the home) were claimed for politics in a new way and sometimes for the first time. These places were already present as objects of policy, through law, welfare, and social administration. But now they were claimed as sites of political identification and contestation, too, as places where power was organized and embodied. This perspectival shift moved politics away from the conventional arenas (the state, the parties, and public organizations in the narrower sense) into a much broader and less manageable societal domain.

3. Katznelson uses the concept of critical junctures primarily within the context of institutional transformation. This permits a deeper insight into the way that shifting levels of power intersected and permeated each other throughout both the formal and informal structures of the waterfront labor process. He argues, "This approach to periodicity and the formation of preferences links institutions, identities, and problem-solving. It treats institutions as parametric constraints on the behavior of actors while placing human agency at the center of accounts of how the crystallized legacies of decisions taken at key historical moments are reproduced." Katznelson, "Strange Bedfellows, Strange Deals," ms, chapter 11, p. 2.

Chapter 1. History as Class Politics on the Docks

1. American Social History Project, *Who Built America?* 2: 209.

2. Stone, "Systemic Power," 980.

3. Schattsneider argues: "It has been assumed that only legal barriers inhibited the disenfranchised. We know better now. The exclusion of people by extralegal processes, by social processes, by the way the political system is organized and structured may be far more effective than the law." Schattsneider, *The Semisovereign People: A Realist's View of Democracy in America*, 108.

4. As Brass points out: "We have been taught to believe that we live in democracies that more or less conform to that model. Political science has devoted itself overwhelm-

ingly to discussions of how far our democracy does conform to that model and how far it deviates from it. . . . It is not a question of whether democracy or constitutional government is better than autocracy . . . but how all these governments actually govern within the spheres in which they undertake to govern." Brass, *Foucault Steals Political Science*, 309.

5. Lichtenstein argues that "the rights of workers, as workers, and especially as workers acting in an autonomous fashion have moved well into the shadows." Lichtenstein, *State of the Union*, 3.

6. Lichtenstein, *State of the Union*, 4.

7. Stone argues: "There is also a dimension of power in which durable features of the socioeconomic system confer advantages and disadvantages on groups in ways that predispose public officials to favor some interests at the expense of others. . . . Thus, socioeconomic inequalities put various strata on different political footings." Stone, "Systemic Power," 978.

8. Dahl argues that the exercise of power was primarily the reflection of the internal workings of pluralistic democracy, which reflected an ongoing process of perfecting the prevailing political system. "Power," he writes, "is here defined in terms of a relation, between people, . . . from this definition is developed a statement of power comparability, or the relative degree of power held by two or more people." Dahl, "A Concept of Power," 201.

9. Dahl, *Who Governs?* 11.

10. Dahl, *Who Governs?* 62.

11. Dahl argues that "in recent years control over jobs by both private and public employers has been further restricted by unionization, professionalization, job security and the rise of a new group, the trade union leaders. The resources of this group in terms of numbers . . . are sufficient to guarantee that many private employers will bargain with them on matters important and relevant to their roles as trade union leaders." Dahl, *Who Governs?* 255.

12. In *Political Economy*, Bensel argues that a significant aspect of the American political economy was its regional development and dependency. This process created regional protective tariffs and other devices that made political autonomy highly unlikely.

13. Lindblom argued that "unionism's large membership and its growing coordination of policy, taken together with its tactic of controlling the buyer instead of alternative suppliers, provide the solid foundation of its monopoly power." Lindblom, *Unions and Capitalism*, 99.

14. Lindblom defined responsible unionism as a reflection of the "unification of the labor movement, centrally defined wage policy and the practice of industrial statesmanship where morality and tradition formed the basis for societal constraints inhibiting the all out use of the unions' accumulated power." Lindblom, *Unions and Capitalism*, 195–99.

15. Lindblom argues: "With strong national unions, and large corporate organizations both parties will ordinarily compromise long before the struggle becomes one of solvency or survival." Lindblom, *Unions and Capitalism*, 115.

16. According to Lindblom, "The employer often has a choice; what he does not wish to grant in managerial functions he can preserve by 'buying off' the union. He knows too

that wage concessions can often be regained in price increases; power lost to the union is often gone forever. The tables are turned; the struggle for power now lowers rather than raises resistance to wage increases." Lindblom, *Unions and Capitalism*, 120.

17. Lichtenstein writes: "[The postwar period] reflected the shifting relations between unions, state, and corporation, based on depoliticized unions and an insular collective bargaining process. . . . [R]ather than a mutual agreement between labor and employers, Taft-Hartley set the terms for the new relationship." Lichtenstein, *State of the Union*, 115.

18. Lichtenstein, *State of the Union*, 100.

19. Rueschemeyer argued: "If the bourgeois vision of peaceful commerce and industry, fair deals and voluntary cooperation among equals, and the rule of law and decentralized self-government acquired a social reality—which it undoubtedly did . . . this change took place primarily among new urban middle classes, transforming old elites in the process. It did *not* transform in the same way relations between dominant and subordinate classes." Rueschemeyer, *Power and the Division of Labor*, 9.

20. Wartenberg argues that "alignments are not limited to permanent and fixed modes of social interaction; they come to exist for specific purposes and for limited amounts of time. In such cases, alignments may function in an interventional rather than a systemic manner." Wartenberg, *Rethinking Power*, 86, 90.

21. Wartenberg states: "The appearance of freedom in the relationship between the workers and the capitalist, which has been emphasized by liberal theory, conceals a deeper level at which power is exercised. Only because the options facing the worker have the structure that they do will the worker be willing to work for the wages he does in the conditions he faces." Wartenberg, *Rethinking Power*, 99.

22. Stone, "Social Stratification," 286.

23. Non-decision-making, Stone argues, is shaped by "the larger political landscape that is a different order of questions from the influencing of a particular decision. It influences the capacity to exploit the larger social context and deploy resources on matters that provide indirect and long-term payoffs rather than just immediate and concrete benefits." Stone, "Social Stratification," 285.

24. This differs from the notion of powerlessness defended by John Gaventa, who similarly posits three levels of power. For Gaventa, however, acquiescence plays a fundamental part of his power structure. Stone, "Social Stratification," 293.

25. Stone argues that "the formal equalities of citizenship are countermanded by inequalities in (a) wealth (b) organizing position (c) social status/life style." Stone, "Social Stratification," 284–85.

26. Stone argues that nonelites "are positioned to do little more than try to influence narrow decisions of immediate impact." Stone, "Social Stratification," 285.

27. The first level of power reflects the distribution of rewards through formal and informal policy-making. The second level reflects the mobilization of bias, which is the outcome of both explicit and obscure non-decision-making fashioned by the propensity of political actors. The third level of power refers directly to "systemic constraints," which he defines as both the "general and diffuse strategic activities," that is, qualities and procedures of power holders that do not necessarily demonstrate the implementation of political power. Stone, "Social Stratification," 286.

28. Stone argues that there are four major systemic constraints, which are the char-

acteristics of power and form the basis for inequality: "1) legal or formal-political, 2) economic, 3) associational, and 4) social." Stone, "Social Stratification," 289.

29. Stone argues correctly that "Public officials form their alliances, make their decisions and plan their future in the context in which strategically important resources are hierarchically arranged. That is, officials operate in a stratified society. The system of stratification is a motivating factor in all that they do; it predisposes them to favor upper over lower strata interests. Systemic power therefore has to do with the impact of the larger socioeconomic system on the predisposition of public officials." Stone, "Social Stratification," 289.

30. Etzioni-Halevy writes, "The state legitimizes the select few by granting them a representational monopoly and by making them part of the economic policy-shaping process. In return, it obtains their support for its policy and expects the main organization to deliver the compliance of their member organizations with the dictates of these policies. . . . These arrangements generally bypass parliamentary, democratic procedure." Contrary to my argument above, Etzioni-Halevy defends the idea that elite groups are highly autonomous in modern political life. While she recognizes that they are damaging for the democratic process, she also believes that they can play a positive role. Etzioni-Halevy, *Elite Connection*, 85.

31. Richard Bensel correctly points out, "New York clearly stood apart as the primary entrepôt linking the European and American economies. The dominance of the Port in the import/export trade of the United States conferred on the city's financial markets a dominant role in managing domestic and foreign investment . . . among the leading trade centers, New York City alone was responsible for almost half of the (380 of 840) financial capital addresses in the cable directory." Bensel, *Political Economy*, 77.

32. Bensel writes, "Beyond the activity of the waterfront lay the vast commercial districts and warehouse facilities that underpinned the wholesale collection and distribution of goods and capital in both foreign and domestic trade." Bensel, *Political Economy*, 79.

33. Bensel, *Political Economy*, 77.

34. "Political agents," Bensel argues, "representing New York, whether elected officials or financiers, often assumed the leading role in the design and operation of the financial system—a role that relegated often capital-rich regions and representatives to a limited supporting position." Bensel, *Political Economy*, 8.

35. Stone writes: "Business influence is embedded in the imperatives of the situation in which local government operates. And business interests prevail not because a ruling-class network promotes business proposals, but because governments are drawn by the nature of underlying economic and revenue-producing conditions." Stone, "Systemic Power," 983.

36. Examining the long-term existence of anticommunism as a unique facet of American political life, Ruotsila writes, "Paternalist social reforms seemed, to laissez-faire eyes, perilously close to collectivism itself, and the resulting fundamental disagreement between these parties was never erased. But there was an even more fundamental agreement that allowed two strands of conservatism to cooperate in the twentieth-century attack on collectivism." Ruotsila, *British and American Anticommunism before the Cold War*, 14.

37. Ruotsila, *British and American Anticommunism before the Cold War*, 15.

38. The best analogy outside of the New York waterfront was the reign of terror perpetrated by the Ku Klux Klan in the American South and their embedded existence within state and local political structures that shielded them from legal prosecution.

39. Goldstein defines repression in American political life as "government action which openly discriminates against persons or organizations viewed as presenting a fundamental challenge to existing power relationships or key government policies, because of their perceived political beliefs." Goldstein, *Political Repression*, xxvii.

40. Goldstein writes: "Labor was probably repressed more consistently during the twenties than during any other decade in American history. Because business and business mentality thoroughly dominated not only the federal government, but also most state governments, virtually all labor activity was viewed and treated as somewhat subversive by most governmental agencies." Goldstein, *Political Repression*, 183.

41. Stone states: "Systemic power refers to something more fundamental than recruitment. It refers to the circumstance that office holders (regardless of personal background, nature of electoral support, network of associations, etc.) are by virtue of their position more situationally dependent on some interests than others. Because this dependency is inherent in the situation, officials are inescapably predisposed to favor some interests over others." Stone, "Systemic Power," 982.

42. Using recently declassified FBI archives, Schrecker reveals in detail how during the New Deal, in spite of the conservative view that Roosevelt was soft on communism, labor leaders who posed any sort of threat were kept under surveillance, and Roosevelt enjoyed a good relationship with Hoover, who informed him of his surveillance of labor leaders, including Harry Bridges of the ILWU. Schrecker, *Many Are the Crimes*, 88–89, 90.

43. As Schrecker notes, "Dies's attacks on the CIO ensured the backing of businessmen and AFL leaders alike. Henry Ford even offered to supply automobiles to HUAC and its staff." Schrecker, *Many Are the Crimes*, 92.

44. Schrecker suggests that if not for World War II, it is probable that "some form of McCarthyism" would have appeared in American politics much earlier, since all of the repressive devices were already in place. "When Joe McCarthy came onto the scene in 1950," Schrecker argues, "brandishing his inaccurate and ever changing list of supposed communist agents within the federal government, the 'ism' with which he was identified was already in full swing." Schrecker, *Many Are the Crimes*, x, xvi.

45. "It took teamwork," Schrecker argues, "to create such timidity. The anti-communist crusade was, above all, a collaborative project." Schrecker, *Many Are the Crimes*, xiv.

46. U.S. Chamber of Commerce, *Communists within the Labor Movement*, 52.

47. Plotke points out: "For all of their passions, labor and other opponents of Taft-Hartley could not stop Republicans and Democrats in Congress from supporting the measure." David Plotke, *Building a Democratic Political Order*, 236, 239.

48. McAdams argues that Landrum-Griffin represents "the result of an all-out power struggle among various groups in our society; it does reflect the underlying conservative bias of our national legislature; it does reflect certain misconceptions of power relationships, actual and potential, by leaders of the labor movement." McAdams, *Power and Politics in Labor Legislation*, 7.

49. Sexton points out: "Some 13.5 million people or about one in five people in the

labor force were affected by loyalty-security programs as a condition of employment. Some 10,000 were fired from their jobs. . . . Besides those fired over 20,000 were formally charged between 1947 and 1953 under the federal program alone, most charges involving association with a suspected person. . . . At a federal cost of some $350 million during that period, not a single spy was uncovered by the loyalty-security programs." Sexton, *The War on Labor and the Left*, 152.

50. Schrecker writes, "Nearly three thousand longshoremen and seamen failed to pass the screening test. Invoking the traditional image of the communist saboteur, the Coast Guard commandant explained that these workers had been denied clearance in order to protect the nation's waterfronts from anyone who might engage in sabotage . . . [by] inducing unrest, strikes and slow-downs or espionage." Schrecker, *Many Are the Crimes*, 89.

51. Schrecker, *Many Are the Crimes*, 268.

52. "Coast Guard examiners," Schrecker notes, "were quite explicit about the labor politics that drove the program. One longshoreman was actually told that he would be cleared [of charges] if he could prove that he had supported the anti-communist factions within the ILWU. Other maritime workers got the message: activists and ordinary seamen alike kept a low profile and reduced their demands on employers." Schrecker, *Many Are the Crimes*, 269.

53. In reality the threat of job loss for New York dockworkers was also a mechanism built into the waterfront labor process, and the "shape-up" was a daily reminder for those who sought to contest the domination exercised by ILA union officials. The political power of the shape-up is explored in greater depth in chapter 2.

54. Bensman writes: "Once the denial of equality of access to the state machinery is undertaken, together with the delimitation of substantive rights and privileges, the society commits itself to a system in which violence and political assassination become normal means of political action. In such situations it is the by-product of a defective political process." Bensman, "Social and Institutional Factors," 387.

55. Woodiwiss, *Organized Crime and American Power*, 150–51. Early studies of business practices by Gordon Hostetter and T. Q. Beasley illustrate how elite political and economic interests supported and converged with those of organized crime. They write: "Businessmen wanted monopolies in their trades and services, control of their labour forces, the power to fix prices in their favor, and control over the enactment or application of regulatory laws. The corrupt leader of organized labour also wanted to control the labour force for this ensures to the treasury the dues of all men in the trade. . . . Moreover, it enables him to manipulate his man forces to the advantage of his co-conspirators, the businessman or the politician, or both."

56. Lipset identified the emergence of occupational communities whose distinct culture was a reflection of specific craft traits or geographical isolation, such as that experienced by miners, sailors, and longshoremen. Lipset, *Political Man*, 408.

57. Miller defined subculture as a "culture within a culture [with] an identifiable human group sharing some of the characteristics of the surrounding dominant culture, but separated from it by the special set of behavior, norms, loyalties, beliefs, etc." He writes, "The dock laborers' loyalties belong predominantly to his gang, to his fellow dockworkers. . . . The longshoremen operate on a one in trouble, all in trouble principle." Miller, "The Dockworker Subculture," 305, 308.

58. Marx argued: "The owners of mere labor-power, the owners of capital, and land-lords, whose respective sources of income are wages, profit, and ground-rent, in other words, wage laborers, capitalists, and landlords, form the three great classes of modern society, resting on the capitalist mode of production." Marx, *On Society and Social Change,* 15.

58. Giddens argues: "While there may be a multiplicity of cross-cutting interests created by differential market capacities, there are only, in a given society, a limited number of classes." For him, the development of class relationships emanates from three sources: "The division of labor within the productive enterprise, the authority relationships within the enterprise, and the influence of what I shall call distributive groups." Giddens and Held, *Classes, Power, and Conflict,* 159, 160.

60. Schneirov wrote: "Class is therefore best understood as a contingent, multidimensional social construct, developing over time within the context of industrial and political change (and this applies to capitalists as well as workers)." Schneirov, *Labor and Urban Politics,* 3.

61. Thompson's concept of class is useful. He argued that "class happens when some men, as a result of common experience (inherited or shared) feel and articulate the identity of their interest as between themselves, and as against other men. . . . The class experience is largely determined by the productive relations into which men are born—or enter involuntarily." Thompson, *The Making of the English Working Class,* 9.

62. Katznelson correctly notes, "Non-class patterns of social division also affect class formation. Class, society, and politics cannot be conflated; their relationships are contingent. Class disposition and behavior are not fixed by interests but shaped by relationships." Katznelson, "Constructing Cases and Comparisons," 9.

63. Zweig writes, "Class has its foundation in power relations at work, but it is more than that. Class also operates in the larger society: relative power on the economic side of things translates, not perfectly but to a considerable extent, into cultural and political power." Zweig, *Working-Class Majority,* 4, 122.

Chapter 2. Who Controls the Waterfront?

1. Kimeldorf explains that "longshore employment posed the question of control in the sharpest possible terms, for whoever controlled the hiring process quite literally ran the waterfront, deciding who would work, for how long and under what conditions." Kimeldorf, *Reds or Rackets?* 29.

2. In his early study of dock labor on the Port of New York, Barnes reported: "The entire hiring of the Port is based on a system of hourly employment. The longshoreman is on a more casual basis than the ordinary day laborer, who, when he is hired, is at least assured of a day's work. After work has begun, men are knocked off and rehired at any hour according to the demands of work. . . . A savings of even fifteen minutes' pay of several hundred men is a considerable item to the company." Barnes, *The Longshoremen,* 57.

3. Barnes, *The Longshoremen,* 60–64, Barnes argues that "not only are the hours of hiring irregular and uncertain, but the men do not know with surety whether they will be chosen at the shape-up. The duration of work, when obtained, is uncertain" (69).

4. Barnes, *The Longshoremen,* 69.

5. Winslow's examination of the Port of New York gives a broad panorama of the problem. "In New York, in 1915, there were three longshoremen for every job. On a 'normal day' on the Chelsea waterfront twenty-five hundred men might be hired, but five thousand would shape-up." Winslow, "Men of the Lumber Camps Come to Town," 7.

6. Exploring the characteristics of dock labor, Hobsbawm argues: "It follows that the habitual picture of an industry comprised overwhelmingly of casual and unskilled laborers is highly misleading. On the contrary: the specialized wheat or grain porter, the coal heaver and salt porter, the stevedore who stowed export cargo on board a ship, had to have at least the qualities of an iron-puddler—strength and dexterity within a limited range, and very frequently the qualities of an all around craftsman." Hobsbawm, *Labouring Men*, 245.

7. As Winslow points out, "The power of the longshoremen, then, was not simply strategic. It was also the product of a 'system' in which competition had to be overcome because survival depended on cooperation and a sense of common identity. The most experienced as well as the least skilled dockers depended on others—in perilous settings their lives literally depended on their cooperation." Winslow, "Men of the Lumber Camps Come to Town," 7.

8. Citing a Senate subcommittee hearing, Colin Davis wrote: "[A] union leader successfully maintained his power because he is able to discipline any man who dares to raise his voice in a union meeting. . . . That man does not work anymore. The shape-up system and its corresponding surplus of labor guaranteed subservience and ensured employment insecurity." Davis, "All I Got's a Hook," 133.

9. Montgomery, *The Fall of the House of Labor*, 105–6. Also see Winslow, "Men of the Lumber Camps Come to Town," 62.

10. Marcantonio Papers, report from Mary Testa to Marcantonio regarding the Panto case. Also see letter from Lally Lange, executive secretary of the Pete Panto Memorial Committee to Commissioner Herlands, March 12, 1941. New York Public Library.

11. Axelrod, "Government Covers the Waterfront," 54.

12. Axelrod, "Government Covers the Waterfront," 58.

13. Tarrow defined a social movement as "collective challenges based on common purposes and social solidarities in sustained interaction with elites, opponents and authorities." Tarrow, *Power in Movement*, 4, 5.

14. Tarrow, *Power in Movement*, 7.

15. Tarrow writes: "The outcomes of such waves of contention depend not on the justice of the cause or of the persuasive power of any single movement but on their breadth and on the reaction of elites and other groups." Tarrow, *Power in Movement*, 7.

16. While the hourly wages of New York's longshoremen were considered high for the period, the casual nature of longshore work made the annual wages extremely low. In *Divided We Stand*, Nelson writes, "The dynamics of the casual labor market resulted in the anomaly of high hourly wages and low annual earnings. In 1946, when Atlantic and Gulf dockworkers received a week's vacation with pay for the first time if they had worked a total of thirty-four weeks in a year, 70 percent of the men in New York did not qualify."

17. Kimeldorf argues: "The threat of physical violence hung like a cloud over anyone who dared to speak out. Dissidents were routinely 'dumped' or worse. In one case, two rank-and-file activists were found murdered, gangland style, in different parts of the

city only hours after meeting with Communist leader Sam Madell." Kimeldorf, *Reds or Rackets?* 125.

18. *Daily Worker*, July 26, 1939. Also see *Daily Worker*, August 3, 1939.

19. The Brooklyn port received mainly bulk cargo such as 'Banana Boats' that were known to have tarantulas among the cargo, whereas Manhattan received passenger ships whose cargo was much lighter, and the longshoremen received tips from the passengers.

20. *Daily Worker*, July 26, 1939.

21. *Daily Worker*, July 26, 1939.

22. Kimeldorf wrote: "Panto's open and increasingly bold attacks on organized crime and union corruption galvanized his followers into a real movement." Kimeldorf, *Reds or Rackets?* 124.

23. *Daily Worker*, July 25, 1939.

24. Morris, *A Tale of Two Waterfronts*, 13.

25. *New York Times*, December 19, 1952: Marcy Protter testimony to the New York State Crime Commission Hearings, December 18.

26. Kimeldorf, *Reds or Rackets?* 124.

27. Turkus and Feder, *Murder, Inc.*, 470, 473. Also see Morris, *Tale of Two Waterfronts*, 9.

28. Marcantonio Papers. Also see *Daily Worker*, July 26, 1939.

29. Morris, *Tale of Two Waterfronts*, 12.

30. *New York Times*, December 19, 1952: Albert Tannenbaum testimony to Asst. D. A. Heferman entered as evidence to the New York State Crime Commission Hearings.

31. Turkus and Feder, *Murder, Inc.*, 472.

32. *Daily Worker*, July 23, 1939.

33. Kimeldorf, *Reds or Rackets?* 124–25.

34. Marcantonio Papers.

35. Marcantonio Papers.

36. Marcantonio Papers.

37. Marcantonio Papers.

38. Axelrod, "Government Covers the Waterfront," 30.

39. Axelrod, "Government Covers the Waterfront," 30.

40. Sam Madell, oral interview, New Yorkers at Work Collection, Tamiment/Bobst Library, NYU. Interviewed by Deborah Bernhardt and Joe Doyle.

41. Armstrong, Glyn, and Harrison, *Capitalism since 1945*, 72.

42. Armstrong, Glyn, and Harrison, *Capitalism since 1945*, 73, 74. Armstrong points out: "Marshall aid affected the U.S. economy most directly in the export field. The rise of net exports in 1946 had accounted for nearly one fifth of the total rise in non-governmental spending. This rise prevented the fall in military spending from generating a major recession. . . . In 1946, 16 percent of agricultural machinery, 20 percent of freight cars and motor cars, 10 percent of steel products, and 40 percent of wheat were exported."

43. Preis notes: "The demonstration for Marshall and the retreat on Taft-Hartley were two sides of the same coin." Preis, *Labor's Giant Step*, 340.

44. Schrecker, "McCarthyism and the Labor Movement," 145. Also see Rosswurm, *The CIO's Left-Led Unions*, 15. He notes: "In the case of the port security program, not only did the CIO acquiesce, but its affiliates helped initiate and administer what Murray's

Report in 1950 promised would be the 'most effective maritime security program ever devised.'"

45. *Dockers News*, ca. 1949.

46. New York State Crime Commission Hearing for Remedying Conditions on the Port of New York, June 8–9, 1953.

47. U.S. Senate Subcommittee on Interstate and Foreign Commerce, 83rd Cong., 1st sess., 1953.

48. Report by Cleophas Jacobs, secretary-treasurer of Local 968, to the New York State Crime Commission, June 8–9, 1953. Also see Davis, "All I Got's a Hook," 133. Davis argues: "Daily competition with white longshoremen at the shape-up exposed black longshoremen to the racism of the hiring boss and attendant union official. One black longshoreman described the humiliating experience: 'Sometimes standing on the pier with my union button and my union book, the hiring boss acts like he hates me. . . . It happens all the time.'"

49. Davis, "All I Got's a Hook," 140.

50. Citizens' Waterfront Committee membership list in the Vernon Jensen Papers, Kheel Center, Cornell University.

51. Letter from the Citizens' Waterfront Committee to Capt. William Bradley, ILA, September 23, 1955, in Jensen Papers.

52. Kimeldorf, *Reds or Rackets?* 143.

53. The dockworkers refused to handle sling loads weighing more than 2,240 lbs.

54. Jensen, *Strife on the Waterfront*, 37.

55. *New York Times*, October 4, 1945.

56. *New York Times*, October 3, 1945.

57. *New York Times*, October 2, 1945.

58. *New York Times*, October 5, 1945.

59. *New York Times*, October 10, 1945.

60. *New York Times*, October 10, 1945.

61. *New York Times*, October 4, 1945.

62. Jensen, *Strife on the Waterfront*, 39.

63. *New York Times*, October 11, 1945.

64. As Jensen notes, "When Ryan appeared at a somewhat disorderly meeting, at Prospect Hall in Brooklyn on October 10, he was booed and hissed off the stage. The rank-and-file leaders declared that Ryan was trying to shove a settlement down their throats, and said they were sick and tired of the dictatorial attitudes of the ILA leaders." Jensen, *Strife on the Waterfront*, 40. Also see the *New York Times*, October 11, 1945.

65. *New York Times*, October 16, 1945.

66. *New York Times*, October 12, 1945.

67. *New York Times*, October 15, 1945.

68. *New York Times*, October 11, 1945.

69. *New York Times*, October 16, 1945.

70. Jensen noted that toward mid-October "it was reported that the men of Local 856, of the lower tip of Manhattan, and Local 920 of Staten Island returned to work, and that the shipping officials were pleased with the 'Back to work' movement." Jensen, *Strife on the Waterfront*, 42.

71. *New York Times*, October 17, 1945. Also see Jensen, *Strife on the Waterfront*, 45.

72. Jensen, *Strife on the Waterfront*, 45.

73. *New York Times*, October 16, 1945.

74. *New York Times*, October 19, 1945.

75. *New York Times*, October 21, 1945.

76. *New York Times*, October 21, 1945. Also see Jensen, *Strife on the Waterfront*, 46.

77. *New York Times*, October 22, 1945.

78. *New York Times*, October 27, 1945.

79. *New York Times*, October 4, 1945.

80. *New York Times*, August 27, 1947.

81. Davis, "All I've Got's a Hook," 140.

82. Davis, "All I've Got's a Hook," 141.

83. *New York Times*, August 17, 1948.

84. *New York Times*, October 2, 1948.

85. *New York Times*, August 20, 1947.

86. *New York Times*, August 23, 1947.

87. *New York Times*, August 23, 1947.

88. Davis points out: "Experience had shown that Ryan and other ILA officials had generally taken what was offered by the shippers, usually settling for just enough to quiet rank-and-file opposition." Davis, "All I've Got's a Hook," 143.

89. *New York Times*, November 7, 1948.

90. *New York Times*, November 13, 1948.

91. *New York World Telegram*, November 10, 1948. Also see Davis, "All I Got's a Hook." He writes: "Ryan with ILA goons and members of the AFL's Seafarers Union attempted to storm the building. Although they were able to leave leaflets declaring the meeting a 'communist plot' to gain control of the ILA . . . Ryan's forces were outnumbered and had to beat a hasty retreat."

92. *New York World Telegram*, November 10, 1948.

93. *New York Times*, November 16, 1948.

94. *New York Times*, November 25, 1948.

95. *New York Times*, November 28, 1948.

96. *New York Times*, September 21, 1951.

97. *New York Times*, September 26, 1951.

98. *New York Times*, October 9, 1951. Also see *Longshore News*, Newsletter of the ILA, Special Edition, October 10, 1951.

99. *New York Times*, October 16, 1951. Also see *Federated Press*, News Release Eastern Bureau, October 16, 1951.

100. *New York Times*, October 25, 1951.

101. *New York Times*, October 25, 1951. Also see *March of Labor*, December 1951, p. 23.

102. *New York Times*, October 17, 1951.

103. *New York Times*, October 18, 1951.

104. *New York Times*, October 18, 1951.

105. *New York Times*, October 19, 1951.

106. *New York Times*, October 20, 1951.

107. Pamphlet of the Strike Committee, 1951, Jensen Archives.

108. *The New Deal*, 1951 bulletin, Jensen Archives.

109. *Weekend Worker,* October 25, 1951.

110. *The March of Labor,* December 1951, 23.

111. *New York Times,* October 20, 1951.

112. *New York Times,* October 24, 1951.

113. *New York Times,* October 26, 1951.

114. *New York Times,* October 26, 1951.

115. *New York Times,* October 24, 1951

116. *New York Times,* October 23, 1951.

117. *Dockers News,* special edition, October 25, 1951.

118. *New York Times,* October 24, 1951.

119. *New York Times,* October 25, 1951.

120. *New York Times,* October 21, 1951.

121. *New York Times,* October 23, 1951.

122. *New York Times,* October 27, 1951.

123. *New York Times,* October 28, 1951.

124. *New York Times,* October 28, 1951.

125. *New York Times,* October 30, 1951.

126. *New York Times,* November 1, 1951.

127. *New York Times,* November 2, 1951.

128. Order Establishing Board of Inquiry, State of New York, Department of Labor, November 2, 1951, Jensen Archives.

129. *New York Times,* November 6, 1951.

130. *Federated Press,* Eastern Bureau, press release, November 8, 1951, Jensen Archives.

131. *Dockers News,* December 8, 1951.

132. Reply by Mr. Dean Alfange, member of the NYS Board of Inquiry into the longshoremen's strike of 1951, to the recent statements made by Mr. Joseph P. Ryan, press release, July 10, 1951, Jensen Archives.

Chapter 3. Who Speaks for New York's Dockworkers?

1. *New York Times,* May 9, 1953.

2. Maud Russell wrote: "The Commission is financed by assessments levied on firms employing waterfront workers, and thus it really comes from the wages of the longshoremen since shippers must figure Commission assessments as part of labor costs. . . . It is not tax supported, but neither is it free." Russell, *Men along the Shore,* 275.

3. Annual Report of the Bi-State Waterfront Commission, 1956–57.

4. Commerce and Industry Association of New York, news release, June 11, 1953, in Vernon Jensen Archives, Kheel Center, Cornell University, Ithaca, N.Y.

5. Axelrod argues: "To investigate subversive elements the Commission has worked with the Office of Naval Intelligence and the local police agencies as well as with the Coast Guard and has set up a unit solely devoted to this task." Axelrod, "Government Covers the Waterfront," 234.

6. Letter from U.S. Coast Guard to Servio Mello, in possession of author.

7. Interview with Servio Mello, November 29, 1994

8. DiFazio, *Longshoremen,* 49.

9. Russell argued: "Among the thousands of men working the port, in a year [1963–64] of intensive investigation [the Commission] had unearthed a total of two loan sharks." Russell, *Men along the Shore*, 275.

10. An alternative to the Waterfront Commission is the practice of union-controlled hiring halls that rotated work based on a seniority system, such as was developed on the West Coast with the ILWU.

11. *New York Longshore Data Book*, NYSA Research Department, June 6, 1962, 6, Jensen Archives.

12. *The Longshore Industry in the Port of New York*, confidential report, NYSA Research Department, 7, in Jensen Archives; *Impact of the Longshore Strikes on the National Economy*, U.S. Department of Labor, January 1970, 44.

13. Jensen, *Strife on the Waterfront*, 134.

14. Raymond, *Waterfront Priest*, 143. Also see *New York Times*, October 3, 1953.

15. *New York Times*, September 26 and October 15, 1953.

16. Hutchinson, *The Imperfect Union*, 231.

17. *New York Times*, October 20, 1953.

18. Jensen Archives.

19. *New York Times*, September 29, 1953.

20. *New York Times*, October 18, 1953.

21. *New York Times*, January 2, 1954.

22. *New York Times*, December 4, 1953.

23. *New York Times*, December 4, 1953.

24. *New York Times*, October 7, 1953.

25. *New York Times*, October 15, 1953.

26. *New York Times*, December 2, 1952.

27. *New York Times*, September 5, 1953.

28. *New York Times*, October 9, 1953.

29. *New York Times*, September 22, 1953.

30. *New York Times*, September 22, 1953.

31. *New York Times*, September 24, 1953.

32. *New York Times*, September 25, 1953.

33. *New York Times*, September 24, 1953.

34. *New York Times*, September 29, 1953.

35. *New York Times*, September 30, 1953.

36. *New York Times*, October 27, 1953.

37. *New York Times*, September 27, 1953.

38. *New York Times*, September 29, 1953.

39. *New York Times*, September 30, 1953.

40. *New York Times*, September 30, 1953.

41. *New York Times*, October 1, 1953.

42. *New York Times*, October 2, 1953.

43. *New York Times*, October 4, 1953.

44. *New York Times*, October 14, 1953.

45. *New York Times*, October 13, 1953.

46. *New York Times*, October 15, 1953.

47. *New York Times*, October 14, 1953.

48. *New York Times,* December 12, 1953.

49. *New York Times,* December 18, 1953. The ILA's failure to comply with the Taft-Hartley regulation was not because of any left-leaning political tendencies, but rather that the measure also demanded scrutiny of the unions' financial records, which was a problem for the dock union given its long history of financial impropriety.

50. *New York Times,* December 12, 1953.

51. *New York Times,* December 18, 1953.

52. Hearing of the National Labor Relations Board, December 17, 1953, cases NYSA-2-R-6282, 2-R-C-6392, and 2-R-M 5561.

53. *New York Times,* December 18, 1953.

54. *New York Times,* December 22, 1953.

55. *New York Times,* December 22, 1953.

56. Pamphlet in possession of author.

57. *Waterfront News,* vol. 2, no. 44 (July 20, 1956): 1. This is an AFL waterfront newsletter that reported this as an indication of the "growing communist influence" in the ILA; however, Velson's activity was also confirmed in the interview with CP rank-and-file dockworkers such as Servio Mello.

58. *New York Times,* May 23, 1954.

59. Annual Report of the Bi-State Waterfront Commission, 1957–58, 25–26. Also see Waterfront Commission of New York Harbor (Velson), NYLJ, May 22, 1958, 6 (Sup. Ct., NY, Co).

60. CP labor analyst John Swift argued, "Every right-led union has two sides to it: its elementary class struggle origin and nature, and its class collaboration policies and leadership. These two opposites exist side-by-side, interpenetrate each other, and express themselves in the contradiction between the strivings and needs of the rank and file on the one hand, and the official policy and aims of the top leadership, on the other." Swift, "Some Problems of Work in Right-Led Unions," 34.

61. *Dockers News,* April 2, 1954, in Jensen Archives.

62. *New York Times,* December 23, 1953.

63. *New York Times,* December 23, 1953. Also see *New York Times,* December 24, 1953.

64. *New York Times,* December 25, 1953.

65. *New York Times,* December 27, 1953.

66. *New York Times,* December 28, 1953.

67. *New York Times,* December 28, 1953.

68. *New York Times,* January 1, 1954.

69. *New York Times,* December 24, 1953.

70. *New York Times,* January 9, 1954.

71. *New York Times,* January 29, 1954.

72. *New York Times,* January 13, 1954.

73. *New York Times,* January 13, 1954

74. *New York Times,* January 18, 1954.

75. *New York Times,* January 12, 1954.

76. *New York Times,* January 4, 1954.

77. *New York Times,* March 4, 1954.

78. *New York Times,* March 9, 1954.

79. *Dockers News,* April 4, 1954. On file in the Jensen Archives.
80. *New York Times,* March 10, 1954.
81. *New York Times,* March 11, 1954.
82. *New York Times,* March 12, 1954.
83. *New York Times,* March 16, 1954
84. Interview, Servio Mello, November 26, 1996.
85. *New York Times,* March 16, 1954.
86. *New York Times,* April 2, 1954.
87. *New York Times,* April 3, 1954.
88. *New York Times,* April 2, 1954.
89. *New York Times,* April 3, 1954.
90. *New York Times,* April 3, 1954
91. *New York Times,* April 3, 1954.
92. *New York Times,* April 6, 1954.
93. *New York Times,* April 5, 1954.
94. *New York Times,* April 3, 1954.
95. *New York Times,* May 7, 1954
96. *New York Times,* May 6, 1954.
97. *New York Times,* May 6, 1954.
98. *New York Times,* May 6, 1954.
99. *New York Times,* May 24, 1954.
100. *New York Times,* May 25, 1954.
101. *New York Times,* May 25, 1954.
102. *New York Times,* May 21, 1954.
103. *New York Times,* May 25, 1954.
104. *New York Times,* May 21, 1954.
105. *New York Times,* May 25, 1954.
106. *New York Times,* May 26, 1954.
107. *New York Times,* May 25, 1954.
108. *New York Times,* May 27, 1954.
109. *New York Times,* May 28, 1954.
110. *New York Times,* May 27, 1954.
111. *New York Times,* May 28, 1954.
112. *New York Times,* June 4, 1954.
113. *New York Times,* December 1, 1955.
114. *New York Times,* December 1, 1955.
115. *New York Times,* October 1, 1954.
116. *New York Times,* October 5, 1954.
117. *New York Times,* June 4, 1954.
118. *New York Times,* June 29, 1954.
119. *New York Times,* November 29, 1955.
120. *Waterfront News,* nos. 1, 2, 20, 23, 26, 34, 44, and 45, in the Jensen Archives.
121. *New York Times,* August 3, 1956.
122. *New York Times,* August 24, 1956.
123. *New York Times,* September 25, 1956.
124. *New York Times,* October 17, 1956.

125. *New York Times,* August 1, 1956.

126. *New York Times,* August 9, 1956.

127. *New York Times,* August 9, 1956.

128. *New York Times,* August 14, 1956.

129. *New York Times,* October 18, 1956.

130. *New York Times,* September 25, 1956.

131. Jensen, *Strife on the Waterfront,* 134.

Chapter 4. Port Automation and Control of the Dock Labor Process

1. *New York Longshore Data Book,* 14. Jensen points out, however, that when examining statistical data of wages and hours of longshoremen, some allowance has to be made for overtime work, which accounts for 25–30 percent of all waterfront work. Hence 1,500 work hours could in reality be equal to 1,750 hours of straight time employment. By 1960, Vernon Jensen argues, "20 percent of the longshoremen (4,373) still worked less than 700 hours in the year, the level of employment required for establishing eligibility for vacation, pension and welfare benefits. Another 15 percent (3,470) worked between 700 and 1,200 hours. One might argue, therefore, that one fourth to one third of the longshoremen received insufficient earnings. . . . The men who receive less than 1,200 hours experience hardship." Jensen, *Hiring of Dock Workers,* 89.

2. Jensen, *Hiring of Dock Workers,* 58–59.

3. Axelrod, "Government Covers the Waterfront," 253.

4. U.S. Department of Labor, *Impact of Longshore Strikes on the National Economy,* 44.

5. Annual Report of the Bi-State Waterfront Commission, 1959. Also see Axelrod, "Government Covers the Waterfront," 235.

6. "In several cases," Axelrod wrote, "the evidence is also turned over to the local District Attorney for the initiation of criminal proceedings." Axelrod, "Government Covers the Waterfront," 236–37.

7. Axelrod, "Government Covers the Waterfront," 236.

8. Axelrod, "Government Covers the Waterfront," 236.

9. Axelrod, "Government Covers the Waterfront," 241–42.

10. Axelrod, "Government Covers the Waterfront," 243.

11. *New York Longshore Data Book,* 6.

12. *New York Times,* September 20, 1956.

13. Vernon Jensen argued, "Anastasia's presence was felt in another matter, although it was not solely of his making. Top leadership of the ILA had never really settled with Captain Bradley's succession to Ryan. He tried hard and meant well, but in the relatively anarchistic internal situation, with locally controlled 'Empires,' his lack of leadership acumen or authority was pronounced." Jensen, *Strife on the Waterfront,* 231.

14. Jensen, *Strife on the Waterfront,* 232.

15. *New York Times,* September 25, 1959.

16. *New York Times,* September 25, 1959.

17. *New York Times,* November 20, 1956.

18. *Dockers News,* April 1956.

19. *Dockers News,* April 1956.

20. *Waterfront News* 2, no. 34, June 1, 1956.

21. *The Great Ships: The Freighter,* A&E Television Network (1996).

22. *The Great Ships: The Freighter,* A&E Television Network (1996).

23. *New York Times,* August 2, 1956.

24. *New York Times,* August 3, 1956.

25. ILWU *Dispatcher,* supplemental issue, May 25, 1956. Also see *New York Times,* August 27, 1956. Bridges, however, also had specific interests in the success of the ILA's contract negotiations. Recently concluded contract negotiations on the West Coast had provided only a 2 cent hourly wage increase with the understanding that if the ILA's contract provided an increase above 2 cents, it would automatically be passed on to West Coast dockworkers.

26. *New York Times,* August 31, 1956.

27. *New York Times,* September 26, 1956.

28. *New York Times,* September 20, 1956.

29. *New York Times,* October 23, 1956.

30. *New York Times,* October 23, 1956.

31. *New York Times,* October 25, 1956.

32. *New York Times,* October 26, 1956.

33. *New York Times,* November 8, 1956.

34. *New York Times,* November 16, 1956.

35. *New York Times,* November 16, 1956.

36. *New York Times,* November 18, 1956.

37. *New York Times,* November 17, 1956.

38. *New York Times,* November 21, 1956.

39. *New York Times,* November 18, 1956.

40. *New York Times,* November 20, 1956.

41. *New York Times,* November 21, 1956.

42. *New York Times,* November 22, 1956.

43. *New York Times,* November 23, 1956.

44. *New York Times,* November 25, 1956.

45. *New York Times,* November 24, 1956.

46. *New York Times,* November 25, 1956.

47. *New York Times,* November 27, 1956.

48. *New York Times,* November 30, 1956.

49. *New York Times,* November 30, 1956.

50. *New York Times,* December 1, 1956.

51. *New York Times,* December 3, 1956.

52. *New York Times,* December 28, 1956.

53. *New York Times,* January 23, 1957.

54. *New York Times,* January 31, 1957.

55. *New York Times,* January 31, 1957.

56. *New York Times,* February 8, 1957.

57. *New York Times,* February 11, 1957.

58. *New York Times,* February 13, 1957.

59. *New York Times,* February 13, 1957.

60. *New York Times,* February 14, 1957.

61. *New York Times,* February 16, 1957.

62. *New York Times,* February 16, 1957.

63. *New York Times,* February 18, 1957.

64. *New York Times,* February 19, 1957.

65. Jensen, *Strife on the Waterfront,* 227.

66. *New York Times,* November 19, 1958.

67. *New York Times,* November 19, 1958.

68. *New York Times,* November 27, 1958.

69. *New York Times,* October 8, 1959.

70. *New York Times,* September 4, 1959.

71. *New York Times,* September 17, 1959.

72. *New York Times,* September 19, 1959.

73. Jensen wrote, "They wanted a three-year agreement, flexibility in use of labor—both in number and in assignment, and in shifting gangs from ship to ship and in shifting men within the gangs between hold and dock—a flexible noon meal hour, elimination of paid travel time, reduction of absenteeism, right of cancellation in the event of non-arrival of a ship, removal of restrictive customs and practices, review of the pension and welfare funds." Jensen, *Strife on the Waterfront,* 237.

74. *New York Times,* September 24, 1959.

75. *New York Times,* September 26, 1959; Jensen, *Strife on the Waterfront,* 243.

76. *New York Times,* September 29, 1959.

77. *New York Times,* January 21, 1959.

78. Jensen notes, "The *Dockers News* had also been stirring up the longshoremen." Jensen, *Strife on the Waterfront,* 244.

79. "The basic problem was," Jensen wrote, "that there was no one in the ILA who could control the various factions. It was obvious too, that the AFL-CIO could not step in effectively, for those who opposed re-entry into the AFL-CIO were the fractious ones rebelling in New York." Jensen, *Strife on the Waterfront,* 245.

80. Jensen, *Strife on the Waterfront,* 246.

81. Jensen, *Strife on the Waterfront,* 246.

82. *New York Times,* October 3, 1959.

83. *New York Times,* October 4, 1959.

84. *New York Times,* October 9, 1959.

85. *New York Times,* October 4, 1959.

86. *New York Times,* October 7, 1959.

87. *New York Times,* October 8, 1959.

88. *New York Times,* October 8, 1959.

89. *New York Times,* October 11, 1959.

90. *New York Times,* November 9, 1959.

91. *New York Times,* December 2, 1959.

92. Jensen notes: "The ILA correctly said, 'It is almost impossible to identify the guy that's displaced . . . a man does not lose his job, automation reduces hours.' Besides severance and a closed registrar would reduce the local's members; this, some ILA leaders did not want." Jensen, *Strife on the Waterfront,* 248.

93. Jensen, *Strife on the Waterfront,* 251.

94. Jensen, *Strife on the Waterfront,* 252.

95. Jensen, *Strife on the Waterfront,* 253.

96. *New York Times,* December 10, 1959.

97. *New York Times,* December 18, 1959.

Chapter 5. "The Health and Safety of the Nation"

1. *Brooklyn Longshoreman,* March 1964, 4.

2. DiFazio wrote: "The reaction of the union to *Dockers News* has been to claim it is a communist paper that the great majority of workers have ignored. The attitude has been to view *Dockers News* as subversive to the best interests of the men and the union." DiFazio, *Longshoremen,* 47.

3. Regarding the 1959 election for Local 1814, historian Colin Davis notes, "The Unity Ticket came under violent attack. Tony Anastasia with '25 other men' had attempted to break up a unity meeting at the home of longshoreman Clyde Blue." Davis, "Shape or Fight?" 153.

4. Interview with Servio Mello, November 29, 1994.

5. Interview with Gus Johnson, December 29, 1994.

6. Interview with Frank DiLorenzo, December 29, 1994.

7. Interview with Johnson.

8. Interview with DiLorenzo.

9. *New York Times,* April 16, 1962.

10. Traditionally negotiations began in the month of August, proceeding the October 1 contract expiration date.

11. New York Times, April 19, 1962.

12. *New York Times,* April 27, 1962.

13. *New York Times,* May 16, 1962.

14. *New York Times,* June 11, 1962.

15. *New York Times,* June 14, 1962. Also see *New York Herald Tribune,* June 14, 1962.

16. *New York Times,* June 14, 1962. Also see *New York Herald Tribune,* June 16, 1962, and *Baltimore Sun,* June 17, 1962.

17. *NYSA Research and Information Bulletin #7,* July 1962. Vernon Jensen Archives, Kheel Center, Cornell University.

18. *New York Times,* July 17, 1962.

19. *New York Times,* August 2, 1962. Also see *New York Times,* September 6, 1962.

20. ILWU *Dispatcher,* October 19, 1962.

21. *New York Times,* July 17, 1962.

22. *New York Times,* August 21, 1962.

23. *New York Times,* August 23, 1962.

24. *New York Herald Tribune,* September 16, 1962.

25. *New York Times,* August 22, 1962.

26. *New York Times,* August 22, 1962.

27. *New York Times,* August 24, 1962.

28. *New York Times,* August 24, 1962.

29. *New York Times,* September 5, 1962. Also see *New York Times,* September 14, 1962.

30. *New York Times,* September 15 and 17, 1962.

31. *New York Times,* September 20, 1962.

32. *New York Times,* September 21, 1962.

33. *New York Times,* October 2, 1962.

34. *New York Times,* October 2, 1962.

35. *New York Times,* October 5, 1962.

36. *Dockers News,* October 1962.

37. *New York Times,* December 24, 1962.

38. *New York Times,* October 2, 1962.

39. *New York Times,* December 27, 1962.

40. NYSA, "An Open Letter to Striking Longshoremen, Their Families, and the Public," January 10, 1963. Jensen Archives.

41. Dockworkers Rank and File Committee, "An Urgent Appeal to Trade Unionists and All People of Our City," January 1963, Jensen Archives.

42. *New York Times,* December 29, 1969.

43. *New York Times,* December 31, 1962.

44. *New York Times,* January 2, 1963.

45. *New York Times,* December 31, 1962.

46. *New York Times,* January 7 and 8, 1963.

47. *New York Times,* January 17, 1963.

48. *New York Times,* January 23, 1963.

49. *Business Week,* January 19, 1963.

50. *New York Times,* January 18, 1963.

51. *New York Times,* January 22, 1963.

52. *Wall Street Journal,* February 20, 1963.

53. *Wall Street Journal,* February 20, 1963.

54. *New York Times,* January 23, 1963.

55. *New York Times,* July 2, 1963.

56. *Dockers News,* January 1963.

57. *Dockers News,* January 1963.

58. *Dockers News,* January 1963.

59. *New York Times,* July 6, 1964.

60. *New York Times,* July 15, 1964.

61. *New York Times,* July 8, 1964.

62. *New York Times,* July 29, 1964.

63. *New York Times,* August 13, 1964.

64. *New York Times,* August 14, 1964.

65. A dockworker was considered hired if he was contracted for at least four hours work.

66. *New York Times,* August 13, 1964.

67. *New York Times,* July 15, 1964.

68. *New York Times,* August 3, 1964.

69. *New York Times,* August 19, 1964.

70. *New York Times,* October 1, 1964. Also see *New York Herald Tribune,* October 1, 1964.

71. *New York Times,* October 2, 1964.

72. *New York Times,* October 2, 1964.

73. *New York Times,* October 2, 1964. Also see Report to the President by the Taft Act Board of Inquiry in the East Coast–Gulf Longshoremen's Dispute, October 2, 1964.

74. *New York Times,* October 2, 1964.

75. *New York Times,* October 2, 1964.

76. *New York Times,* October 3, 1964.

77. *Dockers News,* October 8, 1964.

78. *New York Times,* November 11, 1964.

79. *New York Times,* November 25, 1964. Also see *New York Times,* December 2, 1964.

80. *New York Times,* December 3, 1964.

81. *New York Times,* December 17, 1964.

82. *New York Times,* December 18, 1964.

83. *New York Times,* December 18, 1964.

84. *New York Times,* December 22, 1964.

85. *New York Times,* December 22, 1964.

86. *New York Times,* December 24, 1964.

87. *New York Times,* January 1, 1965.

88. *New York Times,* January 9, 1965.

89. *New York Times,* January 10, 1965.

90. *New York Times,* January 16, 1965.

91. ILA, "Letter to All ILA Members on the Port of New York," January 13, 1965, Jensen Archives.

92. *New York Times,* January 21, 1965.

93. *New York Times,* January 23, 1965.

94. *New York Times,* January 27, 1965.

95. *New York Times,* January 28, 1965.

96. *Washington Post,* January 29, 1965.

97. *Washington Post,* January 29, 1965.

98. *New York Times,* February 6, 1965.

99. *New York Times,* February 4, 1965.

100. *New York Times,* February 4, 1965. Also see *New York Times,* February 10, 1965.

101. *New York Times,* February 11, 1965.

102. *New York Times,* February 11, 1965.

103. *New York Times,* February 20, 1965.

104. *New York Times,* March 6, 1965.

105. *New York Herald Tribune,* January 3, 1964.

106. *New York Times,* March 9, 1966.

107. *New York Times,* September 21, 1966.

108. At this time, automation of the port work process was increasing rapidly, which further reduced the amount of work hours available.

109. *New York Times,* April 3, 1966.

110. *New York Times,* April 3, 1966.

111. *New York Times,* November 9, 1964.

112. *New York Times,* April 5, 1966.

113. *Journal of Commerce,* April 5, 1966.

114. *New York Times,* April 9, 1966.

115. *New York Times,* April 11 and 12, 1966.

116. *New York Times,* April 15, 1966.

117. *New York Times,* May 6, 1966.

118. *Journal of Commerce,* May 16, 1967.

119. *Journal of Commerce,* May 16, 1967. Also see *New York Times,* May 15, 1967.

120. The "hot cargo" provision prohibits a strike against employers because of their use of struck goods from another company.

121. *Baltimore Sun,* May 15, 1967. Also see *New York Times,* March 14, 1968.

122. *New York Times,* March 19, 1968.

123. *New York Times,* March 21, 1968.

124. *New York Times,* March 28, 1968.

125. *New York Times,* March 27 and 28, 1968.

126. *New York Times,* March 29, 1968.

127. *New York Times,* April 2, 1968.

128. *New York Times,* July 11, 1968.

129. *New York Times,* September 5, 1968.

130. *New York Times,* September 25, 1968.

131. *New York Times,* September 28, 1968.

132. *IFT Newsletter,* no. 6 (June 1967). Also see *New York Times,* September 29, 1968.

133. *Dockers News,* September 27, 1968.

134. *New York Times,* October 1, 1968.

135. *New York Times,* October 2, 1968.

136. *New York Times,* October 1, 1968.

137. *New York Times,* October 2, 1968.

138. *Dockers News,* October 1968. Also see Jensen, *Strife on the Waterfront,* 378.

139. *Journal of Commerce,* November 1, 1968.

140. *New York Times,* November 1, 1968.

141. *Wall Street Journal,* November 5 and 6, 1968.

142. *Wall Street Journal,* November 5, 1968.

143. *New York Times,* November 2, 1968.

144. *New York Times,* November 5, 1968.

145. *New York Times,* November 5, 1968.

146. Interview with Johnson.

147. DiFazio, *Longshoremen,* 47.

148. *New York Times,* December 3, 1968.

149. *New York Times,* December 11, 1968.

150. *New York Times,* December 12, 1968.

151. *New York Times,* December 17, 1968.

152. *New York Times,* December 18, 1968.

153. *New York Times,* December 18, 1968.

154. *New York Times,* December 21, 1968.

155. *New York Times,* December 24, 1968.

156. *New York Times,* December 25, 1968.

157. *New York Times,* December 29, 1968.

158. *New York Times,* January 1, 1969.

159. *New York Times,* January 4, 1969.

160. *New York Times,* January 8, 1969.

161. *New York Times,* January 3, 1969.

162. *New York Times,* January 9, 1969.

163. *New York Times,* January 10, 1969.

164. *New York Times,* January 13, 1969.

165. *New York Times,* January 15, 1969. In New York the cost of two extra weeks vacation was 16 cents per hour of the $1.60 package, in Philadelphia, however, the same two weeks of vacation would cost 28 cents.

166. *New York Times,* February 4, 1969.

167. *New York Times,* January 19, 1969.

168. *New York Times,* January 22, 1969.

169. *New York Times,* January 23, 1969.

170. *New York Times,* January 26, 1969.

171. *New York Times,* January 27, 1969.

172. *New York Times,* January 30, 1969.

173. *New York Times,* February 2, 1969.

174. The main reason for declaring a national emergency was not simply to force the return of striking dockworkers but also to enable small business to seek low-cost loans to subsidize their financial losses.

175. Skrentny, *The Ironies of Affirmative Action,* 181. This was more than just political pragmatism. Nixon's policy towards labor reflected what Skrentny defined as the politics of "creative destruction."

176. Skowronek, "Notes on the Presidency in the Political Order," 286. Skrentny's argument draws on Skowronek's concept of the "politics of preemption," where he argued that "the exercise of creative political leadership hinges on expanding and altering the base of opposition support, and here the leader is naturally drawn toward latent interest cleavages and factional discontent within the ranks of the traditional supporters."

177. *New York Times,* February 6, 1969.

178. *New York Times,* February 8, 1969.

179. *New York Times,* February 9, 1969. Also see *New York Times,* February 10, 1969.

180. *New York Times,* February 9, 1969.

181. *New York Times,* February 9, 1969.

182. It was reported that waterfront workers from other professions were also invited to attend the meeting.

183. *New York Times,* February 9, 1969.

184. *New York Times,* February 12, 1969.

185. *New York Times,* February 11, 1969.

186. *New York Times,* February 15, 1969.

187. *New York Times,* February 15, 1969.

188. *Dockers News,* May 20, 1970.

189. Dickman, "The Basic Position of the NYSA," press release, NYSA, October 5, 1971, Jensen Archives.

Conclusion. Class and Power: A View from the Docks

1. Stone, "Social Stratification," 285.

Bibliography

American Social History Project. *Who Built America? Working People and the Nation's Economy, Politics, Culture, and Society.* 2 vols. New York: Worth, 2000.

Armstrong, Philip, Andrew Glyn, and John Harrison. *Capitalism since 1945.* Cambridge, Mass.: Basil Blackwell, 1991.

Axelrod, Daniel. "Government Covers the Waterfront." PhD diss., Syracuse University, 1967.

Barnes, Charles Brinton. *The Longshoremen.* New York: Survey Associates, 1915.

Bensel, Richard Franklin. *The Political Economy of American Industrialization, 1877–1900.* New York: Cambridge University Press, 2000.

Bensman, Joseph. "Social and Institutional Factors Determining the Levels of Violence and Political Assassinations in the Operation of Society: A Theoretical Discussion." In *Assassinations and the Political Order,* ed. William J. Crotty. New York: Harper and Row, 1971.

Brass, Paul. "Foucault Steals Political Science." *Annual Review in Political Science* 3 (2000): 305–30.

Dahl, Robert A. "A Concept of Power." *Behavioral Sciences* 2 (1954): 201–25.

———. *Who Governs? Democracy and Power in an American City.* New Haven: Yale University Press, 1961.

Davis, Colin. "All I've Got's a Hook: New York Longshoremen and the 1948 Dock Strike." In *Waterfront Workers: New Perspectives on Race and Class,* ed. Calvin Winslow. Urbana: University of Illinois Press, 1998.

———. "Shape or Fight: New York's Black Longshoremen, 1945–1961." *International Labor and Working-Class History* 2, no. 2 (Fall 2002): 143–63.

Davis, Mike. *Prisoners of the American Dream: Politics and Economy in the History of the U.S. Working Class.* London: Verso, 1986, 1999.

Dickman, James J. "The Basic Position of the NYSA." Press release, NYSA, October 5, 1971. Vernon Jensen Archives, Kheel Center, Cornell University.

DiFazio, William. *Longshoremen: Community and Resistance on the Brooklyn Waterfront.* South Hadley, Mass.: Bergin and Garvey, 1985.

Dockworkers Rank and File Committee. "An Urgent Appeal to Trade Unionists and All People of Our City." Vernon Jensen Archives, Kheel Center, Cornell University, December 1962.

Eley, Geoff, and Keith Nield. "Farewell to the Working Class?" *International Labor and Working-Class History* 57 (Spring 2000): 1–30.

Etzioni-Halevy, Eva. *The Elite Connection: Problems and Potential of Western Democracy.* Cambridge, Mass.: Polity Press, 1993.

Freeman, Joshua B. *Working-Class New York: Life and Labor since World War II.* New York: New Press, 2000.

Giddens, Anthony, and David Held, eds. *Classes, Power, and Conflict: Classical and Contemporary Debates.* Berkeley: University of California Press, 1982.

Goldstein, Robert Justin. *Political Repression in Modern America from 1870 to 1976.* Urbana: University of Illinois Press, 2001.

Hobsbawm, E. J. *Labouring Men: Studies in the History of Labour.* New York: Basic Books, 1964.

Hutchinson, John. *The Imperfect Union: A History of Corruption in American Trade Unions.* New York: E. P. Dutton, 1970.

International Longshoremen's Association. "Letter to All ILA Members on the Port of New York." January 13, 1965. Vernon Jensen Archives, Kheel Center, Cornell University.

Jensen, Vernon H. *Hiring of Dock Workers and Employment Practices in the Ports of New York, Liverpool, London, Rotterdam, and Marseilles.* Cambridge: Harvard University Press, 1964.

———. *Strife on the Waterfront: The Port of New York since 1945.* Ithaca, N.Y.: Cornell University Press, 1974.

———. Vernon Jensen Papers. Kheel Center, Cornell University.

Katznelson, Ira. "Constructing Cases and Comparisons." In *Working-Class Formation: Nineteenth-Century Patterns in Western Europe and the United States,* ed. Ira Katznelson and Aristide R. Zolberg. Princeton: Princeton University Press, 1986.

———. "Strange Bedfellows, Strange Deals: The New Deal, The South and the Origins of Our Time." Manuscript.

Kimeldorf, Howard. *Reds or Rackets? The Making of Radical and Conservative Unions on the Waterfront.* Berkeley: University of California Press, 1988.

Lichtenstein, Nelson. *State of the Union. A Century of American Labor.* Princeton: Princeton University Press, 2002.

Lindblom, Charles E. *Unions and Capitalism.* New Haven: Yale University Press, 1949.

Lipset, Seymour Martin. *Political Man: The Social Bases of Politics.* Garden City, N.Y.: Doubleday, 1960.

Marcantonio Papers. New York Public Library.

Marx, Karl. *On Society and Social Change.* Edited by Neil J. Smelser. Chicago: University of Chicago Press, 1973.

McAdams, Alan K. *Power and Politics in Labor Legislation.* New York: Columbia University Press, 1964.

Miller, Raymond Charles. "The Dockworker Subculture and Some Problems of Cross-Cultural and Cross-Time Generalizations." *Comparative Studies in Society and History* 11 (1969): 302–14.

Mills, C. Wright. *The New Men of Power*. Chicago: Chicago University Press, 1948, 2000.

Montgomery, David. *The Fall of the House of Labor: The Workplace, the State, and American Labor Activism, 1865–1925*. New York: Cambridge University Press, 1987.

Morris, George. *A Tale of Two Waterfronts*. New York: Daily Worker, 1952. Pamphlet stored at Tamiment/Bobst Library, NYU.

Nelson, Bruce. *Divided We Stand: American Workers and the Struggle for Black Equality*. Princeton: Princeton University Press, 2001.

New York Shipping Association (NYSA). "An Open Letter to Striking Longshoremen, Their Families, and the Public." Vernon Jensen Archives, Kheel Center, Cornell University, December 1962.

New Yorkers at Work Oral History Collection. Tamiment/Bobst Library, New York University.

Plotke, David. *Building a Democratic Political Order: Reshaping American Liberalism in the 1930s and 1940s*. New York: Cambridge University Press, 1996.

Preis, Art. *Labor's Giant Step: Twenty Years of the CIO*. New York: Pathfinder Press, 1972.

Raymond, Allen. *The Waterfront Priest*. New York: Henry Holt, 1955.

Rosswurm, Steven, ed. *The CIO's Left-Led Unions*. New Brunswick, N.J.: Rutgers University Press, 1992.

Rueschemeyer, Dietrich. *Power and the Division of Labor*. Stanford: Stanford University Press, 1986.

Ruotsila, Markku. *British and American Anticommunism before the Cold War*. Portland, Ore.: Frank Cass, 2001.

Russell, Maud. *Men along the Shore*. New York: Brussel and Brussel, 1966.

Schattsneider, E. E. *The Semisovereign People: A Realist's View of Democracy in America*. New York: Holt, Rinehart and Winston, 1960.

Schneirov, Richard. *Labor and Urban Politics: Class Conflict and the Origins of Modern Liberalism in Chicago, 1864–97*. Urbana: University of Illinois Press, 1998.

Schrecker, Ellen. *Many Are the Crimes: McCarthyism in America*. Boston: Little, Brown, 1998.

———. "McCarthyism and the Labor Movement." In *The CIO's Left-Led Unions*, ed. Steven Rosswurm. New Brunswick, N.J.: Rutgers University Press, 1992.

Sexton, Patricia Cayo. *The War on Labor and the Left: Understanding America's Unique Conservatism*. Boulder: Westview Press, 1991.

Schultz, Bud, and Ruth Schultz, eds. *The Price of Dissent: Testimonies to Political Repression in America*. Berkeley: University of California Press, 2001.

Skowronek, Stephen. "Notes on the Presidency in the Political Order." *Studies in American Political Development* 1 (January 1986): 286–302.

Skrentny, John David. *The Ironies of Affirmative Action: Politics, Culture, and Justice in America*. Chicago: University of Chicago Press, 1996.

Sombart, Werner. *Why Is There No Socialism in the United States?* Edited by C. Husbands. White Plains, N.Y.: International Arts and Sciences Press, 1976.

Stone, Clarence N. "Social Stratification, Nondecision-Making, and the Study of Community Power." *American Politics Research* 10, no. 3 (1982): 275–302.

———. "Systemic Power in Community Decision Making." *American Political Science Review* 74 (1980): 978–90.

Swift, John. "Some Problems of Work in Right-Led Unions." *Political Affairs*, April 1952.

Tarrow, Sidney. *Power in Movement: Social Movements and Contentious Politics.* New York: Cambridge University Press, 1998.

Thompson, E. P. *The Making of the English Working Class.* New York: Pantheon Books, 1963.

Turkus, Burton, and Sid Feder. *Murder Inc.: The Story of the Syndicate.* New York: Farrar, Straus and Young, 1951.

U.S. Chamber of Commerce. *Communists within the Labor Movement: A Handbook on the Facts and Countermeasures.* Washington, D.C.: U.S. Chamber of Commerce, 1947.

Wartenberg, Thomas E., ed. *Rethinking Power.* Albany: State University of New York Press, 1992.

Wilentz, Sean. *Chants Democratic: New York City and the Rise of the American Working Class, 1788–1850.* New York: Oxford University Press, 1984.

Winslow, Calvin. "Men of the Lumber Camps Come to Town: New York Longshoremen and the Strike of 1907." In *Waterfront Workers: New Perspectives on Race and Class,* ed. Calvin Winslow. Urbana: University of Illinois Press, 1998.

Woodiwiss, Michael. *Organized Crime and American Power.* Toronto: University of Toronto Press, 2001.

Zweig, Michael. *The Working-Class Majority: America's Best Kept Secret.* Ithaca, N.Y.: IRL Press, 2000.

Reports

Annual Reports of the Bi-State Waterfront Commission, 1953–60.

Impact of Longshore Strikes on the National Economy. Washington, D.C.: Department of Labor, 1970.

Longshore Industry on the Port of New York. New York: New York Shipping Association, 1962.

New York Longshore Data Book. NYSA Research Department, June 6, 1962.

New York Shipping Association Research Bulletin no. 7, 1962.

New York State Board of Inquiry into the Longshoremen's Strike of 1951.

New York State Crime Commission Hearings for Remedying Conditions on the Port of New York, June 8–9, 1953.

Report to the Presidency by the Taft Act Board of Inquiry into the East Coast–Gulf Longshore Dispute, October 2, 1964.

U.S. Senate Subcommittee Hearings on Interstate Foreign Commerce. 83rd Cong., 1st sess., 1953.

Union and Rank-and-File Newsletters

Brooklyn Longshoremen. Newsletter of ILA Local 1814 (1964).

Dispatcher. Journal of the International Longshoremen's and Warehouse Workers Union (ILWU).

Dockers News. Newsletter of rank-and-file activists on the Port of New York (1947–81).

March of Labor (1951).

New Deal. Manhattan dockworkers newsletter (1951).

Shape-Up. Newsletter of the Brooklyn Rank and File Committee.

Waterfront News. Newsletter of the International Brotherhood of Longshoremen (1954–57).

Newspapers

Baltimore Sun (1962–67).

Business Week (1963).

Daily Worker (1939).

Journal of Commerce (1967–68).

New York Herald Tribune (1962–64).

New York Times (1945–69).

New York World Telegram (1948).

Wall Street Journal (1968).

Washington Post (1965).

Weekend Worker (1951).

Documentary

Great Ships Series: The Freighter. A&E Television Network (1996).

Index

Page numbers in italics refer to illustrations.

Shipping elites: and political authorities, 27, 154–55, 197; power wielded by, 13–17, 27. *See also* Shipping companies
Shultz, George, 192
Skowronek, Stephen, 225n176
Slowdowns, 140–41, 182
Smalls, Freddy, 158
Smith, Chatman "Smitty," *117*
Smith Act (1941), 20
Social stratification, 6, 12–13, 206n29. *See also* Class; Inequality, socioeconomic
Southern and Gulf ports, 152, 155, 191; and ILA demand for coast-wide bargaining, 134–35, 141–42; and strikes of 1956–57, 138–39, 140; and strikes of 1964–65, 174–75, 176, 177, 178, 179. *See also* Charleston; Galveston; Miami; Mobile; New Orleans
Stanley, Bernard, 87
Staten Island, 46, 65, 181, 182
Stone, Clarence N., 204–7nn7,23,25–29,41
Strikes:
—official: in 1953–54, 83–85, 93–97, 101, *108*; in 1956–57, 137–40, 142–44; in 1959, 148–52; in 1962–63, 164–69; in 1968–69, 186–94
—wildcat, 22–23, 70–71; in late 1940s, 44, 45–52, 53–54, 56–59; in early 1950s, 59–67; in 1953–54, 80–81, 91–92; in 1960s, 174–75, 176–79, 181–82, 184, 187–88
Subculture of resistance, 24–26
Sugarman, Sidney, 178
Sukhovitch, Mary, 44
Swift, John, 216n60

Taft-Hartley Act (1947), 21, 27, 41, 53, 91, 183, 216n49; weakening of unions by, 10, 15, 21, 198; and CIO, 41–42; anticommunist oath required by, 86, 88, 99. *See also* Taft-Hartley injunctions
Taft-Hartley injunctions, 71, 83, 153–55, 188, 199, 202; Truman administration and, 55–56, 64; Eisenhower administration and, 83–85, 91, 93, 138–40, 142, 149–50; Kennedy administration and, 165; Johnson administration and, 172–73, 174, 186, 187–88
Tarrow, Sidney, 210nn13,15

Teamsters union. *See* International Brotherhood of Teamsters
Tegnell, G. G., 190
Terranova, Benny, 158
Testa, Mary, 37
"Them and us," 24, 32
Thompson, E. P., 209n61
Tinkham, George, 31
Tobey, Charles, 70
Tobin, Austin J., 97, 171, 184
Truman, Harry S., 55–56, 64, 65
Turkus, Burton, 36–37, 182, 184

"Unfair labor practice" charges, 155; against ILA, 16, 65–66, 137, 178, 191, 193
Unions: political repression and, 24–29, 207n40. *See also specific unions and federations*
United Mine Workers of America (UMWA), 69, 87
U.S. America Line, 54
U.S. Chamber of Commerce, 21
U.S. Coast Guard, 73
U.S. Congress, 20, 72, 154, 166, 207n47; committee hearings of, 49–50, 70, 135
U.S. Department of Labor, 46, 68, 163, 172. *See also specific Department of Labor officials*
U.S. Lines, 43
U.S. Supreme Court, 53

Vandiver, Ernest, 167
Van Kleeck, Mary, 44
Velson, Charles, 88, 216n57
Violence, 19, 64–65, 188, 208n54; against rank-and-file movements, 13, 14–15, 23–24, 34, 35–39, 49–50, 188, 210–11n17; between ILA and ILA-AFL, 78, 90, 94–95

Wages, 124, 210n16. *See also* Guaranteed Annual Income
Wage Stabilization Board, 64
Wagner, Robert F., Jr., 31, 95, 166
Wagner Act (1935), 15, 21, 85, 86
Wainwright Commission on Unemployment, 29
Waldman, Louis, 138, 140, 142, 173
Walker, James, 31

www.ingramcontent.com/pod-product-compliance
Lightning Source LLC
Chambersburg PA
CBHW020659270326
41928CB00005B/200